TONY HARRISON

Yorks*sshhh*ire

Him drawing those lines, me composing these,
our breathing inside louder than the sea's.
Yorks*sshhh*ire . . . *ssshhh*, Yorks*sshhh*ire . . . *ssshhh* they say
the whispering waves on this last day of May.

Pebbles skimmed by two school-skiving kids
bounce on bulky waves that dawdle onto Brid's
bare beaches where a man shouts, "Stay!"
to his disobedient dog who runs away,
the studio clock with its metallic tick,
the craftblade scratching on the charcoal stick,
the gulls' cries and the crows' dry caws
as I compose, stock-still, and David draws,
and Brid's grey ocean, lisping and then lush
shuffles into one long silent *ssshhh*!

TONY HARRISON

Bridlington
31 May 1996

TONY HARRISON
LOINER

EDITED BY
SANDIE BYRNE

CLARENDON PRESS · OXFORD
1997

Oxford University Press, Great Clarendon Street, Oxford OX2 6DP
Oxford New York
Athens Auckland Bangkok Bogota Bombay
Buenos Aires Calcutta Cape Town Dar es Salaam
Delhi Florence Hong Kong Istanbul Karachi
Kuala Lumpur Madras Madrid Melbourne
Mexico City Nairobi Paris Singapore
Taipei Tokyo Toronto
and associated companies in
Berlin Ibadan

Oxford is a trade mark of Oxford University Press

Published in the United States
by Oxford University Press Inc., New York

British Library Cataloguing in Publication Data
Data available

Library of Congress Cataloging in Publication Data
Data available
ISBN 0–19–818430–1

1 3 5 7 9 10 8 6 4 2

Typeset by Hope Services (Abingdon) Ltd.
Printed in Great Britain
on acid-free paper by
Biddles Ltd.,
Guildford & King's Lynn

Foreword

GREY GOWRIE

ALONG with Ted Hughes and Geoffrey Hill, Tony Harrison strikes me as the most English poet working today. Whereas Hughes taps a vein of nature, mysticism, and the occult, and Hill is immersed in the detritus of human cultures, Harrison is social and gritty. He has taken the grand iambic beat of English poets and all the literary luggage that comes with it, and made it new for a generation. T. S. Eliot's phrase, 'tradition and the individual talent', has real meaning here.

If we are moving, crablike, towards a much more classless society, Harrison brings the old wound of the working class to the surface of his raw music. People left the land, where they were at least rooted, for new industrial towns. Having built, with great difficulty, a culture in these unpromising places, they are now dispersed once more into the television, plastic and supermarket, oil and electronic wilderness of mass consumerism. 'Don't forget,' he seems to be saying. 'If we forget, we are lost.'

Like the others, Harrison is in no sense provincial. He is sharply aware of England as one kingdom of our offshore islands, the one closest physically, most distant emotionally, to the continental mainland. Harrison's translations, Greek tragedies, and classical French drama in particular have the texture and fascination of a civilization looking through the windows of its origins from outside. Who else can make, has ever made, classical drama a force for North Country speech?

Poetasting critics of the early twentieth-century 'Georgian' period were castigated by modernists for being insufficiently analytic. Yet metaphor has at least the merits of speed and conclusion. In French culinary terms, Harrison's poetry is a 'cuisine du terroir'. Auden said that poets should be like cheeses, local but prized elsewhere. When you read Harrison's work you have to leave quite a long interval before you read anyone else's. The rhythms, the flavours, penetrate the skin. He is more than a poet. He is a writer of the first rank.

Acknowledgements

THE editor, contributors, and publisher would like to thank Tony Harrison for kindly allowing us to quote from his poems, and David Hockney for the stunning portrait of Tony Harrison on the front cover.

Acknowledgement is made to Bloodaxe Books for permission to quote from Neil Astley (ed.), *Bloodaxe Critical Anthologies 1: Tony Harrison*, and to Faber and Faber for permission to quote from *Tony Harrison*, *Theatre Works*, *The Trackers of Oxyrhynchus*, and *Plays 3*.

Grateful thanks to Jason Freeman, Commissioning Editor, Literature, at OUP for his enduring patience and support, to T. W. Bartel and Sophie Goldsworthy for making a manuscript out of a mess, and to Clare Harraway for reading and commenting on part of the typescript. Thanks also for their great helpfulness to Sophie Byrne of the Arts Council of England, Gordon Dickerson, the librarians of the English Faculty Library of Oxford University: Sue Usher, Andrew Mackinnon, and Mark Allcock, and Sarah Whalley of London Weekend Television.

Front cover illustration: Tony Harrison, conté crayon drawing © David Hockney, 1996.

Contents

Abbreviations

Ew	Tony Harrison, *Earthworks,* Northern House Pamphlet Poets Series (Leeds: Northern House, 1964).
Newcastle	Tony Harrison, *Newcastle is Peru* (Newcastle-upon Tyne: Eagle Press, 1969).
Loiners	Tony Harrison, *The Loiners* (London: London Magazine Editions, 1970).
Phaedra	Tony Harrison, after Racine, *Phaedra Britannica* (London: Rex Collings, 1975).
School	Tony Harrison, *From 'The School of Eloquence' and Other Poems* (London: Rex Collings, 1978).
Continuous	Tony Harrison, *Continuous: Fifty Sonnets from 'The School of Eloquence'* (London: Rex Collings, 1981).
Mysteries	Tony Harrison, *The Mysteries* (London: Faber and Faber, 1985).
TW	Tony Harrison, *Theatre Works 1973–1985* (London: Faber and Faber, 1986). First published as *Dramatic Works 1973–1985* (Newcastle-upon-Tyne: Bloodaxe Books, 1985).
SP	Tony Harrison, *Selected Poems*, 2nd edn. (London: Penguin, 1987).
v.	Tony Harrison, *v.*, 2nd edn. (Newcastle-upon-Tyne: Bloodaxe Books, 1989).
Trackers	Tony Harrison, *The Trackers of Oxyrhynchus* (London: Faber and Faber, 1990). Contains both Delphi and National Theatre versions of the play.
Coming	Tony Harrison, *A Cold Coming* (Newcastle-upon-Tyne: Bloodaxe Books, 1991).
Chorus	Tony Harrison, *The Common Chorus* (London: Faber and Faber, 1992).

Gorgon   Tony Harrison, *The Gaze of the Gorgon*.
                        (Newcastle-upon-Tyne: Bloodaxe Books,
                        1992).
Shadow   Tony Harrison, *The Shadow of Hiroshima and
                        Other Film/Poems* (London: Faber and Faber,
                        1995).
P3   Tony Harrison, *Plays 3* (London: Faber and
                        Faber, 1996).

'School of Eloquence'   Tony Harrison's continuing sonnet-sequence,
                        parts of which have appeared in *School*,
                        Continuous, *SP*, and elsewhere.

Bloodaxe 1   Neil Astley (ed.), *Bloodaxe Critical Anthologies
                        1: Tony Harrison* (Newcastle-upon-Tyne:
                        Bloodaxe Books, 1991).
'Agrippa'   Tony Harrison, 'The Inkwell of Dr Agrippa',
                        introduction to his poetry written for *Corgi
                        Modern Poets in Focus 4*, ed. Jeremy Robson
                        (London: Corgi Books, 1971), reprinted in
                        Bloodaxe 1.
'Conversation'   Richard Hoggart, 'In Conversation with Tony
                        Harrison', in *Bloodaxe 1*.
'Interview'   John Haffenden, 'Interview with Tony
                        Harrison', in *Bloodaxe 1*.
'THL'   Rick Rylance, 'Tony Harrison's Languages',
                        in Antony Easthope and John O. Thompson
                        (eds.), *Contemporary Poetry Meets Modern
                        Theory* (Hemel Hempstead: Harvester
                        Wheatsheaf, 1991). A version of this essay
                        also appears in *Bloodaxe 1*, 114–28.
Poetry TH   Luke Spencer, *The Poetry of Tony Harrison*
                        (Hemel Hempstead: Harvester/Wheatsheaf,
                        1994).

In quotation, punctuation and italics are original unless stated.

Loiners: 'citizens of Leeds, *citizens* who bear their loins through the terrors of life, "loners" '.

Tony Harrison, 'Agrippa', *Bloodaxe 1*, 34

Introduction: Tony Harrison's public poetry

SANDIE BYRNE

SOME of the claims made for Tony Harrison's work on the cover-copy of his books sound like the worst kind of promotional puff: 'one of the most prodigiously gifted and accessible poets alive today [. . .] "our best English poet" ';[1] 'Bold and brilliant [. . .] the work of a major social poet and a radically innovative dramatist'.[2] Harrison's publishers are, however, no more hyperbolic than less partial sources: *The Times*: 'our finest theatrical translator'; *Punch*: 'our greatest modern theatrical poet';[3] and Stephen Spender: 'Poems written in a style which I feel I have all my life been waiting for'.[4] Even the moderate *TLS* called Harrison 'a major dramatic poet'.[5] Meanwhile, in the book whose cover proclaims him 'the most important poet writing in Britain today',[6] Tony Harrison writes of boarding the Belfast–Newcastle plane anonymously, and reflecting:

> The rowdy squaddy, though he doesn't know it [. . .]
> is sitting next to one who enters 'poet'
> where he puts 'Forces' [. . . .]
> Being a photographer seems bad enough.
> God knows the catcalls that a poet would get![7]

If one aspect of Harrison does acknowledge that copy-writers' claims and critics' praise for his work are justified, another seems instantly compelled to turn that work against the 'poetry lovers', and thus himself, by giving a voice to those who find no value in it, or for him. In the last scene of his *Labourers of Herakles* the published text has the portentous direction *'Enter* **Tony Harrison** *to speak as* **The Spirit of Phrynichos**'. At the first (and thus far unique) performance of the play, the respectful silence following the playwright's highly referential as well as moving speech on war, genocide, and Greek drama was broken by the querulous and irritated voice of one of the labourers: 'Who the fuck was that?'[8]

Complacency is averted at all costs. Our most literate as well as our most technically accomplished poet, Harrison is never in danger of falling into preciousness and pretension while aspects of himself detach themselves to shout: '*A book, yer stupid cunt, 's not worth a fuck!*'[9] Nor is he in danger of overrating his intellect at the expense of his roots or his feelings. His writing can be a roller-coaster ride through one of the most exciting minds we are ever likely to encounter, but it is never sophistical nor arid. It is as visceral as it is cerebral, and as emotional as it is sensual. It is also unique. As Peter Forbes argues in 'In the Canon's Mouth', Harrison belongs to no school, and has no followers.

Harrison has written of his quest for 'a public poetry', which I take to mean both poetry made available to the public through publishing or performance, and poetry on public themes; from which he would 'never want to exclude inwardness'.[10] Through 'what Yeats called "sedentary toil and the imitation of great masters" ';[11] Harrison has hammered out a poetic which embeds the personal in the public, in which 'the public address of the one makes a clearing for the shared privacy of the other'.[12] Shared privacy and public address in Harrison's work are discussed elsewhere in this collection, particularly in N. S. Thompson's 'Book Ends'. The main purpose of this introduction is to chart the progress of this poetry into the public domain, and to record the ambivalent feelings about that progress expressed in the poems on the way.

Harrison's first published poem, 'When Shall I Tune my "Doric Reed"?', appeared when he was an undergraduate reading Classics at the University of Leeds, in a small magazine, *Poetry and Audience*, produced by the university's School of English.[13] The magazine consisted of a variable number of single leaves cyclostyled, stapled together, and sold for a penny. Harrison regularly contributed poems and reviews to the magazine both before and after he took over its editorship, and continued to write for it until 1961. The poems of this stage in Harrison's career, and their relationship to his later work, are discussed by Desmond Graham in 'The Best Poet of 1961'. By 1961, Harrison's work was regularly being accepted by *Stand*. This was not a leap into commercial publishing. *Stand*, edited then as now by Jon Silkin, was consciously provincial and anti-metropolitan, and was hand-distributed in universities and similar outlets rather like a broadsheet, but it was progress. *Stand*'s impressive and prescient list of contributors included Dannie Abse, Geoffrey Hill, and Alan Brownjohn, among others, and the achieving of national distribution (and a circulation of 2,000) was matched by the promotion from cyclostyled typescript to print; from flimsy covers to a heavier weight of paper; from a price of 1d to 9d.

Harrison's first publication in a book came in 1958, with the inclusion of six of his poems in a Leeds University School of English anthology, *Out on the Edge*.[14] This was followed by the inclusion of two poems in *New Poems 1960*,[15] and of four poems in a *Poetry and Audience* anthology.[16] Aware as he is of the divisiveness of canons,[17] it might seem inappropriate for Harrison's poems to appear in the contemporary 'big' anthologies, and on the whole, they have not. There are none in *The Oxford Book of Twentieth-Century English Verse*,[18] *The Oxford Book of Contemporary Verse*,[19] or *The Rattle Bag*.[20] Harrison is represented in *The Faber Book of Twentieth-Century Verse*[21] by one poem, 'The Hands', and in *British Poetry Since 1945*[22] by four poems, 'Voortrekker', 'Study', 'Long Distance II', and 'Clearing I', but his appearances elsewhere have, until recently, been mostly restricted to specialist and thematic collections.[23] The sixth edition of Palgrave's *Golden Treasury*,[24] and the fourth edition of *The Norton Anthology of Poetry*, however,[25] both include a generous selection of his poems, though the former, significantly, has only 'School of Eloquence' poems, and neither prints selections from the dramatic verse.

The next significant stage in the progress of Harrison's work was the publication of *Earthworks*, under Jon Silkin's imprint, Northern House. Though not a bound book, *Ew* is clearly a step up from the little magazines: the paper is heavy white wove, the poet's name stands out in red type on the cover, and, above all, it is devoted to Harrison's work. The austerity of the edition (16 pages, saddle-stitched) was suitable for a young poet's first collection, as was the publication price of two shillings, and it is perhaps as good an indicator of an established poetic reputation as any other that the book now sells for £45.[26]

The first edition of the single-poem pamphlet *Newcastle is Peru*, though not luxurious, was evidently designed to have value in excess of that of a notionally transparent vehicle of text. The type was handset (by Harrison, among others), the poem illustrated by woodcuts, hand-printed on laid paper—all of which is clearly significant because readers are told so.[27] Twenty-six of the 200 copies of the first edition were numbered and signed. Harrison's name now conferred value on the intangible text;[28] when the name was manifest, as a signature, it conferred monetary value on the material artefact. The poet had become a commodity, and was being given wider exposure. Alan Ross had been printing his work in *London Magazine* since July 1967[29] (which presumably led to the subsequent publication of *Loiners* under the London Magazine Editions imprint); he was the first Northern Arts Fellow at the Universities of Newcastle-upon-Tyne and Durham, from 1967–8, and was awarded the UNESCO Fellowship in Poetry in 1968. *Newcastle* is a remarkable poem for many reasons, one of which is that it signals the achievement of Harrison's mature, entirely distinctive poetic voice. More remarkable still, however, is that 'Ghosts: Some Words Before Breakfast'—equally distinctive, equally mature; the earliest poem to be collected beyond *Earthworks*—was published when Harrison was 23.[30]

> I'll have my portrait done, and then I'll show it,
> to prove I've really made it as a poet[31]

In *Loiners* we can look upon Harrison's picture, as well as his book. On the dust-jacket of the hardcover the author, slouching, smoking, is an archetypal angry young urban man.[32] The poems have all the energy and outrage of such a figure, but none of his solipsism. These are not songs of lovelorn or angst-ridden youth, but large-minded, engagé observations; unsparingly observant, yet compassionate; wide-ranging, polyglottal, and polymorphous; truly cosmopolitan.

Loiners had propelled Harrison upward by the distance from two shillings and twenty-five grams to twenty-five shillings and 235 grams: the weight of cloth-covered boards and sewn-in signatures, emblem of solid worth and long shelflife, and harbinger, perhaps, of financial security, whose complicated production processes preclude broadside instant reaction, carries the crushing weight of canon. The poetry evinces a pained awareness of this weight. 'Thomas Campey and the Copernican System', a poem for a down-at-heel scavenger of dispossessed *lares* and *penates*, whose diseased spine is bowed by the weight of old, crack-spined volumes as he pushes his handcart through the Leeds streets, is placed first in his first 'proper book', and—later—in *SP*. The plate in his own books is said to be a woodcut of Thomas Campey, bent almost double in flat cap and mackintosh, with a quotation from the poem:

> And every pound of this dead weight is pain
> to Thomas Campey (Books). . .[33]

—and many years later, in *Poetry or Bust*, the poet John Nicholson is, literally, dragged down by the weight of 'three vast volumes of LITERATURE', and drowns.[34] Harrison writes as if he were aware that '[t]here is no cultural document that is not at the same time a record of barbarism'.[35] Just as Thomas Campey is before him when he opens his books, and Patience Kershaw when he looks into a coal fire,[36] so, perhaps, the trace of the burden of volumes bound in heavy boards, the metaphorical weight of the capital-intensive publishing industry upon its workers, and the moral responsibility of the writer for his or her words, are present in each 'sonnet for the bourgeoisie'.[37]

Loiners received excited and enthusiastic reviews, and won the 1972 Geoffrey Faber Memorial Prize, but when his version of Molière's *The Misanthrope* (commissioned after Adrian Mitchell had shown *Loiners* to the director John Dexter) was performed the next year, Harrison was less well known than the leading actors,[38] so they rather than he are featured on the front cover. Inside the second edition is another significant note: 'All applications to perform this play should be made to Fraser and Dunlop (Scripts) Ltd'.[39] Harrison had been taken on by an agency, and it was theatrical rather than literary. This was not Harrison's first dramatic translation/adaptation. In Nigeria from 1962–6, he had worked with James Simmons in the Ahmadu Bello University at Zaria, and collaborated with him on *Aikin Mata*,[40] a version of the *Lysistrata* of Aristophanes which used Standard and Pidgin English to re-create the linguistic and social division between Attic and Doric Greek.[41] *The Misanthrope*, however, was a landmark. As Rosemary Burton noted, verse drama had been 'languishing—a pale and effete thing.' Harrison's 'shimmering rhyming couplets' gave it new life.[42] The National Theatre production was 'etched in the minds of all who saw it and left critics fighting for superlatives [. . . . It] was an international success and for a while Harrison's phone never stopped ringing with offers of work—mostly film scripts.'[43] One of those offers eventually became his *Oresteia*, which Oswyn Murray called 'the classic account for our generation [. . .] against which we continue to judge all attempts to stage ancient Greek tragedy'.[44] Greek literature has continued to be an ever-renewing source for Harrison, providing not only material for translation/adaptation, narrative frameworks, and formal models, but also precepts for life.[45] Oliver Taplin discusses the importance of Greek drama to Harrison's work, in particular the chorus of women, in 'The Chorus of Mams', and Rick Rylance discusses Harrison's *Oresteia* and other poems of war in 'Doomsongs'.

Just when Harrison had become better known as a (verse) dramatist than as a poet, and he could have made a good living as a translator/adapter, or as a playwright, he began to publish sonnets from the 'School of Eloquence' continuing sequence in periodicals and anthologies.[46] Jem Poster examines these poems of celebration and elegy (among others) in 'Open to Experience: Structure and Exploration in Tony Harrison's Poetry'. The Rex Collings edition of *From 'The School of Eloquence' and Other Poems*, with its black cloth-covered boards; cream laid, watermarked paper with coloured endpapers and stained top edges; dust-jacket in a chaste design of black and white with restrained typography in a serif fount, has a classical, almost eighteenth-century feel. The design could seem appropriate for a rationalist school of eloquence, rhetoric, and linguistic decorum—an impression which would be contradicted only by the reader's encounter with the opening epigram.[47] Here Harrison's work began to achieve the complex publishing history necessary for an *œuvre* to provide satisfactory labour for bibliographers, textual critics, and booksellers. The inside front leaf of the dust-jacket has a notice: 'Half of this new collection is a selection from a work in progress,' while the acknowledgements page has: 'Ten Poems from *The School of Eloquence* was privately printed in an edition of 150 copies as the Rex Collings Christmas Book 1976', and 'Two poems from *Sentences* were published in *The Loiners*, but as they belong with the poems that accompany them, I have chosen to reprint them here.'[48] Harrison, however, avoided the conventional slow passage to a *Collected Works*, just as he had avoided the progress to popular playwright, initially by leaving both behind. After his return from Africa in 1967, he soon took up the first of three British literary fellowships,[49] but continued to travel frequently and extensively. His home base had become Newcastle, but between 1969 and 1977 he visited and worked in Prague, Cuba, Brazil, Senegal, Gambia, Mozambique, Wales, Leningrad, and New York, and between 1979 and 1990 he divided his time between Newcastle, New York, and Florida.

Collaboration on *Stand* and the north-eastern poetry-reading circuit brought Harrison into contact with Neil Astley, the founder (in 1978) of Bloodaxe Books, who was eventually to become the main publisher of his non-dramatic poetry. Bloodaxe issued their first two Harrison titles as a pair in November 1981. *A Kumquat for John Keats* and *U.S. Martial*[50] were described as 'one-off pamphlets published in addition to his book-length collections'.[51] *U.S. Martial*—twenty-four pages, saddle-stitched, with a laminated cover—is more like a low-budget paperback, but its page layout is almost a parody of a 'quality' slim volume. Each of *Martial*'s epigrammatic poems (translated into modern New York English), few of which have more than four lines, is given a page to itself and set close to the top of the printing area, leaving conspicuous acres of white. This reverent framing might seem appropriate were the poems testaments of beauty or philosophical meditations, but, in the context of irritated snappings at poseurs, drunkards, misers, and misfits, it could be read as the poet's (or typographer's) gesture of contempt for pretension and poetry punters, or for himself as their hireling.

Harrison has never been a hack, but he has apostrophized himself as a busker. The first of the 'turns' in the poem of that name is the fatal 'turn' (attack of illness, or fit) of the poet's father, Mr Harry Harrison.

> Dad was sprawled beside the postbox (still VR),
> his cap turned inside up beside his head,
> smudged H A H in purple Indian ink
> and Brylcreem slicks displayed so folk might think
> he wanted charity for dropping dead.

The second is the son's 'turn' (act, performance) as a poet.[52]

> He never begged. For nowt! Death's reticence
> crowns his life's, and *me*, I'm opening my trap
> to busk the class that broke him for the pence
> that splash like brackish tears into our cap.[53]

Many of the 'School of Eloquence' sonnets compare the super-eloquent poet to his tongue-tied, reticent, or silenced forebears, and find him wanting. This self-accusation in the bitterness of grief could also be a variation of 'T. W.'s revenge', in which the poet this time enjoys the irony of his Château Lafitte's[54] being provided by the class which broke his ancestors. Harrison certainly speaks of himself as an independent thinker and writer, describing the production of political poetry in terms of a struggle to avoid being too comfortable either with himself or his audience: 'the moment I become "poet" in that unpoliti-cised way I am in collusion with the reader, and part of the struggle is not always to be in collusion'.[55] Whether or not the poem suggests an ambiguous attitude towards its readers, in performance Harrison's behaviour is neither that of an abusive alternative comedian nor a slavishly ingratiating turn busking for pennies. He is unfailingly courteous and self-deprecating, his stage presence powerful but projecting constraint. Both the poems and the performance suggest someone who is his own man, who signs his own words, resisting the oblivion to which are consigned those whose work remains anonymous, or who become a mouthpiece for others' words. 'The Earthen Lot'[56] compassionately describes stonemasons fated to nameless graves because they spent their lives building the dreams of their betters. In *Poetry or Bust*, John Nicholson rescinds his attack on the mill owners who employ child labour in return for the 'chink chink' of cash:

John Nicholson
In true sobriety, I wrote this poem that reviled
all those who had enslaved the Yorkshire child.

.   .   .   .

Edward Baines
                 Chink! Chink!
Chink! Chink! Chink! Chink! Chink!
Twenty guineas (Chink!), if you rewrite
your version of the factory children's plight
Couldn't you change your mind for a commission?

.   .   .   .

John Nicholson
Perhaps I did exaggerate. Thank you, Mr Baines.

And he is despised for it:

> **John Nicholson**
> Come on, lads, let's sing my drinking song!
> **Wool-sorter 5**
> Piss off, Nicholson, you don't belong.
> **Wool-sorter 2**
> You couldn't compose a song now if you tried.
> **Wool-sorter 3**
> You've long crossed over to the other side.[57]

Harrison writes only in 'my *name* and own voice'.[58]

By the early 1980s, Harrison's poetry was achieving consistent sales, and his work had been performed at the New York Metropolitan Opera, in the National Theatre, and on national radio and television.[59] His strong northern affiliations notwithstanding, he could not be seen as a 'local interest' poet. Like many other writers at this stage of his career, he appears to have found that he could no longer satisfactorily be served by small presses such as Northern House and Anvil Press. Faber and Faber took over the plays in 1985, and in 1984 Penguin became the publisher of the collected editions of both dramatic and other poetry. The move had symbolic as well as financial implications, representing an affiliation to a metropolitan publishing industry which Harrison had seemed until then to avoid. (Anvil Press, Rex Collings, and London Magazine Editions, though based in London, were all relatively small presses.) Harrison's work was now subject to 'poëbusiness', the nexus of production, distribution, promotion, evaluation, and criticism which depends upon and supports poetry, and the systems which accumulate at its margins (the reading circuits, small magazines, grants, writing schools, workshops, and other programmes). Nicolas Tredell reminds us that

Auden once remarked in a radio interview that a poem is a public object. We could add that its nature as a public object makes it always available to whatever systems of publicity exist at any given time, from the word-of-mouth of the coterie to the electronic waves of the modern media. But without those systems a poem will only be a public object ideally or potentially.[60]

'[D]espite the fact that the range of poetry has been diminished by the apparently effortless way that the mass media seem to depict reality',[61] Harrison's publishers needed to tap into those media in order to publicize, and thus make public, his poetry.

The cover of *Mysteries*, in Faber's house style of a small illustration on white, framed, on a background of the 'ff' logo, might have represented the end of Harrison's position as an independent writer indentured to no publisher and untrammelled by corporate image in book design or poetic content, but his books show signs that he has preserved his freedom. The covers of *Trackers* and *Chorus*, for example, are uniform editions, expensively designed, but not the standard Faber house style; *Black Daisies* has a photograph by the author, and the more recent *P3* has a photograph of Barrie Rutter in full Herakles cross-dressing kit.

The association with Neil Astley perhaps brought the work its most intensive packaging and marketing. Astley's attention to modes of (book) production is part of his policy of promoting a corporate image and creating brand-loyalty—establishing a market identity so strong that buyers will recognize, perhaps shop for, or impulse-buy, a Bloodaxe paperback as they do a Penguin or OUP edition.

Our intention was to present all our poetry books as bright, lively, contemporary, relevant, etc, but we've rejected the Faber-type uniform style approach in favour of individual designs for each book which still reflect a Bloodaxe image, with an emphasis on straightforward imagery, an imaginative use of colour, and clarity of type.[62]

He believes that this approach has been successful:

The end result is that the people responsible for ordering our books from sales reps order more copies . . . often books by authors they've never heard of, because the covers are such a draw. Once the books are on display in the shops, people are drawn to pick them up and browse them, and then you're half-way towards getting a sale.

Market-oriented design can generate profit, but if an audience is targeted, the product must fit it. Astley proudly recalls that 'One marketing person described Bloodaxe poetry books as "Waterstones-friendly" '—though perhaps that was not intended as an unqualified compliment. Book buyers do not necessarily make a conscious distinction between popular, down-market, and 'highbrow', up-market poetry, but too novel or over-finished designs, and 'witty' blurbs, can be counter-productive of sales of books which are perceived as inappropriate for such treatment. The Bloodaxe formula must be at least partially right because they have 'become Britain's fourth biggest poetry publisher; according to a recent market-ing report only Faber, Penguin and Oxford University Press achieve higher poetry sales'.[63]

Fire-Gap was issued in a limited edition by its designer, the fine-art printer Michael Christopher Caine, and by Bloodaxe in a trade edition which was described as a 'poster-book',[64] and which thus spans the cultural gap between fine-art/book and pop-art/mass-market paperback.[65] If those who relished the scholarliness of his translations of the work of the Alexandrian poet Palladas,[66] and the translation/adaptation of *Phaedra* and *The Oresteia*,[67] were scornful of the novelty value of a con-certina-folded poster-poem printed in the form of a snake, they would probably have seen it as consistent with the house style of Bloodaxe Books. The Bloodaxe logo, based on a medieval wood cut of the Viking chieftain, but cartoon-like in style; the overlapping upper-case Os and the ragged set of the lettering (artwork rather than type), suggest a less than highbrow, acad-emic, or up-market image. Few poets can grace the lists of both young, dynamic Bloodaxe Books and old, established Faber, fewer still write poetry which is not simply 'able to fit', but tailored for different media: poster, poster-book, pamphlet, private-press special edition, opera house, theatre, television, newspapers, and, soon, audio and video cassettes.[68] High and low, ephemeral and enduring, available to both football and classical drama fans.

Despite his resistance to branding, the strategies of poëbusiness had an effect upon Harrison's work during 1985–7. The first edition of *v.*, a poem written during the miners' strike of 1984, sold a reasonable but not spectacular 2,130 copies. The Channel 4 film of *v.* transmitted in November 1987 more than doubled the sales—or rather, the attempts to prevent transmission and the outrage following the transmission did (a controversy recollected by Melvyn Bragg in '*v.* by Tony Harrison'). The poem was included in the second edition of Penguin's *SP*, but was 'unavailable when all the publicity was happening'.[69] To take advantage of that hiatus, Bloodaxe Books could have produced a second impression of either their cloth or paper first editions of *v.*, or have reissued the book with a TV tie-in cover. Instead, they produced, in paperback only, a 'New edition: with press articles' which annotated the controversy surrounding the film.[70] Half of the first edition's fourteen black-and-white photographs by Graham Sykes were dropped to make room for thirty-five new items: tabloid abuse, disgusted letters, the House of Commons motion attacking the film, a piece by its director, Richard Eyre, even a transcript of the telephone calls logged by Channel 4's switchboard on the night *v.* was transmitted. As if to emphasize the significance of other texts to the reception of this one, the back-cover blurb is printed over a halftone collage of press cuttings.

The new edition of *v.* did not appear until 1989, thus missing the peak period of interest, and coinciding with the availability of the second edition of *SP*. Nor do any of the articles collected in the new edition, denunciatory or adulatory, mention the Bloodaxe editions at all. The journalists who do seem to be aware that the poem was a book before it was a film script plug *SP*. The first publication of *v.* in the *London Review of Books*[71] was almost overlooked, and the critical notice it had generated was ignored in favour of the furore generated by the IBA's decision to allow the film to be transmitted.[72] The inclusion of the pieces in the new edition is not, therefore, the calculated cashing-in on notoriety that it might seem, since the articles generated no publicity for Bloodaxe. Once in the shops, however, with some public recollection of the row, the Bloodaxe edition stood a better chance of profiting from the exposure than the Penguin *SP*, simply because of the large blue V on its cover. Penguin did not put a flash on their cover: 'Contains the controversial poem *v.*', but they did use a Graham Sykes photograph of Beeston Hill Cemetery, where the poem is set, suggesting that the image is central to Harrison's work, and they did put a notice of the poem's presence on the back cover[73] with a quotation from a review.[74]

Penguin's efforts notwithstanding, 2,204 copies of the Bloodaxe new edition were sold, followed by a further 2,496 copies of its second edition in 1991. The total sales of the second (with press articles) edition (4,700) are lower only than those of *Gorgon*, a TV film tie-in, and winner of the 1992 Whitbread Poetry Book of the Year Award.[75]

In a piece on his part in the making of the film of *v.*, Richard Eyre wrote:

If I had the slightest influence over educational policy in this country, I'd see that v. was a set text in every school in the country, but of course if we lived in that sort of country, the poem wouldn't have needed to be written.[76]

Though not a set text, Harrison's poetry was already on the A-level syllabus of the Joint Matriculation Board when the film of *v.* was transmitted; in 1988 eleven schools in the North-east were reported as having an A-level syllabus which included work by Harrison; and a number of secondary schools in the region which do not set the poem for examinations do read it in class.[77] Harrison has reached GCE (Grand Child Eliminator[78] or Great Canon Entrance). As his Voltaire says, he has

> heard bigots rant, rave and revile
> books of mine which, after a short while
> were canonized as classics.[79]

—and in Harrison's case the reviling and canonizing are simultaneous, as the *Daily Mail* reported:

A Tory MP is demanding an inquiry after teenagers were required to study an A-level text full of obscenities. David Sumberg labelled a collection of poems by Tony Harrison as 'crude, obscene and offensive' [. . . .] He said 'It goes to the root of what our children should be studying in preparation for their future lives.' [. . .] Gordon Dickerson [Harrison's agent] said 'He is [. . .] regarded as one of the finest writers in the English language'.[80]

Though not, perhaps, a best-seller (the term has no absolute criteria, but, like 'canonicity', is a function of difference), *Gorgon* did better than its predecessor, *Coming*, which by 1993 had sold 2,728 copies from a print run of 4,600. It also had a limited edition of thirty-eight copies signed by the author, of which twenty-eight were sold or given away. The title poem 'is his [Harrison's] response to the news photograph of a charred Iraqi soldier on the road to Basra',[81] which is reproduced on the cover. Harrison's signature on a copy of the special edition of *Coming* could be perceived as the affixing of his mark to the poetic *J'accuse*; the counterpart to his printed name's function as a journalistic byline in the first publication of the title poem in the news pages of the *Guardian*. But an author's signature on a special collectors' edition of a book illustrated with a photograph of a real person burned to death could also seem hideously inappropriate. The shocking cover is part of the price which Harrison exacts from 'poetry supporters' who buy such books. He has said that when he is 'conscious of satisfying the literate, cultured reader of poetry [. . .] I know that my next temptation is to take away his satisfaction by evoking the ghosts of the inarticulate, and by quoting them in the scale against poetry'.[82]

It is to be hoped that there will be no *Collected Poems* in the foreseeable future, or, should a publisher persuade Harrison to prepare such a work, that, like Robert Graves, he will swiftly make each new collection redundant. Penguin's *SP* is another matter, convenient for readers, making available poems otherwise out of print, and juxtaposing poems from several different volumes in an edition which is portable and (relatively) cheap to replace. The second edition of *SP*, augmented by several new poems, not only *v.*, but also the longer 'American' poems such as 'Cypress and Cedar' and 'Following Pine', is indispensable, and the edition used throughout this collection, except where contributors refer to poems not collected, or published after *SP*.

Bloodaxe 1 has been the critical counterpart to *SP*, its size and weight an index of the attention Harrison's poems had received by 1991. Despite Harrison's determinedly irreverent preface, more than fifty articles attest to both the seriousness of that attention and the serious matter which critics found to consider. The metonymy of canonization has occurred: 'Harrison' now stands for 'Tony Harrison's texts, and the text that is Tony Harrison', objects which can be interpreted, evaluated, explained, and taught by 'Oxford's anointed'.[83] Though Harrison's gaze in the author photograph on the front cover is direct, and his dress rumpled and casual, his portrayal, not in the flesh-tints of four-colour, but the remove of two-, makes him a product.[84] The stance and the blue-grey halftones are suggestive of earlier volumes of respectful admiration, perhaps Martin Seymour-Smith's biography of Robert Graves,[85] whose subject was predominantly blue and camera-gazing on the cover. The photograph is cropped at the sides so that Harrison fills the visible frame and continues into another which is invisible to the reader—nicely Harrisonian—but I wonder whether Harrison approved the cropping of the bottom half, which cuts off his hands and genitals—surely, from the evidence of the poems, not parts of himself which the author would consider negligible? Harrison responds to this canonization and objectification by reiterating the traditional verse which had appeared as the epigraph to *Loiners*:

> *There was a young man of Leeds*
> *Who swallowed a packet of seeds.*
> *A pure white rose grew out of his nose*
> *And his arse was covered with weeds.*[86]

Genuflect to this poetry at your peril.

Periodicals and newspapers have provided the first public airing of much of Harrison's non-dramatic verse, and circumvented the lengthy processes of book production to provide the quick response of 'journalistic' poetry in reaction to current affairs, for example the miners' strike (*v.*) and the Gulf War (*Coming*).[87] The context of 'Deathwatch Danceathon'[88] in a national daily newspaper (though not within the news pages) might lead us to expect another hard-hitting and passionate engagement with war, violence, and death. When the occasion of the poem is seen to be allegations of royal infidelity, and the poem itself no terse, economical statement but 154 lines of juggling with the activities of the death-watch beetle, perhaps the frustration of expectations is more severe than if the poem had been encountered in a book. Just as certain expectations are set up by the *Guardian*'s informing readers that 'Deathwatch Danceathon' is the first of a series of poems on 'current themes', so the body of Harrison's work, for those who know it, generates certain preconceptions which make this poem seem anomalous. While superficially akin to the mordant misanthropy and irony of *Palladas* or *U.S. Martial*, and utilizing many of the familiar devices (to the extent of self-parody), 'Deathwatch Danceathon' is different. Not only is its wit turned on straw targets, but its political point might seem to be masked by its catalogue of synonyms for beetle, and by its series of connections equating beetles' tapping with the pulse, the ticking of time that leads to death, and the beat of a line of poetry. The theme is linked to the stated subject-matter in the closing stanzas:

> spurned, pampered Princess, squire in spurs,
> and as fourposter bedposts rock
> we hear the deathwatch: knock. . .knock. . .knock. . .
> and though too gentle for the axe
> quicker than Anna Pasternak's.

But as beheading is not a likely outcome, even of royal divorce, and the nation is not 'divided' between Prince/Princess supporters or advocates of 'they should/they shouldn't', in the sense that it was divided by the Civil War, the correspondence might seem trivializing. Instead of developing the theme of

> the tapping crown
> of cruising bug brings churches down

into time and scandals perhaps bringing down the crown, Harrison looks at 'Their "grubby passion", his and hers', and the rocking of the bed. Had the poem appeared in an 'occasional' or 'light verse' series, this might not have mattered. In this context, however, the association of the poem's style and themes with large headlines, editorial advertisement, author photograph, and biographical notes make the poet seem closer to one of the royal *paparazzi* than to political journalists. And that, surely, is the point. One division in still-divided Britain is between writers who see the public as morons who can under-

stand public events only in terms of soap, and who need only
regular fixes of prurient tabloid titillation to remain conveniently passive, and writers who want to preserve 'the urgency
of what poems say', even though they are acutely aware that
the beat of time will wipe it away. Harrison is quite prepared to
make a straightforward declaration of republican principles, as
he demonstrated in 'A Celebratory Ode on the Abdication of
King Charles III' published in the *Guardian* the following
January. 'Deathwatch Danceathon' is not a judgement on the
morality of princes, however, but an anthem on urgency: *carpe
diem*. The poem's reiterations reinforce its rhythm; they are
about and *are* the pulse which is the measure of life; both all
vitality and its limit:

> Everywhere there is a measure
> heard or unheard of our pleasure.

Poetry, then, becomes the manifestation of this beat; associated
with the blood's pulse and the heart's beat which represent our
striving to live to the last possible moment, and our awareness
of the limited span of life, an awareness which, in Harrison's
poetry, gives zest to life.

> The momentum of this very verse
> drums up the stretcher and the hearse,
> a beat that comes from long before
> the King-beheading Civil War
> divided still divided Britain
> and Andrew Marvell's poem got written.
>
> .   .   .   .   .   .
>
> the metred couplet with its rhyme
> revels in and coasts on time

Harrison's poems for the *Guardian* became more obviously
concerned with current affairs when the paper sent him to
Bosnia, but 'The Bright Lights of Sarajevo' and 'The Cycles of
Donji Vakuf'[89] still refuse to separate public and private, political and personal. The former describes youthful courtship rituals in Sarajevo, the latter victorious Muslims triumphantly
bearing aloft bicycles and other gifts for their children. There is
nothing trite or sentimental about either of these poems. The
Sarajevans' 'flirtatious ploys' take place in unlit streets pot-
holed by mortar shells, and the soldiers' gifts are looted from

Serbian children. Harrison spares us no details of the recent fighting:

> they stand
> on two shell scars, where in 1992
> Serb mortars massacred the breadshop queue
> and blood-dunked crusts of shredded bread
> lay on this pavement with the broken dead.[90]

Neither, however, does he pretend that war is ever total, either in the joy of victory or the misery of suffering. 'The Cycles of Donji Vakuf' is full of people smiling, feeling 'tall', 'happy', 'glad', as well as a child 'with all his gladness gutted', and 'The Bright Lights of Sarajevo' is as full of the urgency of sex and love as 'Deathwatch Danceathon', in spite, if not because, of the closeness of death.

As Harrison's poetry has entered the public sphere, so the poet himself has evolved into a public (as well as private) figure, well known from interviews, readings on stage and radio, appearances in and voice-overs for television films, and his photographic byline as a war correspondent sending back the poetic equivalent of stills from the front (a subject discussed by Alan Rusbridger in 'Tony Harrison and the *Guardian*'). The poet, as much as his poetry, embodies contradictions. Former editor of literary magazines,[91] former president of the Classical Association,[92] polyglot,[93] recipient of many literary prizes and awards, he resists all forms of incorporation to remain a *metoikos*, a foreigner permitted to live in the city-state and observe its customs, but not a native-born citizen, with all the privileges and blind spots which that entails. Harrison's Loiners resemble the *metoikoi* of Greek city-states (residents without the rights of natives); characters divided from one another, and within. These are not simple restatements of the post-structuralist destabilization of the *esse* and displacement of the unique, autonomous individual. Their sense of self is strong, however divided, but they are dispossessed from the very things which, for most people, constitute the sense of self: origin; family; language; culture; rights. Whether citizens of Leeds, expats, nameless travellers, or the narrative 'I', they are internal aliens within insecure communities clotted together by conformity against the threat of outside; often with strong affiliations, but at home nowhere. A Loiner may be dispossessed by politics, economics, or other extrinsic forces, but the resultant change which alienates him from his roots is internal. Harrison does not allow himself the dramatic licence of glorifying or romanticizing those roots. A Loiner's Eden, whether physical place or group of people and their outlook, is usually imperfect, and his feelings about it ambivalent. That was another country, and the man who belonged there is dead, or does not wish to return, but he feels the absence, the disconnection. Like Marvell's, Harrison's poetry is often 'a fugue on separation and connection'.[94] He interweaves the voices of his Loiners with many others: ancestors and role models, harriers and oppressors; always questioning, always undercutting. (See Martyn Crucefix, 'The Drunken Porter Does Poetry'.)

Loiners are no more idealized than their backgrounds. Harrison's central characters (usually male) are characteristically embattled, anguished, neither wholly admirable nor whole-heartedly wicked. The White Queen, 'Professor! Poet! Provincial Dadaist!', is also 'Pathic, pathetic, half-blind and half-pissed'.[95] Witty, perceptive, especially about his fellow colonial expats, and outrageous, he is yet capable of sensitivity:

> I touched her bosom gently just to show
> I *could* acknowledge gestures, but couldn't stroke
> Her leathery, dry skin and cracked a joke
> Against myself about my taste in little boys.[96]

He is also capable of self-knowledge:

> What's the use? I can't escape
> Our foul conditioning that makes a rape
> Seem natural, if wrong, and love unclean
> Between some ill-fed blackboy and fat queen.[97]

None the less, he is as culturally imperialist as his masters, fucking Africans as they fucked Africa. He professes love, but buys sex, in straightforward transactions when he hires frightened black boys, once 'better', with a man who is described in loving lasciviousness:

Things can be so much better. Once at least
A million per cent. Policeman! Priest!
You'll call it filthy, but to me it's love,
And to him it was. It *was*. O he could move
Like an oiled (slow-motion) racehorse at its peak,
Outrageous, and not gentle, tame or meek—
O magnificently shameless in his gear,
He sauntered the flunkied restaurant, queer
As a clockwork orange and not scared.
God, I was grateful for the nights we shared.
My boredom melted like small cubes of ice
In warm sundowner whiskies. Call it vice;
Call it obscenity; it's love; so there;
Call it what you want. *I just don't care.*

This lover's inferior status in the unequal relationship is, however, indexed by the Queen's ventriloquial protest. The white
man narrates this story; the hegemony of the narrative voice
enables him to attribute thoughts and feelings to the characters
with whom he populates his anecdotes, just as his coins give
him the power to manipulate the actions of the rent boys. (For
an exploration of the antecedents of this poem, see Sandie
Byrne, 'On Not Being Milton, Marvell, or Gray'.)

You'll call it filthy, but to me it's love,
And to him it was. It *was*.

The Queen's description of true love, however, turns into
another chapter of self-dramatization:

I come back raddled to the campus bar
And shout out how I laid a big, brute
Negro in a tight, white cowboy suit.[98]

This paradoxically self-centred polyvalency is characteristic of
the Harrison subject. The reference to Wyatt's sonnet ['They fle
from me'][99] is perhaps a clue to a reading of 'The White Queen',
and the Queen himself. Though at first we share the narrator's
bitterness, sympathizing with the steadfast lover against the
newfangled, changeable woman in her 'straunge fasshion of
forsaking', on a second reading we might wonder whether the
two are so neatly opposed as victim and perpetrator, hero and
villainess. We realize that the narrator is reproaching the
woman for ceasing 'to take bred' from his hands, and thus provide the occasions when for him it was 'twenty tymes better'

and for her, and perhaps him as well, there was danger. In spite
of this evident self-centredness it is the lover in his erotic reverie
and unheroic desire for revenge who is the centre and unseen
focus of the poem, while the woman, powerful though her
image is, remains a wraith of his remembrance. Harrison handles our sympathies as skilfully as Wyatt. When the Queen
shouts 'And to him it was. It *was*' he protests too much—
almost—just as when Wyatt's narrator insists: 'It was no dream.
I lay broad waking', though he is clearly convincing himself: we
do believe him, or at least believe that he believes it.

Greek tragedy gives Harrison further source material for this
kind of characterization, both compromised hero (Orestes) and
semi-justified villain (Medea). The nearest thing to a hero in the
satyr play *Trackers* is the communal characters of the satyrs, but
their leader, Silenus, could be said to stand for them all.[100] His
final speech shows him in an ignominious light:

> I didn't mind a bit of inferior status
> as long as there was Bacchus to inebriate us.
> I didn't mind a bit of lowly forelock-tugging
> as long as it went with retsina-glugging.
> To social inequality I turned a blind eye
> if that guaranteed the liquor supply.
> Some sort of pattern seemed to exist,
> get a bit pissed on then go and get pissed.
> I didn't mind conniving with gods and their greed
> if my modest wants were guaranteed.
> Unlike my poor flayed brother, Marsyas,
> I never yearned to move out of my class.
> Better we satyrs stay where we are
> with Bacchus at least there's a buckshee bar.
>
> .   .   .   .
>
> So don't make waves, boys. Don't rock the boat.
> And add up the pluses of being man/goat.[101]

If the Delphi text gives a faint impression of authorial self-
disgust, echoing Harrison's self-accusation in 'Turns',[102] in the
National Theatre text, at the foot of a palpable ladder of aspiration, Silenus achieves near-heroic stature. His slightly more
sophisticated language, and the honesty with which he faces
his limitations, including his own fatalism, make him a less
comic, and, though he denies it, more tragic figure:

> We've all served our time with that weight on our heads
> but no satyr ever trod where tragedy treads.
> God, heroes and kings are all who walk there,
> high and low divided just by a stair.
> This is my big chance. But I don't dare.
> A lifetime's conditioning makes me refrain
> from attempting, a satyr, the high tragic strain.
> A lifetime's conditioning makes me afraid
> that to step a rung higher will get misself flayed.
> And I'd never know the right words to speak
> after 2000 years I've forgotten my Greek.[103]

Scotty Scott, hunchbacked Victorian comic and the Prince of Wales's sycophant, victim, and (would-be) murderer, achieves a similar status in the more recent *The Prince's Play*.

William Empson highlights the significance of this kind of ambivalent hero, 'outside society because too poor for its benefits', and thus 'independent, as the artist claims to be'. He

can be a judge of the society that judges him. This is a source of irony both against him and against the society, and if he is a sympathetic criminal he can be made to suggest both Christ as the scapegoat [. . .] and the sacrificial tragic hero, who was normally above society rather than below it, which is a further source of irony.[104]

On the outskirts of their respective societies, Silenus and his satyrs, the skinhead of *v.*, and the Luddites of 'On Not Being Milton' are dispossessed from their benefits. They do, to an extent, express their judgement of the societies which judge them. Other of Harrison's characters, Patience Kershaw and Thomas Campey, for example, can only judge implicitly, through their lives as described to us. They do not articulate their grievance and judgement, through aggressive acts or words, because their dispossession has extended to (recorded) language. Less ambiguous than the satyrs, they belong in the same category because they are both oppressed and dispossessed. Harrison, dispossessed from a class which was itself dispossessed, takes on the task of voicing their social judgement.

The characters based on historically documented people are similarly drawn. The guests invited to dine at Harrison's table in the Omar Khayyam restaurant had little in common but their blasphemy, or scepticism, and their shadowy identities.

We cannot be certain who and what they were, not only because their stories come via many hands, not all of them reliable, but also because the facts we do have do not add up to clear portraits of either hero or villain but could be either or both. All of the guests, alive or dead, were, however, outside their respective cultural norms. All, seen from this side of history, resist categorization. The connection between Harrison and the other blasphemers, Bruce Woodcock writes, is that 'they were writers on and from the margins',[105] but in his first example he touches upon something more significant. He describes 'Rushdie, with his contradictory Indian-Muslim and English public school background, all of which he has "rejected" in a certain sense, and with his current "outlaw" status'. Although the others are described as straightforward protesters ('Molière, who was buried with no religious rites for refusing to abjure the stage; Voltaire, persecuted for his enlightened godless rationalism'), the common link between them is not simply that they are 'renegades against bigoted holiness' but that they had conflicting interests and divided loyalties. They embodied polarities: margin and centre, orthodoxy and heresy, privilege and dispossession, but polarities in confusion. Voltaire, denouncer of religious bigots and corrupt monarchs, but also author of fawning flattery; Molière, satirist and comedian of manners, accused of irreligion, but a beneficiary of royal patronage; Lord Byron, satirist, freedom fighter, and freethinker, but also aristocrat, self-dramatist, and misanthrope; Omar Khayyam, mathematician, astronomer, and famous agnostic poet, or, the counter-argument runs, no poet, but mere anthologizer. The respective identities are complex, oppositional, but also indeterminate—'outside' even a definitive persona. There are no unambiguous heroes in Harrison's work; only victims and protagonists—agents of *agon*—Loiners.

Even in his most apparently unambiguous avatar, Harrison himself is projected as one of his own dubious heroes. 'The Heartless Art', an offering to and in memory of an American neighbour, Seth Tooke, might be expected to depict the poet in an uncomplicatedly positive light—in loving remembrance, in grief, in anguish at witnessed suffering, in friendship. Harrison promises:

> I'll show you to distract you from the pain
> you feel, except when napping, all the time
> because you won't take drugs that dull the brain,
> a bit about my metre, line and rhyme[106]—

and begins:

> In Arthur Symons' *St Teresa* Nazaréth
> is stressed on the last against its spoken flow
> to engineer the contrast Jesus/Death.

Instead of explaining the significance of stressed and unstressed syllables, however, he breaks off from metrics to discuss the content of the line, or more specifically, his feelings about and opinion of its meaning:

> Do I endorse the contrast? I don't, no!
> To have a life on Earth and then want Heaven
> seems like that all-night bar sign down below
> that says that *Happy Hour*'s from 4 to 7.

We never are given insights into Harrison's 'engineering'. A lesson in the craft of poetry is abandoned in favour of the explanation that its practice involves the earmarking of material, including people, for future use, as when the narrator first learned the name of his neighbour, and 'stored away this rhyme'. Such a demystification of poetic composition would not necessarily offend, but the poem's 'I' not only explains the process but reveals, in the language of direct address to his dying friend:

> that stored rhyme
> that has the same relentlessness as death
> and comes to every one of us in time
> and comes to you this April full moon, SETH!

The bumptious, almost comic relish for the rhyme, and for the ingenuity of the poet in achieving it, which is suggested by the capitalization and exclamation mark, is distasteful in the extreme, especially as until the reader reaches the last stanza s/he does not realize that the direct address is a fiction within a fiction, and Seth Tooke, at least within the context of the poem, was never shown it. The narrative 'I' hesitates, not because the line is in dubious taste, but because

> The last thing the dying want to read,
> I thought, 's a poem, and didn't show it.[107]

The first two stanzas depict the poet in heroic attitudes: protecting delicate plants; taking part in communal rituals of husbandry; milking the day of its last drop because it will be the last day of his friend; pitting his vigour against the fast-coming dark, the looming abyss, significantly filling a hole (which had been cleared by Seth). Stanzas three to five exhibit his sensitivity to his friend's pride and pain. The appalling sixth stanza reveals anti-heroic traits, not the intellect which enables the 'I' to calculate the effect of a rhyme and make matter of a dying friend—that characteristic is offset by its coexistence with the evident tenderness and respect for that friend—but the self-congratulation and self-centredness of the artist absorbed in his art. The direct address and slow pace,

> by finally revealing that stored rhyme
> that has the same relentlessness as death
> and comes to every one of us in time
> and comes to you this April full moon,[108]

leads up to that comma, which foregrounds the final name like a punchline—boom!—a capitalized, depersonalized, objectified signifier: SETH! (pause for laughter/applause). In this, Harrison seems callous. The heartless art, poetic composition (or Harrison's version of it), with its dramatic tensions and oppositions, precludes simple virtues. The straightforward hero of the opening stanzas is turned to show other sides, other aspects, and like many of his other creations, the PWD man, the White Queen, Silenus, 'Tony Harrison' is shown to be composed of 'opposing valencies':

> But he was a poet and he'd probably follow,
> when it came to the crunch, the laws of Apollo.

Several contributors to *Bloodaxe 1* link the names of Tony Harrison and Richard Hoggart, and Ken Worpole takes one of Hoggart's chapters, 'Scholarship Boy', as the title of his piece.[109] While it might be tempting to regard Harrison as typifying Hoggart's 'scholarship boy', and thus to see the divisions in the poet's persona as products of the scholarship system—the result of the pressures upon those in transit from the working class to a 'declassed' state—neither Harrison nor Hoggart closely resembles the exam-obsessed, lonely plodder of Hoggart's book, and that notional character the scholarship boy is himself a generalized abstraction. The sense of hopelessness, cynicism, and alienation described in Hoggart's anecdotes and analyses of the states of mind of those whom education has made upwardly mobile might be excerpts from a parody of the 'modernist angst' text.[110] Harrison's sense of alienation is, however, more than mourning for an undissociated past, or educated distaste for the populist. Aware that the school of eloquence which enabled him to articulate social division was also a safety-valve for directing the articulate working-class child into the harmless channels of art, he came round to his father's position on the arts, for a time. He also harnessed his anger and his education to produce, among other things, the powerful indictment of linguistic, artistic, and social division which was staged in two temples of high art, the ancient stadium at Delphi and the National Theatre in London.[111] The catch is that the protest is part of the problem. The medium which exposes the cultural hegemony is a product of it when 'I put it down in poems, that's the bind',[112] and the one responsible for 'breaking the chain' of ancestry, class, and city has only the 'dividers' of eloquence and education with which to articulate his fragile sense of 'one continuous US'.[113] Christopher Butler considers these questions in 'Culture and Debate'.

While the mass reproduction of film removes the aura of elitism from a work of art, and makes it, potentially, the property of all, it also fixes a text for mutable or ephemeral works, and, Harrison suggests, robs the audience of a vital experience, because 'the current obsession with televising and videoing stage performances almost inevitably undermines the true nature of the theatrical'.[114] In this spirit, the company of *Trackers* 'prevented three rather peeved TV crews from filming what we then thought would be the first and final perfor-'mance'. Harrison, of course, writes for television and film, and is acutely aware of how few can afford to attend play productions in Carnuntum, Delphi, and elsewhere. But no celluloid can transmit the excitement and risk of his one-off staging. He notes: '[h]ow differently the energies of performer and audience are concentrated if they know there is only one chance to give or receive the occasion', and reanimates the spirit in which 'the papyrus of the ancient play [*Trackers*] was in that version literally destroyed by fire'.[115] Private and public recordings, published scripts, and the schools' selection of his work[116] may eventually make all Harrison texts available for editing, analysis, and assimilation into canon, but their author is a playwright as well as a writer of plays, and his productions will always have qualities which defy reproduction. *P3* collects three poems written for particular spaces and particular occasions, and Jonathan Silver writes about the fruitful association of Harrison and Salt's Mill in 'Poetry or Bust'.

Like the plays, the non-dramatic works are being hailed 'as classics', but if 'they' try to preserve Harrison beneath deep permaverse, no doubt he will resist. This collection neither canonizes nor buries with valedictory praise. It salutes Harrison at sixty, in mid-stride; bard and Loiner, scholar and satyr, playwright, film-maker, director, performer; always and only, poet.

1

The Best Poet of 1961

DESMOND GRAHAM

IT was the bullfrogs' mating season. I was newly arrived as an Assistant Lecturer and in that colonial way, just one year from my BA, was invited to give a lecture to the English Association of Rhodesia and Nyasaland on 'Poetry in England Today'. For an hour I put the whole of poetry in perspective, told them, chapter and verse, what to read and look for. I knew. I had been there, in the centre of poetry, and for all my modesty knew what the real thing was! It was hot and humid. That was why the bullfrogs were mating. Beside the lecture hall with all its windows open for the breath of air was an ornamental pond. Throughout my lecture the frogs roared, and as I held to my theme with more and more intensity, so the frogs roared the louder. Over, through, and beyond them, I disposed of Eliot—what had he given to poetry in the past eighteen years (almost the whole of my lifetime)? I disposed of Auden in a sentence or two. I patronized Graves; had great fun with the indulgent comfy 'Movement'; mentioned the Mavericks and Thomas Blackburn, Ted Hughes (a bit excessive), Gael Turnbull and R. S. Thomas, and proved the inadequacy of the supposedly current view of contemporary poetry—'How can I dare to feel?' indeed. I was ready to say then who were the writers people should take note of in this outpost where they wore dinner jackets to go to the cinema, and were mostly as racist as hell. Writers who felt, writers who didn't trivialize—like Jon Silkin in his 'Death of a Son', like Geoffrey Hill in his recent *For the Unfallen*, like one or two others maybe, but above all, like Tony Harrison.

The next day, the colleague whose intelligence I most valued, John Reed, drove round, bewildered but quite positive, in hope of reassurance. 'I enjoyed the lecture . . . but why did you make so much of Tony Harrison? Who is he?' So I played him a tape I had of Tony reading the poem I had made the centrepiece of my conclusion, 'The Flat Dweller's Revolt'. 'Just listen,' and I sat back and enjoyed the proof of my conviction. John had that confusion of someone who feels outside something someone else has discovered and wants genuinely to share, but at the same time comes with a feeling of superiority and exclusion. He was puzzled, bewildered, and we left it at that.

Now, having looked at the poem for the first time after thirty-four years, I want to do what I couldn't do then; to prove why Tony Harrison was the greatest poet of 1961: at the beginning, no doubt, but at the beginning of things only he was doing and he was doing with mastery. But first a word on how Tony Harrison had discovered me.

Between 1959 and 1960, as a graduate student researching on translations of Virgil, Tony edited *Poetry and Audience*. As a student within the Classics Department, and as a Postgrad, he was inevitably outside the snug community of the undergraduates' English Department, where Wilson Knight would pop in for a chat and hand round Woodbines while we stapled five hundred copies of the magazine every Thursday afternoon. Fridays we sold *P & A*, as it was called, at tables in the Union and the Parkinson Building, the main building of the university. Meanwhile, the magazine's Secretary (a science student, I believe, when Tony was Editor) sent out about a hundred copies to our subscribers—it cost one penny (about ½p) for its weekly eight folded sheets of poems. Between about ten in the morning and one-thirty or two we sold perhaps three hundred copies. The Secretary then took the proceeds to the bank (about £1 5/0 [£1.25] in pennies), and we went to the pub till three. On Saturday mornings we had the Editorial Board meeting, in the *P & A* room in the department. There, Tony sat in the Editor's chair (*it* had arms and an intact seat); we went over the poems which had come in and we each had marked with initials for the next issue. Then off to The Eldon to drink till three, with the man in the passage between the lounge and the bar who if you crossed him would aver: 'I'll see you in Lawnswood'—he worked in the crematorium there. And in the evenings the Eldon's other spirit, Lotte, after a half or two would fix you in the eye and sing deep into your soul: *'I only have eyes for you'*.

During my second year as an English student, as just about the only newcomer who had shown hard-working interest and had produced poems which the magazine printed, I was brought on to the *P & A* board by Tony. The system was simple: an Editor lasted a year, chose his own committee, and ran everything, but then, like Cinderella or a mayfly, he had to hand over. His last act of power was to choose his successor, who in turn would choose his own board, and had the single year. There was a snag. Hugh Dalwood, the Gregory Artist-in-Residence, had made a wonderful sculpture for *P & A*, inscribing on the back that this was to remain for one year the property of the Editor on condition that he would not sell it but pass it to his successor. In the event of the magazine collapsing, it was to be sold and the proceeds spent entirely on drink. I, then, had the awkward task of going to Tony's flat to remove the sculpture for the duration of my editorship.

Tony was a hero and a friend, though more a hero—because of the way he could write: he rhymed, he used strict forms, and yet wrote passionately. He already carried a great past which he would talk about, the time of the former Gregory Fellow in Poetry, Thomas Blackburn, an influence on all of them in Leeds at the time, and Tony's friends, now left, James Simmons and Barry Cryer. With John Hearsum he would go to the Union Bar for the Saturday night Hop. Alan Page, quiet and self-contained, who contributed beautiful, strange poems to the magazine, was an equal. Jane Barr (I discovered only recently she had shared with Tony a schooling in Leeds) was a highly sophisticated female presence on the magazine's board. But I, within that stratified world of students, three years younger, only second/third-year, was of a different generation. In any case, Tony was already very much his own man. He had no interest in a following. However, I was it. His opinion mattered, his misanthropic pronouncements, his misogynistic challenges to girls, his declaration that he would die young—which seemed inevitable to me, given his talent and his way of life, his combining of a morbid, deathly dark humour and a personal warmth, kindness, and generosity which made him a figure of note, of charisma.

He was way ahead—or maybe I was just way behind—talking of Dryden and Gavin Douglas as translators (his research topic), but more often of Casaubon as doleful warning, of *The Heart of Darkness*, often of Joyce and the tower and Dublin, which sounded the place where life and freedom were, of Rimbaud and Baudelaire, of Beckett (especially of *Waiting for Godot*), and often of *The Brothers Karamazov*, *The Idiot*, and *The Possessed*: all perfect texts for him—obsession and intellect and sex; obsession and corruption and Africa; waiting for no God, but with plenty of mordant commentary on His absence and the pains He inflicted; the outcast, freed, peripatetic urban outsider, companionable intellectual Irishman, Joyce; the Dostoevsky of impossible dilemmas.

Marvell's 'To His Coy Mistress' was probably the most famous and most remembered poem at that time, and it was most definitely Tony's poem. Its worms and virginities and graves; its fatalism and anger you couldn't be quite sure about; its impenetrably black Yorkshire sense of humour—or was it all dead straight after all? Its control and power through the perfecting of verse. Tony's one concession to being social was to 'do' his T. S. Eliot, and we used to get him to favour us with this—or maybe some of his board humoured him with it—at editorial meetings. Tony would borrow glasses, perch them on the tip of his nose, sit back in his editorial chair, take up a book, and recite some Eliot, making it sound even more gloomy, caustic, and superior than Eliot could manage himself.

Tony read 'The Flat Dweller's Revolt' (notice the singular) for a programme I had been invited to set up for BBC Home Service North, in Leeds, in the spring of 1961, one of three on 'Northern Universities' Poetry'. I asked him for the poem for *P & A*, and it appeared there. It was included in his Northern House pamphlet of 1964, *Earthworks* (published, like his poems in *P & A*, under 'T. W.', not 'Tony' Harrison), but has not been included in subsequent collections of his work and as it is difficult to obtain now, I have printed it in full at the end of the chapter.[1] Tony, then, may not be too pleased with my resurrecting it here. It is in some senses untypical of his work at that time. Beside the other poems in *P & A* and *Ew*, it is comparatively simple and emotionally open, and carries more disturbance than power. Perhaps I specially liked it because it seemed to be Tony's less guarded voice, or because I wanted this to be his less guarded voice? In any case, I believe its positive impulses, its affirmation, however surrounded by ironies, reminds us of the current which underlies the creative anger and wit of much of his writing. This may not be what he often wrote about, but it is what he is writing from.

The poem is a plea for fertility, an implicit rewriting of *The Waste Land* forty years on. My main task here, however, is to demonstrate the poem's mastery of its art.

> Dogs in mangers feel, he thought, like this;
> He cast bread on the pavement for the birds.
> Their claustrophobic voices, hers and his,
> Their guarded actions louder than their words,
>
> The booming, morning wind brought back tenfold

The quatrains of the poem will be in iambic pentameter, that rising pattern of unstress/stress most common in English poetry. Yet the very first line announces a different form, a falling pattern from stress to unstress (for simplicity, I will italicize stressed syllables): '*Dogs* in/ *man*gers/ *feel*'. So we have two reversed feet, trochees, not iambs. Tony was to do the same in the start to his now justly famous 'Book Ends I':[2] '*Baked* the/ *day* she', two falling feet, trochees, which also lead to a line of nine not ten syllables. I will come back to that opening later.

The opening syllables of 'The Flat Dweller's Revolt' pause on 'feel', drawing attention to that word and accommodating the change of rhythm which will take place in the second half of the line. There we will have two rising feet, iambs—'he *thought*,/ like *this*'. Pronouns are crucial to the interplay of metre and rhythm, and are often difficult to measure with certainty. Here, however, the pattern and pause of the metre encourage stress to fall on 'thought' rather than 'he', and through this stress 'meaning' is artfully negotiated. The emphasis is shifted from doubt—*he* thought this, it was his idea though it may not be true—to a statement of what he was doing—he was engaged in thought—and a sympathetic realization—so, dogs felt like this. The metre of the final foot in turn confirms the emphasis: he felt 'like *this*'. Identification is completed. The focus is on how the person felt, the 'he' which in the course of the poem's intimacies reads very much as a distanced 'I'.

Such skills and catches can be tedious to read about because one must slow everything down so. But what Harrison's handling of the metre has already helped to do is establish the subject and location of the poem. *His* thoughts are the subject and their concern is with his feelings. The poem will be a narrative of emotions felt through and meditated on at a specific moment in a specific place—like Coleridge's 'Dejection', or Keats's Odes thinking of birds not born for death, or Urns defying mortality—it will be a Romantic Ode. Yet its rhetorically patterned syntax and metre will, in the language of the early sixties, be classical.

Coupled with the play of metre, rhythm, and syntax, within this meditation Harrison plays on the contrast between more and less elevated modes of thought, more intimate and more general ideas, more commonplace and more special locations. So, in the second line, 'He' didn't throw bread to the birds, but 'cast bread on the pavement for the birds.' In that 'cast' there are echoes of Jesus, perhaps, of pearls before swine, of seed sown, of bread rather more significant than this. Yet the action itself is no more than a gesture, the hand moving to do something because the mind and consciousness are so trapped, and the pavement is very much in Leeds, as we shall see.

Within this line there is also another important metrical issue. One can make an iambic pentameter of it—'He *cast*/ bread *on*/ the *pave*/ment *for*/ the *birds*'—but this is rather awkward. Stress would have to fall on 'on' rather than on 'bread', and on the comparatively insignificant word 'fall'. Certainly, in the latter case, such a diminishing of the expected stress would reduce the tension which had been established by the first line of the poem, which possessed more stressed than unstressed syllables. In doing so it would reflect the releasing of tension with the action of putting the bread out. There is, however, a different way of looking at the metre of the line.

I have been scanning by stress, as is customary in English verse. The metre of classical verse, however, is length-based, each foot being made up of long and short rather than stressed and unstressed syllables. At the time of writing this poem (and ever since) Harrison was steeped in classical poetry. Scanned in a classical way, by length, the problem of 'bread' in this line disappears: the line is now pretty regular iambic pentameter—

short long/ short long/ short long, and so on. There are tensions between length and stress in all English verse, but
Harrison's ear, throughout, is acutely aware of them. The final
line quoted above, for example—'The booming, morning wind
brought back tenfold'—plays on the length of vowel in 'booming' and 'morning' so as to slow down the poem with an effect
which is onomatopoeic not so much of the wind as of the
sounding of the two voices in his head. At the same time,
within these particular words the poem's early interplay
between trochee and iamb is echoed: the words would themselves be trochaic, '*boom*ing', '*morn*ing'; their place in the line
ensures that they are part of the regular iambic metre.

They are also part of a play between words of differing
syllable length, essential to formal, metrical verse.

> The booming, morning wind brought back tenfold;
> Time after time their suffocated talk
> Filled and left, like rats a sodden hold,
> His keeling mind: he had to go and walk,
>
> To think of all he still had chance to save
> And claim the open spaces of the park

In the previous stanza we had 'claustrophobic' and 'guarded
actions'. Now, after 'booming' and 'morning', we have 'suffocated', 'sodden', and 'keeling'. The verse is not stilted or
clogged because of these polysyllabic words, but it is elaborate.
Then, when the poem tells of the narrator's decision to take
action to get away from his impasse, the verse turns to the sim-
plest monosyllables: 'he had to go and walk'. Through its
simple regularity the metre sustains the monosyllables' meanings and even in detail works in the cause of their expressive-
ness, emphasizing necessity—'he *had* to'—and stressing 'go' so
that 'he had to *go*, get away,' is included in 'he had to go and
walk'. The beat in these lines—in contrast to that in part of the
second line—falls naturally on the important words: 'think',
'all', 'still', 'chance', 'save', 'claim': each is an emphatic term of
the decision which had to be made. And immediately following on them, the two-syllabled words come when the place of
release is described: 'open spaces', and another diminished
stress follows at once with 'of', as tension is relaxed—'of the
park'.

This is the same kind of care for simple words and their interplay with more elaborate ones as Harrison shows at the start of 'Book Ends'. There, two of the polysyllabic words are epithets giving crucial information—'suddenly' and 'slowly'. They are surrounded by simple monosyllables: 'Baked the day she suddenly dropped dead | we chew it slowly that last apple pie'. The third polysyllabic word, 'apple', takes part in the expressive slowing down at that line's end. Again, though, the interplay between rhythm and metre, stress and length is instructively complex.

The regular iambic feet of the second line here actually sound like a falling rhythm—'*chew* it/ *slow*ly/ . . . *ap*ple/'. The word 'last', which metrically should be unstressed, attracts stress through its weight of meaning. In the first line, the metrical pattern which reduced the significance of the pronoun 'he' in 'The Flat Dweller's Revolt' does the same to 'she': '*Baked* the *day* she *sud*denly': the suddenness is stressed. The line feels as if it has moved from being trochaic to being iambic: 'Baked/ the *day*/ she *sud*/'. No sooner is it iambic than stress seems to diminish from the next foot with the 'ly' sound and to be drawn into the final foot, with the alliteration encouraging the stressing of both its words, making a spondee instead of an iamb: 'she *sud*/denly/ *dropped dead*'.[3]

It is difficult enough to write of metre and syntax without losing the reader. To write of sound patterns always courts exaggeration, though Harrison here is certainly writing a poem which is highly concious of its aural patterning:

> He kicked the fuzzy stalks of London Pride,
> Unfettered hairy seeds on tended plots:
> That fallow night he hoped the wind had died
> And, like unwanted children in cheap cots,
>
> Between proud dahlias and hollyhocks,
> On half-built sites the length and breadth of Leeds,
> Neat crematorium, demolished blocks,
> Like risen men, would stand the purple weeds

The alliterations, assonances, and echoes really do speak for themselves here, in writing which is a rhetorical *tour de force*: the sentence actually has another whole stanza to go before it will be complete. But I will pick on one tiny pattern of sound from earlier in the poem and one pattern from later to complete my case on Harrison's mastery.

The central figure of the opening lines of the poem was a personal pronoun, masculine, singular. In the third line another pronoun entered, 'hers'. When it came in it had already been (unknowingly) anticipated and at once it could be accommodated because it picked up the preceding end-rhyme: 'He cast bread on the pavement for the birds | Their claustrophobic voices, *hers* and his'. Much could be said about the relationship implied in that emphasis, but none of it is revealed or defined. The second sound pattern is in the last three stanzas of his poem. There, Harrison moves across two related rhyme sounds for one of his alternate rhymes. He had already set up certain echoes by making many of his rhyme words plurals, and moving from the rhymes 'talk/walk' to 'park/dark'. Now, however, we have 'own . . . stone . . . bone . . . moon . . . rooms . . . wombs'.

Here I encounter a limit to my analysis. What am I hearing as the sounds of these words? We know from the 'School of Eloquence' poems that a decade or two later Harrison sets traps and catches in rhyme and sound so as to 'occupy' the lousy leasehold poetry colonized by RP speakers like me. He is a poet whose work stops you short when you try to read him aloud in public and encounter head-on those 'matter/water' rhymes which work for him and Wordsworth, the direct speech of father and son, the Northern and specifically Leeds voices you are not sure whether to get something of your tongue round or ignore. From the direct challenge of those 'School of Eloquence' sonnets we can learn, perhaps, but the issue is far more pervasive than we may think. In the first line of 'Book Ends' the pronoun 'she' has no stress, but maybe it is also a short syllable rather than the long one of RP; it chimes with an equally short vowel in the muted stress at the end of 'sudden*ly*'; 'that', 'last', and 'apple' create an assonantal effect unheard in RP.

In 'The Flat Dweller's Revolt', then, what are we to do with those final rhymes: are there two groups of rhymes, or does 'moon' rhyme with 'bone' as Harrison would hear it, and then rhyme on with 'rooms' and 'wombs'? And come to think of it, most of those plurals would be voiced rather than unvoiced;

the opening, 'Dogs in mangers feel', would have different terms of length and nasalization than I use, highlighting the contrast in the word 'feel'. In the sixties, the aim was to find a voice. One talked of poets having a voice. Normally it meant one which was distinct. Already, for Tony Harrison, it was his own.

I suggested earlier that in 'The Flat Dweller's Revolt' we can also meet, more clearly than usual perhaps, a positive impulse, an affirmative desire underlying Harrison's art. This poem's ancestral connections, in contrast to those of Eliot's poems, are familial—in terms which fascinatingly foreshadow *v.* and other, later elegies. It presents a waste land which is literal—in the 'redevelopment' of the fifties the terraces are being demolished. The urban landscape may be full of metaphorical significances, but it is the place where the subject of the poem lives, and he is intimately involved in it. He hopes that:

> Like risen men, would stand the purple weeds;
> And most profusely spread where common earth
> Combined more spacious parents than his own,
> Where such as he thought grimly on one birth
> And ageing sons laid flowers on one stone.

It is '*common* earth', communal, shared, for all of us; and in that play between levels of language—the public, general, and classical (dictionary language) and the personal, local, and private (what is heard and said)—it is 'common' in other senses. This common earth is the 'common land'—the people's unowned spaces. There is therefore a body of human knowledge and memory, political and historical, which affirms the right to freedom against oppression.

Just as Harrison in 'The Flat Dweller's Revolt' takes up a different relationship to the societal from that of Eliot, or, for that matter, that of his own 'Movement' contemporaries, so he takes up a different relationship to the specifically personal or intimate. 'Common earth' carries within it a dark joke at the expense of two respectabilities: one, that of his own class, particularly its parents in relation to their children: 'Don't do that, it's common'; the other, that of those who would deny the humanity of his class: 'they're common'. The apparently direct comment, 'More spacious parents than his own', establishes an unequivocal personal significance at the same time as it leaves much unsaid. How are his parents 'less spacious' than others'? Private, first-hand experience sounds as if it lies behind this just as much as awareness of class. The poem keeps many of its secrets, but that they exist is made plain, for they are part of the poem's credentials, part of what measures the depth of what is felt.

So Harrison's whole role as poet is different: the degree to which he is present and responsible is antithetical to the impersonality aspired to by Eliot. He is not trying to extinguish himself in some sought-after impersonality; he is trying to look at himself in terms which make sense, and those terms are given by the formalities and art of poetry. In this Harrison is also sailing straight between the Scylla and Charybdis which, it was claimed, faced the poet at that time: emotionalism and formlessness which were attributed (inaccurately) to the forties; and a distrust of emotion, concentration on intellect, and detached formality which (absurdly) it was claimed were bringing new life to poetry through 'The Movement'.

Blasphemy also sets him apart, relieving him from the whole transcendental clutter of religion at the same time as it enables him to invoke the historical and spiritual territories long occupied by religion. (He writes, oddly, a little like an ex-Catholic—the attraction of Joyce and, in a different way, of Dostoevsky becomes a little clearer.) Rebirth, resurrection, was, after all, to be the cure to *The Waste Land*. Here, 'Like risen men, would stand the purple weeds': the weeds are unmistakeably phallic in colour and vulgar in idiom ('stand'). The 'rising' of Christ is not mocked by the pun 'risen men', just rewritten in a demythologized, secular world. Yet, at the same time, 'such as he' thinking 'grimly on one birth' would clearly be remembering the appalling story of Jesus, what he promised and what was done to him, as well as thinking of his own birth and whatever private context of pain from an unnamed event this poem about conception may carry. Equally, the flowers laid on one stone can quite properly suggest a mourning for a Jesus for whom no angelic presence rolled back the stone.

The terms and memories of religion are there, but transformed or emptied of their powers of transcendence or consolation. Gods there may be, but they are best not interfered with, though they may be invoked. The self is what one has:

> That night he learnt himself by heart, his prayers
> Unsaid for safety, summoned flesh and bone,
> His ripe autumnal love and climbed the stairs
> And in the bathroom, washing, begged the moon

Pagan prayers may have meaning, if only because their invocations are gestures which measure need rather than the expectation of an answer.

The peroration which Harrison will continue in his next stanza holds the central affirmation of the poem. The plea has been for the free growth of the uncultivated, the revolt of the common weed or wild flower against the demolition of terraces where people lived. The problem here has not been Eliot's one of impotence or barrenness. It has been the impeding of fertility.

The final images Harrison uses may, today, seem less than appealing if we take them on a literal level to refer to contraception: '*protected* brides' relating to '*guarded* talk' at the poem's start. Through its formalities and dictions, however, the poem has built up a wider theme of repression. What is at stake is a whole pressure towards growth against the dead hand of denial. Andrew Marvell, with a related dilemma in 'To His Coy Mistress', still played with guns, even if they were big: 'Let us roll all our strength and all | Our sweetness up into one ball, | And tear our pleasures with rough strife | Thorough the iron gates of life'. Harrison wishes only for the moon:

> The queen of female courses and of tides,
> To shine on insured love in rented rooms
> And break the dykes of all protected brides
> And flood the little land of fertile wombs.

Aggression is certainly there and the image is in fact of ejaculation but it is none the less the female principle which is summoned to bring the fertility, and it is a fertility which will release to growth the defiant energy of life against the forces of oppression. And this was only the beginning.

The Flat Dweller's Revolt

Dogs in mangers feel, he thought, like this;
He cast bread on the pavement for the birds.
Their claustrophobic voices, hers and his,
Their guarded actions louder than their words.

The booming, morning wind brought back tenfold;
Time after time their suffocated talk
Filled and left, like rats a sodden hold,
His keeling mind: he had to go and walk,

To think of all he still had chance to save
And claim the open spaces of the park,
The earth that held his birthright and his grave,
And strictly meditate the fruitless dark.

He kicked the fuzzy stalks of London Pride,
Unfettered hairy seeds on tended plots:
That fallow night he hoped the wind had died
And, like unwanted children in cheap cots,

Between proud dahlias and hollyhocks,
On half-built sites the length and breadth of Leeds,
Neat crematorium, demolished blocks,
Like risen men, would stand the purple weeds;

And most profusely spread where common earth
Combined more spacious parents than his own,
Where such as he thought grimly on one birth
And ageing sons laid flowers on one stone.

That night he learnt himself by heart, his prayers
Unsaid for safety, summoned flesh and bone,
His ripe autumnal love and climbed the stairs
And in the bathroom, washing, begged the moon,

The queen of female courses and of tides,
To shine on insured love in rented rooms
And break the dykes of all protected brides
And flood the little land of fertile wombs.

2

Tony Harrison the Playwright

RICHARD EYRE

WHENEVER the litany of names is invoked to justify an assertion of the vigour of post-war playwrighting in Britain, there is
one name that is consistently absent, and it is the one name that
seems to me to justify the claim that there is an unbroken tradition in the British theatre going back to the fifteenth century.

The missing name, of course, is Tony Harrison, who is as
prolific a writer for the theatre as, say, his contemporary and
fellow native of Leeds, Alan Bennett. You could make compar-
isons between the two writers, and they would not be invidi-
ous ones. Both write about sex, class, and death, even if Alan's
mordant wit provides an opaque filter which makes these
themes less conspicuous than Tony's. They share a common
contempt for the merely fashionable, and they are thoroughly
demotic—both making idiosyncratic films for television.
Popular without being populist, they are thoroughly
accessible, and thoroughly and unapologetically elitist—if that
means believing in the absolute values of good and bad art and
refusing to talk down to people from the class you were born
into.

Leaving aside Alan's drollery and Tony's melancholy, and
Alan's concerns with unexpressed longings and Tony's for
unexpressed contradictions, what divides the two writers is
that one writes in prose, the other in verse. Poet and playwright are usually seen as mutually opposed roles—the poet a
solitary figure answerable to no one but his own talent and
conscience, the playwright a collaborator, colluding in the
pragmatism and expediency of production, and the approval
of the audience. This is one of the many paradoxes that Tony
embraces in his work, his life, and his background.

The baker's son from Leeds is probably the most cosmopolitan man I know. Multilingual (Greek, ancient and modern, Latin, Italian, French, Czech, and Hausa), much travelled—a citizen, as they say, of the world, living, often rather precariously, between London, Florida, Greece, and Newcastle. An expert in many cultures, with a curiosity about many others. Fastidiously knowledgeable about food, wine, music, and the theatre. Tender, witty, wry, volatile, living up (or down) to the Yorkshire stereotype only in his rare but formidable stubbornness and intransigence.

The man is the work. It is not so much that it is autobiographical (though much of it is) but that the content invariably dramatizes the ambivalence at the heart of his character and attempts to reconcile the opposed sides. Tony does not deal in the familiar English mode of ellipsis and reticence, but in an unremittingly direct address that is at times almost unnerving. Those opposite valencies that he invokes in *v.* are not a poet's conceits but are the syntax of his daily life— heart/brain, soul/body, male/female, and, if you like, poet/playwright.

Can we forget so easily that our dramatic tradition is founded on verse drama, that our national playwright was a poet? The life of Shakespeare's plays is in the language, not alongside it, or underneath it. Feelings and thoughts are released at the moment of speech, and an Elizabethan audience would have responded to the pulse, the rhythms, the shapes, sounds, and above all meanings, within the consistent ten-syllable, five-stress lines of blank verse. They were an audience who listened. To a large extent, we've lost that priority; nowadays we see before we hear. Verse drama places demands on the audience, but a greater demand still on the actors, habituated by naturalistic speech, and to private, introspective, emotional displays.

Eliot (whom he robustly dislikes) described the kind of theatre to which Tony aspires:

There is a fringe of indefinite extent, of feeling which we can only detect, so to speak, out of the corner of the eye and can never completely focus; of feeling of which we are only aware in a kind of temporary detachment from action [. . . .] This peculiar range of sensibility can be expressed by dramatic poetry, at its moments of greatest intensity. At such moments, we touch the border of those feelings which music only can express.[1]

In Tony's poetry and his plays it's the sense of rhythm that's as important as the meaning. Dramatic language without the sinew of rhythmic pulse is completely inert to him, and he can be violent and unforgiving about performances and productions of verse plays where the actors and directors have been deaf to the pulse of the poetry. 'You should be able to feel the language,' he says, 'to taste it, to conscript the whole body as well as the mind and the mouth to savour it.'

In the same way, Tony wants the whole body of society, not just its head, to be involved in art. He wants art and literature to be accessible to everyone, for the distinction between High and Low art to be annulled, and for art to be removed from the clutches of class distinction. However, his hatred for the pap of popular culture is almost boundless. He has a committed loathing for the propagators and purveyors of this pap and, in spite of his determined compassion, for the consumers as well. He's like Chekhov who, when told by a Narodnik actor that Gogol needed to be brought down to the level of the people, said that the problem was rather that the people needed to be brought up to the level of Gogol.

If ever there was an anthem set to this theme it is *v.*, and I directed a film of the poem in 1987 for Channel 4.[2] Poets who read their work in public can often be maddeningly diffident and awkward. Tony is not of this school. He is a poet who performs rather than reads, without self-regard and without self-indulgence, and without the spurious 'performance' values that actors often bring to the reading of poetry. He does not, however, neglect the demands of volume and articulation, the sense of the event, and the awareness of his audience. He is metrically unnervingly constant. When we were filming *v.*, you could have set a metronome at the beginning of the performance and forty minutes later the poet would still have been in sync with it. In addition, he could accommodate with an actor's instinct instructions about camera movements and eyelines. He could, as we say, 'take direction'.

The film's editor was a man who, like many victims of our educational system, had been turned off poetry at an early age.

'It was not for me,' he said, but I watched him become drawn into the poem so that he felt each nuance, each rhyme, each rhythm, each shift of thought, with an ever-increasing vividness. 'Fucking amazing,' he said. And it is.

I've talked about many projects for the theatre over the last ten years, and some of them have materialized. I've been god-father to two of Tony's plays—*The Trackers of Oxyrhynchus* and *Square Rounds*, and I've talked to him about directing many others. Over the last ten years we've talked about doing *Alcestis* in a Greek café, *Prometheus* on slag heaps,[3] and *The Trojan Women* outside the gates of Greenham Common. We've discussed a production of an unwieldy Hungarian epic, *The Tragedy of Man*, and *Le Bourgeois gentilhomme*, with a seventeenth-century Monsieur Jourdain struggling to become an English gentleman in the late twentieth century.

Tony is one of the few playwrights who is prepared to write for the Olivier Theatre, a big public space that defies naturalistic presentation and demands that the actor acknowledges the audience's presence. It calls on huge resources of energy from the writer and the actor; the timid need not apply. It is an auditorium that might have appealed to the gargantuan imagination and appetite of Victor Hugo, who wanted to overturn the rigid conventions of French classical theatre and, like Berlioz, to emulate Shakespeare.

Hugo said after a play of his had opened and been drubbed by the critics: 'I love it all the more.' Perhaps it's not entirely coincidental that we started talking about doing an English version of *Le Roi s'amuse* shortly after Tony had taken a critical beating with *Square Rounds*. The world of *Le Roi s'amuse* (*The Prince's Play*)[4] that Tony suggested was instantly alluring: the court of a 'Prince of Wales' around the turn of the century, the world of music hall, and the world of Jack the Ripper. Tony leapt on the tirades of Hugo's play like a hungry dog, chewing them into ferociously excoriating attacks on the monarchy, the aristocracy, and the inability of the rulers to feel for those who are ruled.

Unexpectedly—but perhaps not uncharacteristically—Tony acquired a laptop computer with fax modem, and when I was in New York in the autumn of 1995 I started to receive streams of muscular and mercurial rhyming couplets on the hotel fax machine. Tony is as methodical as any writer I know. He collects and collates information about subjects that attract him in a series of quarto-sized notebooks with quotations, newspaper cuttings, photographs, ideas, fragments of lines, all laid out meticulously. The Japanese film director Ozu used to go to his country cottage for weeks to write his scripts. When he emerged he described the script by the number of cases of sake he'd had to consume to write it. With Tony it's notebooks. And postcards. I have vast numbers of cards from Greece, Austria, Florida, Japan, Colombia, Newcastle—even Bosnia; pictures of friezes, of vases, of statues, of satyrs, of ruins, of opera houses, of thoughts and images and ideas and good wishes—the DNA molecule of our friendship.

Preparing the production, Tony's interested and involved in all aspects—the casting, the design, and the music—loving to sit by the piano with the composer working the lyrics like a blacksmith with a horseshoe. During rehearsals he is punctiliously professional, observing the courtesies of the lines of division between director and writer, encouraging, practical, inventive, and always willing to cut or rewrite if it seems to be necessary. He takes delight in sitting in the rehearsal room turning out a new couplet, handing it to the actor, and grinning as the actor tastes the new words, and for Ken Stott (who played the leading role of Scotty Scott in *The Prince's Play*) he loved weaving Scottish rhythms and phrases into the part of the hunchbacked court jester cum music hall comedian. Tony had boundless admiration for his performance: 'I love to write for him.'

As a director of his own work he is wearied by the aspects of the job that often make you feel like a night-nurse, dispensing comfort, advice, treatment, and solace to actors while wondering why they don't just *do* it. Directors are mediators, and Tony is not a natural negotiator. There are few directors, however, who are more conscientious in ensuring that the minds of the actors are concentrated with an almost religious rigour on their performance. He is the only director I know who (in *Trackers*) invites the cast to drink champagne from a three-thousand-year-old cup before going on stage.

If many, or most, of his plays are adaptations, or translations, 'carried across' from another language, I never think of them as

anything but Tony's plays. It is not that he buries or usurps the
voice of the original writer, it is that he mediates in his own
voice between a foreign (or older) language and English verse,
between one culture and another, between the past and the
present. There's no more accurate description of this position
than the epigraph which Tony uses for his first collection of
plays (*TW*). It's a poem by Leon Feuchtwanger, who collaborated with Brecht on a version of Marlowe's *Edward II*:

> I, for instance, sometimes write
> Adaptations. Or some people prefer the phrase
> 'Based on', and this is how it is: I use
> Old material to make a new play, then
> Put under the title
> The name of the dead writer who is extremely
> Famous and quite unknown, and before
> The name of the dead writer I put the word 'After'
> Then one group will write that I am
> Very respectful and others that I am nothing of the sort and all
> The dead writer's failures
> Will be ascribed
> To me and all my successes
> To the dead writer who is extremely
> Famous and quite unknown, and of whom
> Nobody knows whether he himself
> Was the writer or maybe the
> Adaptor.

Every day when I walk down a dark blue corridor to the
rehearsal room at the National Theatre I am reminded of this
poem as I pass the poster for *The Trackers of Oxyrhynchus*, a play
based on fragments of a lost play by Sophocles. I look at the
photographs of twelve Yorkshiremen in clogs dressed as satyrs
with long tails, the ears of pantomime horses, and magnificently gross erect phalluses, and I think this: there is no bolder
or more imaginative playwright working in this country.

v. by Tony Harrison,
or Production No. 73095, LWT Arts

MELVYN BRAGG

THE film is set in a landscape of snow and headstones. The snow was accidental but the director could be forgiven for being pleased that fortune had presented him with the white shroud covering the graveyard which was slowly sinking into the black of the disused mineshaft. The voice over film that we hear at the very beginning is that of the poet, Tony Harrison, whom we see walking, purposefully, towards a rather grand four-sided square solid tombstone.

He tells us that he first came to this place when he was seven, during the war, with his dad, who explained that the graves tilted towards the city of Leeds because they were undermined by a worked-out pit. In 1984, at the time of the miners' strike, he remembered his father's words while he was tending the family grave, and it was then that the poem started. *v.*

In 1987 the poem was filmed, directed by Richard Eyre, through my department at LWT, and from there steered into Channel 4 with no small difficulty. The problem was the language. PISS, CUNT, SHIT, and FUCK featured heavily, and the case had to be made. To the credit of Channel 4 and the authorities, it was finally upheld, and the filmed poem was transmitted.

It is only marginally because of my own association with *v.* that I choose to write about it. There is of course the interest in remarking on the double life of the work—once in print, once in celluloid. But more importantly, *v.* has something of a per-sonally resonant autobiographical echo about it, especially if read in conjunction with those truly fine, woundingly moving poems brooding over the final days and death of his dad and mam. *v.* lists more towards his dad, and the poet's long argument with the man who responded to the scholarship boy's diet of Ibsen, Marx, and Gide with 'one of his you-stuck-up-bugger looks' and *'ah sometimes think you read too many books'*,[1] and yet knew to give him a dialect book at their final exchange,[2] reaches to the roots of the poet's talent, as surely as those rose roots planted by his dad seek out the ashes below.

v. brings in so much. It is an elegy in a city churchyard. The church is unmentioned in the poem, unseen in the film. The dead are mourned but so are the living who prey on them. A voice is given to a 'skin', neither mute nor Milton, nor entirely inglorious. The poet rakes the graveyard, uncovering his past, and that of his parents and previous generations, their times and work and skills—Beef, Beer, and Bread is the Harrison inheritance—and he throws on to the scales the insubstantial stuff of today's dole. Learning clashes not with ignorance but with despair. The poet himself plays two parts—as now he is and as he might have been had he not gone 'on on on' as a boy to complete his Latin prose.[3]

There are numerous 'V's in society, in culture, in the life of the poet, and, most particularly, in the lives of the Leeds football supporters who spray the stones with four-letter desecrations, 'doing the dirt on death'. Then there is his dad whose whole life becomes versus, embattled in his widowerhood. It is a poem which couples *Lulu* and the 300-million-year saga of coal, and embraces a critical late-twentieth-century breakpoint in British society—the fight between the miners and the coal board in 1984. It speaks of the departure from a place, once solid as the ground was once solid beneath the graveyard itself. That departure led to a neglect of the tributes to life carved with the care of poetry for posterity. The poet's own life—the eternal themes—his love, his women, his fame, his falling away from home, and his journey towards death are as pungently evoked as that contemporary phenomenon, the tribe of youth nourished, it seems, on nothing at all save the fate of the local football team and seeing in graffiti a pleasure of revenge.

It is a poem which requires, and will most likely get, a book to unravel it—which is part of what makes it such a great poem, as I believe it is, and the reason why this essay can only sketch out an appreciation. Harrison's epigraph is the words of Arthur Scargill, the defeated leader of the NUM in that tragic/disastrous strike of 1984: 'My father still reads the dictionary every day. He says your life depends on your power to master words.' Everything about those two sentences would appeal to Tony Harrison.

The poem begins with a verse which quietly asserts the poet's self-valuation and sets out one of the themes—how poetry can find its place in the solid world.

> Next millennium you'll have to search quite hard
> to find my slab behind the family dead,
> butcher, publican, and baker, now me, bard
> adding poetry to their beef, beer and bread.[4]

The film, after Harrison's statement about the genesis of the poem, switches into a rapid montage of some images from World War II—dominated by the first image of 'V'—Churchill's two fingers underscored by one of his battle hymns. 'V' for victory, a 'V' picked up in columns of soldiers marching into a V shape and fortified by shots of Spitfires, the miraculously unbombed St Paul's, the friendly 'V's on city walls, and finally a 'V' from Mrs Thatcher clearly signalling that victory had turned to adversarial politics.

In the poem, that first verse is followed immediately by a puckish reference to Byron and Wordsworth, whose graves lie nearby.

> With Byron three graves on I'll not go short
> of company, and Wordsworth's opposite.
> That's two peers already, of a sort,
> and we'll all be thrown together if the pit,
>
> whose galleries once ran beneath this plot,
> causes the distinguished dead to drop
> into the rabblement of bone and rot,
> shored slack, crushed shale, smashed prop.[5]

Wordsworth turns out to be a builder of church organs, Byron a tanner of 'luggage cowhide in the age of steam'. But references peg in the poet's claims to space none the less.

Here, very early in the film, we see Tony Harrison reading the poem to a very small group—there is the atmosphere of a sect, underground, survivors. The scene is low lit, with an undoubted religious overtone as the young preacher stands and delivers the word to the silent transfixed congregation. Harrison conducts himself as he reads, generally with his right hand beating the pulse of the poem as he glances now and then at the book held in his left hand. The effect is of a performance rather than a reading, the performance of someone determined that no syllable will be lost and no punctuation unmarked, and the hand is a wand.

The precise geography is given—Beeston Hill, Leeds before him, the Leeds United Football Club to the left—and then two major themes come in bound together.

> This graveyard stands above a worked-out pit.
> Subsidence makes the obelisks all list.
> One leaning left's marked FUCK, one right's marked SHIT
> sprayed by some peeved supporter who was pissed.[6]

I presume that 'peeve' plays on the fact that 'peevy' also means pissed. Harrison's technique throughout is our best modern example of *ars celare artem*, but it would be to ignore his deep skills for the apparent ease of the lines not to be seen for the lightly worn achievement they are. Look at the seeming simplicity, the comprehensive subtlety of a verse a little way on, talking about one of the youths who sprayed 'V' (as in 'Leeds V. | the opponent of last week, this week, or next').

> Vs sprayed on the run at such a lick,
> the sprayer master of his flourished tool,
> get short-armed on the left like that red tick
> they never marked his work much with at school.[7]

The poem then enlarges on its theme of 'V'.

> These Vs are all the versuses of life
> from LEEDS v. DERBY, Black/White
> and (as I've known to my cost) man v. wife,
> Communist v. Fascist, Left v. Right,
>
> class v. class as bitter as before,
> the unending violence of US and THEM,
> personified in 1984
> by Coal Board MacGregor and the NUM,
> Hindu/Sikh, soul/body, heart v. mind [. . .][8]

And on it goes, the Hindu/Sikh in some way foreshadowing the feeling that his aged father, in permanent grief for his dead wife, experiences as 'his' street, 'his' shops, 'his' daily route is taken over by 'coloured chaps | dad's most liberal label as he felt | squeezed by the unfamiliar'. A key point in this story in the poem is when the poet finds that UNITED has been 'graffitied on my parents' stone'. Is he to wipe it off; take it as a symbol, an omen, a hope even though he himself believes in no future life? It inspires an immediately warm memory of his father.

> When I first came here 40 years ago
> with my dad to 'see my grandma' I was 7.
> I helped dad with the flowers. He let me know
> she'd gone to join my grandad up in Heaven.
>
> My dad who came each week to bring fresh flowers
> came home with clay stains on his trouser knees.
> Since my parents' deaths I've spent 2 hours
> made up of odd 10 minutes such as these.[9]

On the film the sad speculative shrug which accompanies the words '2 hours' could alone justify the argument that seeing can indeed add a rift to reading.

Back to childhood, on to more signs, and the neon signs that royalty and industry use as their licensed graffiti to smear the public air, and then on to the puzzle:

> But why inscribe these graves with CUNT and SHIT?
> Why choose neglected tombstones to disfigure?
> This pitman's of last century daubed PAKI GIT,
> this grocer Broadbent's aerosolled with NIGGER?

He brings up the joblessness but holds fast to the aimlessness of the desecration.

> What is it that these crude words are revealing?
> What is it that this aggro act implies?
> Giving the dead their xenophobic feeling
> or just a *cri-de-coeur* because man dies?

The poet's *cri-de-coeur* instantly provokes a versus *cri-de-coeur* from the *alter ego* whose voice now makes the poem a drama.

> *So what's a* cri-de-coeur, *cunt? Can't you speak*
> *the language that yer mam spoke. Think of 'er!*
> *Can yer only get yer tongue round fucking Greek?*
> *Go and fuck yerself with* cri-de-coeur![10]

Greek, the language of the beginning of so much knowledge foreign to so many in a country whose elite once revered it. Foreign as so much else the elite revered. Now the reference marks a comprehensive exclusion. Tony Harrison knows all this. His well-learned Greek at Leeds University was a passport and an exile's brand. His mother is evoked as yet another regret—Harrison's long lament that he did not write poems his parents wanted to read. But most of all, this is the voice of the skin Harrison left behind.

You come on him slyly in Eyre's film. We hear what seems another voice—the stanza quoted above—clashing out over the faces of the rapt audience. For a moment we think another player has entered the room. But it is Harrison himself, well mimicking his *alter ego*, and the dialogue becomes a fight about poetry and work. The mood of both for Harrison, the lack of both for the other who, finally challenged to sign his name to the graffiti, does so.

> He took the can, contemptuous, unhurried
> and cleared the nozzle and prepared to sign
> the UNITED sprayed where mam and dad were buried.
> He aerosolled his name. And it was mine.[11]

The central pause in the last line and the significance given the last four syllables by Harrison's close-up expression again enriches the words.

Along the way, Harrison has confessed to an act of vandalism just as much at odds with impossible aspirations and the frustration of reality as those found in the condition of the skin. But his equation will not do. Sans work, sans pride, sans place, the skin is sans the reach of poetry. '*A book, yer stupid cunt, 's not worth a fuck!*' It is part of Harrison's basic struggle that this is a challenge he has tried to meet throughout his career, to make it worth a fuck, to those he left behind.

The film then leads into its final movement. First, perhaps to salve the brutality of that encounter, he recounts younger innocent times when he and his team could have played football together, bawling 'Here comes the bride'. Then he turns towards home. Not the final home of the grave, but the home of himself in a Lawrentian sunset ringing.

> Home, home, home, to my woman as the red
> darkens from a fresh blood to a dried.
> Home, home to my woman, home to bed
> where opposites seem sometimes unified.

But first another farewell to his father seen as the colonized one in the place of his birth, as

> A pensioner in turban taps his stick
> along the pavement past the corner shop
> that sells samosas now not beer on tick,
> to the Kashmir Muslim Club that was the Co-op.[12]

We see all this almost literally on film, and Harrison manages the difficult job, in such prickly territory, of describing the increasing domination and cultural isolation of his father, his slow drowning in foreignness without yielding an inch of decency.

But home, for his son, is high opera and—as we see on the screen in a photograph—life with one of its high practitioners—opera and fire, fire from coal, whose 300-million-year life may never be granted again, whose seams will one day claim the grave he sees thirty years on could well be his. Coal brings him back to the class war and we see that shocking footage of baton-wielding police on horseback racing against unarmed men to club them down for all the world like archive material from a lost, discredited, un-English, oppressive, vicious regime. But it is here. Ours. Talking about who was to blame, earlier in the poem, not wishing to bear down completely on the Leeds United football supporter, he wrote: 'It isn't all his fault though. Much is ours.' Apart from the deep connection with Wordsworth's younger better morality in those last three words, Harrison here is portraying a society deep in fault, indeed, perilously undermined.

As he moves towards his proposed epitaph on the one blank space left on the tombstone, the poet is well served by a frame which takes us to that very blank stone which is an empty frame, as Harrison concludes to those who have sought out his grave, or might pass it by. The last line is superimposed on the screen:

Beneath your feet's a poet, then a pit.
Poetry supporter, if you're here to find
how poems can grow from (beat you to it!) SHIT
find the beef, the beer, the bread, then look behind.[13]

4

On Not Being Milton, Marvell, or Gray

SANDIE BYRNE

RICK Rylance has described 'On Not Being Milton' as 'a stud-iedly literary poem, packed with reference and allusion', whose 'opening self-consciously places it in a literary frame-work'. He finds a difficulty, however, in the poem's attitude to its major literary reference, Milton. It is 'preceded by a sixteen-line epigraph—which therefore looks like a Harrison poem—from Milton's Latin elegy "*Ad Patrem*",' and could therefore 'be saying, humbly, my elegies are not as good as this', but its title puts it in opposition to 'Milton's Latinate language and his learned classicism', which 'stands for that essentially southern English definition of the mainstream which has rejected Harrison's native culture'.[1] Milton is admired, but 'represents what is to be rejected'. Rylance finds that the 'ambivalence about Milton is part of a wider ambivalence in Harrison's work which celebrates the literary as it criticises it.'[2] I would like to talk about that wider ambivalence.

Space restricts this essay almost entirely to Harrison's quo-tation from and allusion to the themes and phrasing of his lit-erary predecessors, but the influence of earlier texts is often more apparent in his form than in his subjects. Harrison is as polymetric as he is polyglottal, which makes him an excellent translator, adapter, and parodist, and enables him to pay homage to 'household gods' such as Keats. Idiosyncratic sound qualities are as deftly reproduced as the conventions of generic form, but his poems are never just glib imitation or pas-tiche.

In his early *Poetry and Audience* poems, Harrison seems to avoid both quotation and imitation,[3] only later trawling his huge literacy for material. An editorial, unsigned, but published during his editorship of *Poetry and Audience*, declares that '[i]t is best not to claim as a poetic ancestor the poet who said:

> A style is found by sedentary toil
> And by the imitation of great masters.'[4]

Twelve years later, however, Harrison states that he 'learned by what Yeats called "sedentary toil and the imitation of great masters".'[5] In the case of most authors such self-contradiction would indicate a rejection of early ideas about poetry, and of early poems, but both statements apply to Harrison. He did not find his style by imitation, it has always been his own. The sedentary toil of a classical education did develop the polymetricality which underpins his work, and he does imitate, or quote, great masters, but not necessarily because he admires and wishes to copy them. He never produces a synthetic Keatsian Ode, or Donnish satire; he imitates in order to be different.

References in the mature work range from self-contained quotation or paraphrase to tone-setting epigraph and wholesale reworking, but few are signposted. It seems unlikely that this is due to carelessness, or to contempt for the reader. Those for whom the sonnet-like fourth stanza of 'The White Queen' does not bring to mind Wyatt's ['They fle from me'][6] are given no direct pointers, and are thus denied access to some of the poem's complexities and tensions, but not to many of its effects. Unlike an authorial intervention or narrator's coy aside, the missing links do not detract from the poem's pace, its touching, comic, tragic effect, or its sheer, awesome nerve. On the other hand, a reading is all the richer for knowing that the section mirrors Wyatt's own inversion of Petrarchan images of the idealized love-object (as huntress rather than hind). Just as the conventions of courtly love depict an only apparent inversion of a power relationship in the servitude of the courtier and the imperious indifference of the Lady, so Harrison's Queen depicts a beautiful object of desire whose superficial power of accepting or rejecting his clients masks far greater inequalities between them.[7]

The pamphlet editions of *Newcastle* are supplemented by a transcript of a radio talk which painstakingly lists the poem's genesis and references.

I was leafing through the Metaphysical Poets, and there in John Cleveland suddenly [. . .] there was:

> *Correct your maps: Newcastle is Peru!* [8]

This describes a spiral of associations behind the poem, a mixture of personal and cultural references: a metaphysical poem, Newcastle and Peru, John Donne, new-found land, making new; Seneca, *ultima Thule*, Zarate, Peru; Durex, Trojan condoms, Aeneas, classical statues, Neptune, Newcastle again; Juanita de Mena, Juan de Mena, *The Labyrinth*, concentric circles, repetition, dullness, rediscovery, celebration, making new, mottos of city, bank, and school, going straight, going in circles. [9] If the line from 'News from Newcastle' was an inspiration, it was not a straightforward antecedent.

> England's a perfect world, has Andes too;
> Correct your maps, Newcastle is Peru! [10]

The tone is ironic; England's 'Andes' are spoil-heaps connoting ugliness and making Newcastle an early industrial wasteland. *Newcastle*'s tone is an excited cry of discovery that the city is made 'new'.

Though the 'School of Eloquence' poems follow the traditional form and (to an extent) subject-matter of the extended or Meredithian sonnet, their adherence to these conventions highlights their disruption of others. The incorporation of material conventionally excluded from canonical forms enables the poet to have it both ways: to use the rhetorical possibilities of the sixteen-line sonnet while implicitly attacking it; to produce a beautifully wrought and moving poem, while refusing to allow the reader acquiescence in the form (in its traditional mode) and the complacent comfort of ignoring the device. This also is characteristic of much of Harrison's writing. Poems such as 'Long Distance' are as much anti-sonnets as sonnets, and in the same way *Trackers* could be said to be an anti-satyr play, the *Oresteia* an anti-tragedy, *Chorus* an anti-comedy, and the longer, more discursive poems such as *Newcastle* anti-metaphysical. Similarly, Harrison both exploits and resists a fruitful poetic convention in the location of some of his poems. Longer works such as *Fire-Gap*, *Kumquat*, and 'Cypress and Cedar' are partly set in gardens, or garden-like

places, which mirror and oppose the Edenic garden and
Arcadian pastoral settings frequented by many medieval and
Renaissance poets, and both exalted and ironized by Andrew
Marvell, while *v.* recollects a reverie in a graveyard which, I
believe, mirrors and opposes the country churchyard of
Thomas Gray.

Harrison incorporates images from a pre-Newtonian universe in the cosmography of *Newcastle* and Thomas Campey's
Copernican astronomy and vision of an Imperial Host, 'Squat
on its thrones of Ormus and of Ind'.[11] Though works such as
Blasphemers' Banquet seem to be trying to bring an Enlighten-
ment rationality to irrational and extreme beliefs, Harrison's
insistence on grounding the intangible and aspirational (love,
art) in the physical and imperfect is Rabelaisian, or perhaps,
given his interest in anatomy, morbidology, Hieronymus
Fracastorius[12] and a sort of social scatomancy, Paracelsian. The
poetry often presents a dialectic between the material and the
spiritual or intellectual. In the shorter, more militant poems
idealism generally loses.

> Think of your conception, you'll soon forget
> what Plato puffs you up with, all that
> 'immortality' and 'divine life' stuff.[13]

Harrison is neither club-wielding materialist nor working-
mens' club comic. 'Cypress and Cedar' suggests that he does
look for spiritual insight, in Sanskrit texts for 'little clues they
offer to life's light'.[14] *Kumquat*, despite a disclaimer to the contrary, obliquely suggests that ideas and ideals might just save
the world from nuclear holocaust.[15] The pragmatic material-
ism does not preclude intangible ideals, aspirations, and imagination.

Harrison's cerebrating never becomes the sophistical
dialectic of the metaphysical style. Where Donne's ventriloquial persona took the conceit of the sun to its limits, defeat-
ing time by arrogant intellect,[16] Harrison pits only the real
extent of his strength, physical and cerebral, against the
material world. Like Marvell, he acknowledges that he cannot
make the sun, symbol of measured time, stand still, but he can
cram more life into a day. He does not make the sun run, he
runs:

When the Southern sun starts setting it sets fast.
I've time to tip one more load if I run.
Because I know this light could be your last
I drain the day of every drop of sun.
The barrow wheel spins round with a clock's tick.[17]

Describing the swinging circle of light cast on his desk from an overhead bulb, he writes:

years of struggle make me concentrate
when it throws up images of planets hurled,
still glowing, off their courses, and a state
where there's no gravity to hold the world.
I have to hold on when I think such things
and weather out these feelings so that when
the wind drops and the light no longer swings
I can focus on an Earth that still has men.[18]

Metaphysical poems displace the concept of knowledge as property to be doled out in rationed but indisputable givens through sophistry and hyperbole, which emphasize the illimitability and play of the individual mind. Harrison rejects superstition and bigotry, and, however powerful the intellectual and cultural baggage, however compelling the rhetoric, his pragmatism prevents it from erupting into the fantastic. Like Copernicus, he inhabits a universe which, though vast and wonderful, is not incomprehensible but only uncharted. While he might enjoy the intellectual appeal of the abstraction of quantum mechanics, or the quasi-mysticism of some recent physics, his focus is on mankind.

Donne circumnavigates the world with his mind, making his little room an everywhere, but Harrison takes planes and trains to the New World—Havana, New York, New Mexico, Florida—and the old—Prague, the Malverns, Dar-es-Salaam, Leningrad. 'The Red Lights of Plenty' starts with art and mythology, personified and endowed with rather unfocused compassion, but 'I stroll round Washington'[19] snaps back to historical and geographical specifics, and a 'real', human perspective which observes details—November, the trees shedding red leaves, Constitution and Independence Avenues, the two museums—in a way which suggests a documentary film sequence. Then the poem's mode of propulsion switches from the physical congruence of the narrator's walk to the poetic association of his imaginative response. Before we arrive at the museums, the simile for the fallen leaves has developed from red welcome carpets (familiar and filmic enough not to stand out from the 'factual' details) to the 'lifeblood' of 'returning warlords [pedestrians] lured inside' to be hacked to death. Before readers become too engrossed in Agamemnon and Clytemnestra, however, 'Buick and Cadillac' bulldozing the blood-red leaves bring them back to Washington, and '[t]hrough two museums, *Science* and *Indian Arts*', until 'something from deep below the car-choked street' is described as 'like thousands of Poe's buried tell-tale hearts'. This, again, is demystified, by 'Japanese in groups come out to stare', prosaically twentieth century and unmysterious with their badges of tourism: 'NASA decals, necklaces by Navajo'.[20] The poem is a barrage of jostling images, visible and intangible, concrete and conceptual, specific and imaginary, one kind redressing the balance disturbed by the other, only to be displaced in turn as the equilibrium is again compromised. 'Plenty' is not only the 'real' stone-carved figure in Washington, but also an imaginary, weeping manifestation, an incarnation of the mask of tragedy in a pumpkin lantern, and the mythical figure representing nature's bounty, here associated with the decadent wastage of late capitalism's beneficiaries, and the want of those at the other end of the cornucopia.

> She chokes back tears of dribbling gasoline
> for the future fates of countries like my own.
>   .   .   .   .
> How many of these children will survive
> crushed through the narrow end of PLENTY's horn?
>   .   .   .   .
> An All Soul's pumpkin rots on someone's porch
> It could be PLENTY's head, about to die.[21]

Next, 'Plenty' becomes that which the flashing of its red lights enumerates, 'the billions the World has in it', and the FBI's record of incidence of serious crime in the USA. The share of the cornucopia of 'Justice, Order, Truth' meted out to the young black man watched by Harrison is pursuit, arrest, and handcuffs. The alternation continues: mysterious, banal; 'actual', 'imaginary'; physical, metaphysical—until the last stanza. This ends on a 'real' image which is yet surreal, and a 'real' place more far-fetched than any flight of fancy: the White House, on whose lawn 'A giant vacuum's Hoovering the Fall'.[22] The poem resists the spin outward into the abstract and metaphorical, and seems to conclude 'Who needs metaphysics, or Disneyland, when they have the White House?' Instead, it drops us at the bottom of the drive, to look up across the lawn at a solid place, a metonymic representation of real culpability.

A more straightforward echo of Donne is apparent in Harrison's itemization of various acts of sex, his unstoppable rhythm, and his ejaculations of discovery.

> This cluttered room, its chandelier
> still spinning from the evening's beer.
>
> .   .   .   .   .   .
>
> this bed, this fire, and lastly us,
> naked, bold, adventurous.
>
> Discovery! wart, mole, spot,
> like outcrops on a snowfield, dot
> these slopes of flesh my fingers ski
> with circular dexterity.
> This moment when my hand strays
> your body like an endless maze,
> returning and returning, you,
> O you; you also are Peru.[23]

The last two lines, reiterating the poem's earlier cry—

> and Newcastle is Newcastle is New-
> castle is Peru!—

of course brings to mind 'O my America! my new-found-land' from Donne's Elegie XIX: 'Going to Bed',[24] as well as 'News from Newcastle', and is prefigured by Harrison's earlier depictions of women as yet-to-be-explored continents.[25] The parallels with Donne go further than paraphrase and pace, however. 'Donne was born into a [religious] terror, and formed by it.'[26] Harrison was born into the terror of Fascism, and lived through war. Religion divided Donne from the stable, given universe of his Catholic background, and further destabilized his personality through the self-loathing which followed his apostasy, and which, with his fears and feelings of betrayal, he displaced on to women and sex.[27] Harrison's social displacement came through education, and did not involve denunciation, but he replaces the stability of his background[28] with sexual love, and sexual energy is the positive aspect of the force he depicts as fire, while its obverse is the destructive fire of war. As Donne responded to religious orthodoxy by exploring the new philosophy yet taking Anglican orders, so Harrison responded to jingoism and fanaticism by opposing war yet remaining sympathetic to male aggression, whether as justified protest, as in *Trackers*, or group display, as in 'The Act'.[29]

'Durham' juxtaposes scepticism, sharp observation, and intimacy; it brings off wonderful metrical effects whilst maintaining the impression of someone speaking; direct address rather than narrative remove.

> They *are* sex, love, we must include
> all these in love's beatitude.
> Bad weather and the public mess
> drive us to private tenderness,
> though I wonder if together we,
> alone two hours, can ever be
> love's anti-bodies in the sick,
> sick body politic.[30]

The cadences and consonants are Donne's, but the voice is twentieth century, and where Donne might have spun out the conceit of 'beatitude', with its overtones of blissful trance, making it an article of love's faith, Harrison is swift to 'wonder if', and undercut it. Both poets celebrate erotic love in defiance of received morality (and in Donne's case, canon law), but Donne presents himself as a martyr to love and thus a founder of a religion, the Christ of all future reckless lovers,[31] while Harrison, though he may see himself as a quintessential Poet, does not equate himself, or his lover, with the Logos, or describe their union in terms of the mystery of omnipresence. He offers love as a respite, consolation, even alternative, but if it is transcendent, it is paradoxically involved in the material.[32]

Marvell, of course, preceded Harrison in using the forms of a genre to resist or subvert its traditional content.[33] *Kumquat* uses pentameter rather than tetrameter, and rhymes in couplets rather than *abab*, but much of the imagery echoes directly or ironically 'The Garden'. Though Harrison describes his kumquat as a 'substitute' for Keats's grape, perhaps the 'older poet'[34] for whom the tart-sweet fruit is so suitable is not only the poet who has lived longer—Harrison—but also one who lived earlier—Marvell. Harrison also shares Marvell's zest for topographies and appetite for small items, preferably bright, scented, or juicy, and exotic either in their newness or by virtue of the contrast between Puritan English drab and the sensual pleasure they afford. Marvell's 'Bermudas' provides a salad of Harrisonian motifs: pomegranates, figs, cedar trees, and Ormus, as well as 'Prelat's rage'.[35] 'To His Coy Mistress'[36] provides a model of tetrameter rhyming couplets sometimes enjambed and sometimes end-stopped, which never fall into formality, stiltedness, or predictable banality, but sustain flexibility and energy; the impetus of both poets' *carpe diem* and *tempus edax* themes.[37]

Following Saint Amant's distinction, Kermode finds that Marvell's is the garden of solitude rather than of *jouissance*.[38] Harrison's Florida garden, characteristically, is both, containing silent meditation and sensual delight; the solitary Stoic and the Epicurean. While Marvell describes the 'happy Garden-state'[39] of man in Paradise alone, Harrison provides his Eden with an Eve, both in *Kumquat*[40] and 'Following Pine'.[41] He describes himself as a Ciceronian Stoic in 'Me Tarzan',[42] and a contemplative in 'Ghosts: Some Words Before Breakfast',[43] but he also relishes kumquats and pomegranates, sex and sensuality.[44] Where Marvell rejects *jouissance* for solitary meditation, Harrison at first rejects solitary intellectualizing and global anxiety for sensual pleasure and love, but kissing and kumquats never become opiates, or Lethe, and he finally refuses to choose between the contemplative and rational, and the active and vegetable, life.

Henry King used tetrameter to bring vigorous dialectic to the elegy,[45] and Marvell, like Donne, continued the progression of ideas from 's/he died—we all must die' to 'we all die—therefore we should gather our rosebuds while we may'; from the evidence of specific and particular death which leads to the assumption of general and universal mortality, to the assumption of universal mortality which leads to the seduction argument. Harrison retains both the elegiac and rhetorical functions of tetrameter couplets, and adapts them to his own dialectic. Like 'To His Coy Mistress', *Newcastle* pits wit and sensuality against both great and small: the universal enemies of time and oblivion, and the particular tribulations of state and politics. Harrison's longer poems argue that our span is short, but our mortality defines us and is an essential part of our love of life; that social living brings social divisions, so any sensitive person is tempted to become a hermit, but that 'the world of night's best born in pairs'.[46] We do not find out whether Marvell's girl said 'yes', but though the poem's ending is to that extent open, the last lines close on a firm determination (to make the sun run). While Marvell resolves to tear with rough strife 'Thorough the Iron gates of Life',[47] Harrison—here, for the moment, a spectator of his life—is determined to be surprised by and to savour it.

> I look out over life and praise
> from my unsteady, sea-view plinth
> each dark turn of the labyrinth
> that might like a river suddenly
> wind its widening banks into the sea.[48]

Newcastle is also one of the most metaphysical of Harrison's poems in its 'Clevelandizing', not in Dryden's pejorative sense, but in the sense of 'the invention of a series of witty hyperbolical conceits, sometimes interspersed with images, and [. . .] erotic statements'.[49] One such series finds Harrison 'dizzy, drunk, alone':

> life circling life like the Eddystone
> dark sea, but lighting nothing; sense
> nor centre nor circumference.[50]

Cunningham describes Clevelandizing as 'a kind of expandable filing system' in which 'conceits and erotic propositions [. . . .] do not develop the syllogism, and they are not required by the syllogism; they are free and extra. There could be more or less of them since there is nothing in the structure that determines the number of interpolated couplets'.[51] In *Newcastle* the impressions of someone half drunk, erratically heightened and occluded, provide the logic of memory's juxtapositions, and I would argue that none of the conceits is redundant. It would be more difficult to make such a claim for the structure of some more recent poems. 'Deathwatch Danceathon', whose nineteen stanzas and final couplet are largely devoted to synonyms for bugs consuming and consummating, does suggest an expandable wallet-file, with conceit folding into conceit.

> Beetle bonkers in the beams
> spell the end of old regimes.
> Down come beams and joists and doors
> to the foreplay of xylovores,
> and ancient truss and cruck
> cracked by fronosaphonic fuck.[52]

Yet it is here that Harrison openly allies himself to Marvell and Horace, associating the driving rhythm of his verse not only with the life-pulse and its affirmation in sex, but with the measuring out of a finite timespan; devouring time.

> So 'never send' and 'had we but'
> And such like thoughts sublimely put
> by poets who've used the tolling bell
> to cast an otherworldly spell,
> or 'time's winged chariot' as a ploy
> to make a mistress act less coy.
> Put less ornately 'we're soon dead,
> my sweetest darling, come to bed!'
> .   .   .   .   .   .
>
> The very verse the poet employed
> to make the virgin see the void
> and be thus vertiginously sped
> into Andrew Marvell's bed,
> is the beat whose very ictus
> turns smiling kiss to smirking rictus,
> the urgent beat that wipes away
> the urgency of what poems say.

The poem ironizes the very genre which it appropriates to such good effect.

A more fruitful source of dissent and resistance is Gray's *Elegy*, a model of difference for *v.*, an anti-pastoral elegy whose bleak depiction of urban Limbo is all the sharper for being cast in the conventions of the picturesque Arcadia. The elegiac pastoral characteristically moves from an observation of the mutability of things to a deduction from that evidence of the poet's (and sometimes the poem's) own mortality. Rather than leading the reader to infer such a progression through an association of images and feelings, as in Wordsworth's 'Lucy' poems,[53] for example, Gray uses 'the strictly Aristotelian form of the enthymeme, or rhetorical syllogism, an abbreviated logic negotiating a move from the general proposition to the particular',[54] and Harrison starts with the fact of his death (and cremation),[55] and moves from there (physically and imaginatively) to his parents' grave. Neither graveyard functions only as a *memento mori*, of course. In the manner of locodescriptive poems, place generates a narrative structure within a more or less static meditation through introduction of the scene before the poet, survey of that scene, contemplation of associations arising from the scene, and departure, while the associations arising from the scene extend the subject-matter beyond the immediately apparent objects.

The neo-classical *abab* quatrain apart, the two poems could hardly be more different.[56] Each of the *Elegy*'s opening lines is rigidly decasyllabic, and though not end-stopped, each contains a discrete unit of sense. The pace is lingering, reaching lines 14-15 before arriving at the 'narrow cell[s]' of the 'rude forefathers' which confirm the location given in the title. The description is cumulative and pathetic, building up to an impressionist picture of the lowering, melancholy, picturesque scene.

The opening of *v.* also shows the locus of the poem to be a burial ground; no rural churchyard at the foot of an ancient parish church, but an urban cemetery, the site of twentieth-century interments which are as decathected from church ritual as the state allows. The landscape is not as picturesque as Gray's, nor is it presented instantly like an unveiled painting.

> Next millennium you'll have to search quite hard
> to find my slab behind the family dead,
> butcher, publican, and baker, now me, bard
> adding poetry to their beef, beer and bread.

> With Byron three graves on I'll not go short
> of company, and Wordsworth's opposite.
> That's two peers, already, of a sort,
> and we'll all be thrown together, if the pit,

> whose galleries once ran beneath this plot,
> causes the distinguished dead to drop
> into the rabblement of bone and rot,
> shored slack, crushed shale, smashed prop.[57]

The attention Harrison pays to the quality as well as quantity of syllables enables him to vary the number per line between six (line 12 only) and eleven. Line 12 gives the 'paragraph' of the first three stanzas a very satisfactory sense of closure with its syllables patterned visually, temporally, grammatically, aurally, and metrically. The visual pattern comes from the apparent arrangement of words in a pattern of two syllables followed by one syllable, though 'shored', 'crushed', and 'smashed' are spoken as one syllable. The temporal pattern consists of the alternation of (conceptually, if not actually) longer and shorter words. The grammatical arrangement is an alternation of adjective and noun. Aurally, the line is patterned by alliteration and assonance, and the opposition of long/short vowels and alveolar/palato-alveolar fricatives. Metrically, the three feet are almost spondees, three strong pillars which support the heavy line, but the elided 'ed's and the slightly lighter stress on 'slack', 'shale', and 'prop' suggest that they are crumbling.

The sense-units vary from a line to a stanza, and the lines are not end-stopped. Harrison does not lead us to the graveyard or explicitly state, 'Here I am in a cemetery,' but the place is implicit from the beginning. Significantly, the graveyard is not anonymous and archetypal as in the *Elegy*, but Beeston Hill, where Harrison's family are buried. Not only is Harrison ostensibly present in, and at this stage evidently the subject of, the poem, but, disrupting the traditional lyric introspection of the elegy, he directly addresses his readers as from the graveyard, taking for granted their interest in locating him, above ground during the readings' durations, and below in the future.

As in the Romantic (even Gothick) poem of place, whose locations are portentous and may 'vividly particularise scenes in which moments of intense, almost mystical, experience have been achieved',[58] the place of *v.* provides an intense experience for one [half] of its protagonist[s], but the experience is neither mystical nor epiphanic, and does not arise from vivid particularization. The *Elegy*'s main dialogue is between poet and landscape, while in *v.* the dialogue is between people, but landscape is significant. This follows the great tradition of British poets with 'a special sense of the importance in human experience of the interaction between the human spirit and the spirit of place',[59] but with the twist that Harrison's interlocutor is the human spirit of blighted Leeds, and the bleak, scarred, desecrated landscape is like a projection of his blighted and blighting spirit.

Behind Gray's *Elegy* is a cultural aesthetic demanding the imposition of order upon nature and the creation of 'exteriors', 'improved' grounds with manufactured vistas and focal points, to complement the interiors.

The career of [. . .] landscape gardeners or estate-planners [. . .] depends upon the same social valuation of 'landscape' one finds in the painting and locodescriptive poetry of the period [. . . and] upon the transformation of the traditional 'common' into private property as a result of a long process of [. . .] agricultural 'improvement'. The invisible grid of property makes possible the reconstruction of the land as 'landscape'.[60]

Representations of eighteenth-century landscape thus reinforce a representation of the national social order as a harmonious totality, and often require that landscape to be depopulated. The *Elegy* begins with a landscape which 'modulates or "fades" into a reflection on the entire social order', and so does *v*. As Harrison wrote more than twenty years ago, 'mining areas are particularly important, for the mines are the classic battlefield between capital and labour in the nineteenth century, where the expense of extracting coal was entirely in the sweated labour of men, women and children'.[61] Mining areas are still important, but now as the classic battlefield between the capital-owning class which is closing them down and the diminishing labour-force. Thus the dead of Leeds have marked out their plots by their gravestones. The whole poem is literally grounded on the worked-out pit which once helped to support the economy of Leeds, and ranges over the churches used as warehouses, the boarded-up shops, the football ground which has become a cockpit for displaced aggression. The skinhead, who resents the lifelong occupations which made the dead part of the social fabric of working Leeds, sprays his graffiti in his own act of territory-marking, reclaiming the city and the working community from which he is dispossessed. Thus the pastoral models of *v.* are subverted to lament the passing of the very industrial institutions (mines) which earlier works deplore as destructive of the rural idyll.

Like the 'me' of Gray's *Elegy*,[62] the 'I' of *v.* does not belong in the company of the living or the dead in the graveyard. Harrison is not as dissociated as Gray from his equivalent of the *Elegy*'s rural poor, the urban unemployed, but neither is he one of them. The difference is that Gray's narrator contemplatively observes the end of the working day, 'a figure just like the idle aristocrat in pastoral disguise', non-contiguous with the characters he sees, who yet 'happens to be, like Milton, the son of a scrivener',[63] while Harrison's narrator, claiming affiliation to the dead, his literal and figurative forebears, and announcing himself the son of a baker, is denied contiguity by the figure he meets, Militant rather than Miltonic, who declares him to be a privileged outsider.

Harrison often reiterates that he has worked hard to become a poet, and earns his living from poetry,[64] and he links it to the occupations of his forebears.[65] He also emphasizes that he makes a living from writing only poetry,[66] however—and not, as Astley remarks, by 'resorting to literary journalism'.[67] Harrison seems to want to be simultaneously 'Maker' rather than money-maker (with a concomitant involvement in commerce) and labourer earning a living through his sweat. Astley suggests that if the earlier poems do not proclaim, they demonstrate (by earning money) the poet's equal worthiness, though not superiority, to manual workers 'in order to prove to himself and to his working-class parents that writing poetry was as much a proper job as being a baker (like his father) or a teacher (a career his mother wanted for him, to make use of his education)'.[68] This would refute ('Blocks')

> all my years of Latin and Greek
> they'd never seen the point of 'for a job',

but by the time *v.* was published, the gesture of solidarity was futile. Not only were fewer working-class people in work, and to be making a respectable living was to be privileged, but few

unemployed people had the luxury of distinguishing between
jobs, respectable or otherwise, and would bracket 'poet' in the
category 'earning'.

> *Ah'll tell yer then what really riles a bloke.*
> *It's reading on their graves the jobs they did—*
> *butcher, publican and baker. Me, I'll croak*
> *doing t'same nowt ah do now as a kid.* [69]

To protest that even though he has a vocation, he still
empathizes with the Leeds skinhead, Harrison adopts a language which paradoxically assaults with invective and
embraces with a common register.

> 'Listen, cunt!' I said, 'before you start your jeering
> the reason why I want this in a book
> 's to give ungrateful cunts like you a hearing!'[70]

Compare this with the stately measures of Gray's convention-
alized address. The skinhead, however, resents this attempt to
transpose him from the realm of popular to high culture, and
replies in kind: '*A book, yer stupid cunt, 's not worth a fuck!*'
Rather than climb the 'ladder of aspiration' his working-class
youth would kick it over and stamp on it.[71] The wish 'on this
skin's words deep aspirations'—which, between two sets of
italicized and exclamatory abuse, gives the impression of the
speaker's having turned away to frame a softly spoken solemn
plea to posterity—is smashed apart by the skinhead's rejoinder:

> *Aspirations, cunt! Folk on t'fucking dole*
> *'ave got about as much scope to aspire*
> *above the shit they're dumped in, cunt, as coal*
> *aspires to be chucked on t'fucking fire.*[72]

This is no 'Haply some hoary-headed swain may say';[73]—
poetic, if quaint, cadences put into a rustic mouth; but direct
speech. Before the skinhead's appearance the poet had been
ready to sympathize and understand:

> What is it that these crude words are revealing?
> What is it that this aggro act implies?[74]

The reception of this liberal-mindedness enrages him, bringing
out profanity (the skin beneath the skin) which reaffirms the

common roots of the two personae: ' "Listen, cunt!" *I* said', but also sentiments which emphasize the widening gulf between them, and between the poet and his younger self:

> 'The only reason why I write this poem at all
> on yobs like you who do the dirt on death
> 's to give some higher meaning to your scrawl.'[75]

That the poet knows his transferred aspirations sound patronizing is suggested by the aggressive nihilism of the skinhead's rejoinder: *'Don't fucking bother, cunt! Don't waste your breath!'* At this point we realize that the dialogue has been two monologues and that, the poet's efforts notwithstanding, communication on neither side is going to be perfect.

> 'You piss-artist skinhead cunt, you wouldn't know
> and it doesn't fucking matter if you do[. . . .]'

This is the last time the poet swears back at the skinhead. Their personae, having split, now jump several feet apart in order to enable some sense of shock to be plausible when we read the name that the skinhead sprays.[76] Even after the skinhead responds to the poet's insistence on their common bond: 'I've done my bits of mindless aggro too',[77] with:

> *You've given yerself toffee, cunt, Who needs*
> *yer fucking poufy words* [78]—

what the poet exclaims is ' "OK!" ' This encounter is as much the collision of two cultures as of two personae or *alter egos*. Though both poet and skinhead employ the *bricolage* 'by which youth subcultures appropriate for their own purposes and meanings the commodities commercially provided', and combine or transform products 'in ways not intended by their users',[79] the skinhead by using aerosols on tombstones, Harrison by incorporating (for example) lager tins into a poem, only the skinhead is still emblematic of both popular and youth culture. The cultures are divided not just by class but by age. The vigorous youth with the Leeds voice has not only 'gone posh' but grown older. The blow is all the more cruel for being self-inflicted.

> *Ah've 'eard all that from old farts past their prime.*
> *'ow now yer live wi' all yer once detested . . .*
> *Old farts with not much left'll give me time.*[80]

Bloodaxe's claim that *v.*'s *'verses* capture the angry, desolate mood of Britain in the mid-1980s'[81] echoes Dr Johnson's claim (in *Lives of the English Poets*, vol. 1) that the *Elegy* 'abounds with images which find a mirrour in every mind, and with sentiments to which every bosom returns an echo', and John Guillory's suggestion that the poem 'seems to be uttered by the *Zeitgeist*, as though it were the consummate expression of a social consensus'.[82] Social consensus in *v.* is perhaps most apparent in the references to a division (employed/unemployed) common to all social strata, to a common demotic (its invective is not dialect-specific), and to the artefacts of common culture. These are not only literary, but also material and mercantile. Harrison's knowledge of the brands of lager which the football supporters might drink,[83] the local bus routes they might take,[84] the advertizing signs they would see and damage,[85] the teams they support, and the words they spray,[86] his wearing a *déclassé* style of outdoor coat, the parka,[87] advertise the poet's solidarity not only with working-class Leeds people, but also with their need to fight to affirm and preserve collective existence. Again, however, affinity is not unequivocal membership. Other cultural references are passwords to another social division. The kids hum 'Here Comes the Bride';[88] Harrison recognizes *Lohengrin*.[89] The stanzas at the end of the poem are presumably addressed not to the skinheads/football hooligans/unemployed of Leeds, but to the mainly middle-class readership of modern English poetry, who will be familiar with *Lulu* and Alban Berg.[90] The poem cannot appeal to an identity common both to football and poetry supporter, the 'UNITED that I'd wished onto the nation',[91] because it is about and confirms the division in their identities. Yet several stanzas are given to a description of the daily difficulties and privations of an elderly working-class man. The bus journey past familiar and changed landmarks enables Harrison to present by recollection and *diegesis* the minutiae of a working-class life he no longer lives. Mr Harry Harrison becomes an indirect, surrogate narrator whose growing frailty and loneliness, and victimization by social imbalance, despite his racism, engage the sympathy of both working- and middle-class reader and, displaced on to his son, bring us back to Tony Harrison as he arrives home, on common ground and with one accord.[92]

Empson describes Gray's *Elegy* as 'an odd case of poetry with latent political ideas' whose 'Full many a flower' section shows 'that eighteenth-century England had no scholarship system or *carrière ouverte aux talents*'.[93] Harrison shows that twentieth-century England has had a scholarship system, but also that selectively awarded superior education has not created a united society. The *Elegy* muses on the different alternatives available to different ranks of society over the necessarily mute corpse of the rural labourer. The dead in *v.* are not described as illiterate, but their words have not survived them. With limited access to cultural capital, they were not able to produce it, and were rendered effectually mute. The skinhead, however, is neither mute nor illiterate. His sprayed words will probably outlast him, and he has not blushed unseen upon the desert air of Leeds, but his writing is anything but prized, and introduces him to no *carrière ouverte aux talents*; he will 'croak' still doing 'nowt'.

The skinhead is at least given a chance to speak, even if, here, it is only to speak of his own death, and *v.* seems to invite a response of informed sympathy to the life of futile monotony he predicts for himself. (Like Gray's 'mute inglorious Milton', he has little, and eventually will have nothing, to do but 'rest'.) In his citation of the *Elegy*, Shelley similarly refused its ineffectual sorrow at the predestination of openings in society—and of closings. Canto v of *Queen Mab* protests its outrage at the repression and frustration of its 'rustic Milton[s]', forced to stifle the 'speechless longings' of their hearts, and its 'vulgar Cato[s]', compelled to harness their energies to manufacture.[94] Again, however, the cause of the complaint is the dehumanizing effect of mechanical, repetitive, badly paid labour, rather than the dehumanizing effect of the unavailability of paid labour. Like Shelley, the skin vents his anger, and the skald does not insult him with false hope.

The *Elegy*'s concern with mortality, humanity's one common characteristic, gives historical particulars an aura of universality and objectivity. The 'truism of the reflections in the churchyard [. . .] claim as if by comparison that we ought to accept the injustice of society as we do the inevitability of death', and the fate of the inglorious Milton is 'stated as pathetic, but the reader is put into a mood in which one would not try to alter it [. . . .] By comparing the social arrangement to nature, he makes it seem inevitable, which it was not, and gives it a dignity which was undeserved'.[95] Harrison echoed this more than a decade before he wrote *v.*, in an article on elegies and epitaphs on workers in the industrial north of England which describes 'the inarticulateness of the dispossessed and the eloquent religious mystification of a class who sought to reconcile them with a fatalistic sentiment to a nature of things laid down by God and/or Law.'[96] It does not necessarily follow that such poems are received as representations of a proper and unalterable arrangement. According to Empson, many readers of the *Elegy*, 'without being communists, have been irritated by the complacence in the massive calm of the poem, and this seems partly because they feel there is a cheat in the implied politics; the "bourgeois" themselves do not like literature to have too much "bourgeois ideology" '. Harrison does not suggest that we accept unemployment and vandalism as inevitable, nor could *v.* be described as calm, complacent, or impersonal. While it does not invite complacency about wasted lives, neither does it pretend that all could be perfectly fulfilled, for 'it is only in degree that any improvement of society could prevent wastage of human powers; the waste even in a fortunate life, the isolation even of a life rich in intimacy, cannot but be felt deeply, and is the central theme of tragedy'. The poet might acknowledge that 'anything of value must accept this because it must not prostitute itself; its strength is to be prepared to waste itself, if it does not get its opportunity'; a statement 'non-political because it is true in any society'.[97] Skin and skald will be 'wasted' both in the sense of 'laid waste', killed, and, perhaps, of 'not used to the full'; it's just that in contemporary Britain wastage among skins is far greater than among skalds.

The link thins, and the two become estranged at the point where the poet's language, incorporating musical references and foreign phrases, is incomprehensible to the skinhead:

> So what's a cri-de-coeur, cunt? Can't you speak
> the language that yer mam spoke.[98]

When Harrison responds to the taunt with the reasonable, if angry, 'She didn't talk like you do for a start!', the skinhead immediately moves his ground:

> *She didn't understand yer fucking 'art'!*
> *She thought yer fucking poetry obscene!*

This is the kind of below-the-belt assault that only a projection from the self can make. Perhaps flinching away from the pain of this, the poet makes the mistake of taking a piously avuncular tone:

> I wish on this skin's word deep aspirations,
> first the prayer for my parents I can't make,
> then a call to Britain and to all the nations
> made in the name of love for peace's sake.

This, delivered, as it were, over the bowed heads of, rather than to its objects, quickly gets the come-uppance it deserves:

> *Aspirations, cunt! Folk on t'fucking dole*
> *'ave got about as much scope to aspire*
> *above the shit they're dumped in, cunt, as coal*
> *aspires to be chucked on t'fucking fire.*

The poet tries to make up lost ground by exhibiting a blokish understanding of skinheads' passionate attachment to their football teams:

> 'OK, forget the aspirations. Look, I know
> United's losing gets you fans incensed

In another rapid twist, however, the skinhead makes this concession seem a superficial explanation of the football hooliganism, while demonstrating his own sensitivity to its deeper determinants:

> Ah'll tell yer then what really riles a bloke.
> It's reading on them graves the jobs they did

Here, the skinhead becomes the one straining to communicate, to make clear, while the poet responds with aggression and invective. ' "Listen, cunt!" *I* said'.[99] With his cry: 'the *autre* that *je est* is fucking you', and anecdote of his own 'mindless aggro' the poet seems to protest too much: 'I still belong'; which would be why the skinhead responds ironically:

> *And then yer saw the light and gave up 'eavy!*
> *Ah've 'eard all that from old farts*

Then he proceeds with his aerosolling, ignoring the poet. His (almost) final words complete the dismissal:

> *Don't talk to me of fucking representing*
> *the class yer were born into any more.*
> *Yer going to get 'urt and start resenting*
> *it's not poetry we need in this class war.*[100]

The poet is hurt. Literally or metaphorically, his words no longer reach the skin, or other Loiners. The divided personality has finally split. Paradoxically, the signing which marked their respective existence and identity, and confirmed their identicality, causes an inner death:

> One half of me's alive but one half died
> when the skin half sprayed my name among the dead.

This acknowledges the final division between his present and his past self; between himself and the young; between himself and the contemporary Loiners. The self is not equally divided, one 'half' is dominant, which is a defeat for the poet who believed his word and wishes could communicate with, do something for, both poetry supporter and United fan:

> The UNITED that I'd wished onto the nation
> or as a reunion for dead parents soon recedes.
> The word's once more a mindless desecration
> by some HARPoholic yob supporting Leeds.

If this is so, it explains why the poet makes an imaginary progression from dead parents to 'the time for ghosts' and 'fears of spooky scaring'. In reappropriating centre stage, moving back from dialogue to monologue, he represses the skinhead:

> I tell myself I've got, say, 30 years.
> At 75 this place will suit me fine.[101]

He seems to be dismissing the encounter as a fancy or hallucination, rather as Scrooge dismisses his first encounter with Jacob Marley. The skin's sudden appearances and vanishings, close-cropped scalp and air of menace, however, make him more like the Ghost of Christmas Yet To Come, Death.[102] After all, he does spray (enlist) Harrison's name 'among the dead', which perhaps parallels the melodramatic indication of Scrooge's future grave by the third ghost's extension of a bony finger. It also echoes the invitation of Gray's 'hoary-headed swain' to

> 'Approach and read (for thou canst read) the lay,
> Graved on the stone beneath yon aged thorn.'[103]

This 'real' epitaph is given a complex counterpart, in the palimpsest of writings, visible and invisible, on the *v.* tombstone. First, there is 'V', 'UNITED', and 'TONY HARRISON' in pointillist-effect paint (itself made of blank spaces as well as marks). Beneath that, in masons' Roman letters carved out of stone (that is, signifying by virtue of absence), the names of 'the dead', the 'continuous [uz]' which to so large an extent defines Harrison's identity. Contiguous with that, in invisible letters, is the 'lay' which is also significant in its absence, the ghostly trace of a poem which Harrison failed to compose. His eloquence is 'blocked' by the very smallest signifying units of written language, letters. The alphabet blocks with which his mother taught him to read mark the entry into linguistic significance, and the lettered block of stone which marks her grave marks the signification of her absence from it (and of her 'presence' in the grave and among the dead).

> I hear the family cry, the vicar drone
> and VALE, MATER 's all that I can spell.[104]

Falling back on the formal distance of Roman capitals and Roman language, the inarticulate Harrison changes places with his father who had fluently berated him in demotic:

> *You're supposed to be the bright boy at description*
> *and you can't tell them what the fuck to put!* [105]

The dignity of carved Latin loses to the ephemeral, illiterate scrawl on a fragment of second-hand paper:

> I've got the envelope that he'd been scrawling,
> mis-spelt, mawkish, stylistically appalling
> but I can't squeeze more love into their stone.

'The stone's too full'—lettered (literate, carved, inscribed) indeed.

As well as the personal associations which gravestones have for him, Harrison may have had in mind other highly charged epitaphs from cemeteries in mining and mill-working areas. His encountering the epitaph of seventeen girls between the ages of 9 and 18 who were burned to death or suffocated when a cotton mill caught fire, because they were locked inside, is a distorting-mirror image of Gray's coming upon his stone-graven lay. 'Near this Place Lie what remains of the bodies of Seventeen Children: *A Striking and Awful instance of the Uncertainty of Life and the Vanity of human attainments.*'[106] Harrison also quotes from a poem on a child mill-worker who died unremarked and unknown:

> An unacknowledged unit of his wealth-creating force,
> That hardly touched the orbit of his high, luxurious course.

Unfortunately, the 'sanctimonious mystification' of municipal epitaphs and canonical poetry finds its way into 'the Uncle Tom tone of some miners' poetry', whose 'love and grief find only the clichés approved by the *status quo*', but sometimes, 'that the exploited dead have no other voice than this makes the form of rebellion linguistic, and often that form of language which most draws attention to itself, poetry'.

Leaving behind municipal and other epitaphs, in *v.*, the poet passes through the graveyard and starts the journey home, training his eyes on reassuring objects: the Town Hall clock, the boys still playing football, the petals on the ground, the tur-baned pensioner, the FOR SALE signs; like someone who thinks they have seen a ghost. His physical condition suggests that this externalization of an interior polyphony is a sign of the poet's sense of defeat, or at least of his own limits. Defeat leaves ashes in the mouth, hopelessness makes us shiver. He thinks of ashes, 'the bits of clinker scooped out of my urn', and notices how cold it has become:

> Home, home to my woman, where the fire's lit
> these still chilly mid-May evenings[107]

Defeat (of a social conscience) is a subtext of this section, as res-ignation is for the *Elegy*, because its confidence in the healing power of love and hope for unification (skald and skin, black and white, man and woman) are never absolute. Home in bed, 'opposites *seem sometimes* unified'.[108] The joys of this fleeting life are not offered as sufficient consolation for a system the poet cannot change, and the sense of unity in personal relationships is rapidly undermined. Opposites do not always fall into pairs, schisms are mostly not refused, and the strands of stories do not always come tidily to resolution.

Perhaps Harrison's attempt to 'knit up male/female feels perfunctory' not because it 'lacks the passion and energy of the encounter between skinhead and poet',[109] but because however loving the pair their union is necessarily temporary, and conditional. We are not Platonic divided souls, and we do slacken and die, even though we love alike. Gray's *Elegy* ends with the dead young man in the 'bosom of his father and his God'.[110] Harrison can offer no such hope to his skinhead. This, then, could be why, after the peaceful interlude of personal love, *v.* ends on uncertainties, irresolution, and trailing possibilities. A possible grave-site, which may or may not be desecrated by football hooligans as yet unborn, on an unstable location which might plunge into the black void of a pit, itself worked-out, non-existent. A choice: whether or not to dissolve the notional graffiti or 'let it stay', offered to putative, perhaps non-existent, readers if, 'having come this far', they read the verses, and if, having come that far, they care for Harrison, or poetry, or both. A suggestion: in the next millennium (which itself has mystical connotations) the notional poetry supporters, in the event of Beeston Hill and its cemetery's (let alone man's) surviving, should 'find out where I'm buried', for which they'll 'have to search quite hard', but are given as a landmark an as yet non-existent brand of beer. A command: successful pilgrims should turn their backs on Leeds (a major signifier as the locus and main theme of Harrison's work), and read the epitaph which Harrison 'has planned', but may not execute—another layer on the stone, another facet of the epitaph (together with the one the seekers may or may not erase with an as yet unknown solvent). Despite these stanzas' resemblance to the stages in a treasure hunt, the final lines do not describe the trove which will be revealed at the end. All the pilgrims will see is the vista before them. All they will learn is what they make of it. The 'answer' is deferred along the chain of signifiers of all the aspects of Leeds and all that might be inferred from the city. Or it might be literally behind, in the poetry supporters' shadows, their own *alter egos*.

> *Beneath your feet's a poet, then a pit.*
> *Poetry supporter, if you're here to find*
> *how poems can grow from* (beat you to it!) SHIT
> *find the beef, the beer, the bread, then look behind.*[111]

Had it closed with a conventional epitaph (which must give the ultimate satisfaction of closure) like the *Elegy*, the whole of *v.* would have been thrown out of kilter. Where *v.* leaves things for the reader to do or to fill in, and the reader–text transaction unfinished, a short, tight, formal epigraph is highly determinate. It draws a moral and issues a warning, a platitude, or piece of gnomic wisdom; it suggests summation or resolution, as well as full stop. A quatrain recording the dead poet's desire for an undivided nation might leave readers admiring his vision, and drained by the emotional pummelling of his experiences in the graveyard. Rather than confronting the causes of Britain's schisms, we might skate over them as products of a natural and inevitable social order, painful but inescapable. It is a pity that the skinhead yells '*Wanker*' at the point where Harrison allows himself to concede that familial (and thus, perhaps, class) affiliations are replaced by romantic and sexual ones:

> The ones we choose to love become our anchor
> when the hawser of the blood-tie's hacked, or frays.

Had the skin's voice sounded in the poet's head at some other point after their division, the latter could have allowed the validity of the former's acts, and maintained the sense of doubt and non-attainment. This way, the tolerant liberal aspect regains ascendancy, because the skin's 'aerosol vocab would baulk at LOVE',[112] while of course the poet is all for it, and the poem comes down comfortably on the 'right' side.

Any comfort extracted by readers is fleeting. The narrative voice is reflective of the social melting-pot, closer in register and accent to his contemporaries, skins and skalds, than Gray to his. (Wordsworth put Gray 'at the head of those who, by their reasonings, have attempted to widen the space of separation betwixt Prose and Metrical composition' for his assertion

that 'the language of the age is never the language of
poetry'.[113]) Harrison's direct address: 'Next millennium you'll
have to look quite hard', in this voice of understandable resentment tempered by an admirable broadmindedness, invites us
to feel part of his 'continuous' [uz]:

> If, having come this far, somebody reads
> these verses, and he/she wants to understand,
> face this grave on Beeston Hill, your back to Leeds
> and read the epitaph I've planned

'They' are responsible for social disorder, vandalism, and
aggro; not 'we', who are empowered to read the epitaph and
choose whether or not to wipe away the graffiti. 'And now it's
your decision: does it stay?' But Harrison beckons us in only to
bite. *'Poetry supporter*[s]'[114] are a cosily exclusive group—cultural capitalists—suddenly we might not be [uz] but [ʌs]. The
poem leaves the choice open. And choice and its lack are crucial. If 'On Not Being Milton' was about being debarred from
the canon, from literacy, from counting—about not being
allowed to be Milton—then I suggest that other of Harrison's
poems are about choosing not to be Milton, or Marvell, or Gray,
or anyone else.

5

Open to Experience: Structure and Exploration in Tony Harrison's Poetry

JEM POSTER

RESPONDING to a remark made by John Haffenden in a 1984 interview, Tony Harrison acknowledged the pessimism of his own poetry, but at the same time drew attention to the celebratory impulse which both challenges and tempers that pessimism. The very act of writing is, he observed, 'a denial of the pessimistic beginning';[1] and if we want to account for the sometimes surprising sense of uplift experienced by the reader of Harrison's work, we might usefully focus on the energy with which the poet prolongs the affirmative act; on his vigorous resistance to conclusion, or, at least, to any simple forms of foreclosure.

It's a resistance most obviously apparent in the open-ended structure of the 'School of Eloquence', the implications of whose publishing history are reinforced by Harrison's complex response to Haffenden's query as to whether he sees 'a final shape' to the sequence. References to a section in which 'a number of things seem to be happening', to the possibility of alternative directions, to 'stirrings of a whole new section' and to 'unexplored avenues'[2] indicate not simply that the sequence was, as Harrison saw it in 1984, far from complete; more significantly, they suggest a marked reluctance even to contemplate its completion.

Harrison's resistance to finality pervades his work at every level. His tacit insistence on the value of formal containment is qualified by repeated acts of subversion, by a series of controlled assaults on his own skilfully fashioned structures. Look, for example, at these lines from 'The Pocket Wars of Peanuts Joe':

> In allotment dugouts, nervous of attack,
> Ambushing love-shadows in the park,
> His wishes shrapnel, Joe's ack-ack *ejac-*
> *ulatio* shot through the dark
> Strewn, churned up trenches in his head.[3]

The characteristically audacious enjambment of '*ejac-* | *ulatio*' sets up a counter-pressure against the formal constraints of rhyme and metre, forcing a breach through which we are hurried on to the next line, a line which, like its successor, resolutely resists the metrical pattern established as the poem's admittedly vulnerable norm.

It's worth insisting on that vulnerability. Harrison has an acute ear, but it's as much in the tremors and dislocations he sets up within his patterns as in the patterns themselves that his mastery is revealed. Again and again we encounter that metrical stutter or hesitancy—the missing foot, the erratic stress—which so fruitfully counterbalances the claims of poise and order. It's there in the conclusion of 'Pain-Killers II':

> I try to pass the time behind such men
> by working out the Latin and Greek roots
> of cures, the *san-* that's in *Sanatogen*,
> compounds derived from *derm-* for teenage spots,
> suntan creams and lotions prefixed *sol-*
> while a double of my dad takes three wild shots
> at pronouncing PARACETAMOL.[4]

There seems to be a certain calculated defiance in Harrison's avoidance of the smoother cadences of the more obvious 'Greek and Latin'; and there's no mistaking the inelegant force of that final line as it half-stumbles in its metrical tracks, its subtle uncertainties of emphasis both underscoring the old man's uncertainties of pronunciation and denying us the inappropriate consolations of balance and resolution. There's a comparison to be made here with the disturbed patterns of some of the sonnets of Gerard Manley Hopkins, though the stagger of a closing line such as 'And hurls for him, O half hurls earth for him off under his feet'[5] is steadied by the final cadence, as the broken rhythms of Harrison's conclusion most emphatically are not.

The closing line of 'Study' functions in a similar if more complex fashion, gesturing towards an alternative to the stasis and enclosure so powerfully established by the body of the sonnet. The curt, end-stopped phrases of the opening line ('Best clock. Best carpet. Best three chairs.'[6]) lead us into the confined space of a room used for deaths and layings-out, and darkly inimical to the developmental processes of life. The punning play on 'Mi aunty's baby still', the glass unclouded by breath, the unwound clock, all insist on that lifelessness which, as so often for Harrison, is associated with voicelessness: 'The dumb-struck mother [. . . .] No babble'. But the isolated closing line ('My mind moves upon silence and *Aeneid* VI') hints, however tentatively, at possibilities of enlargement. The literary allusion is teasingly equivocal in its suggestions: Book VI of the *Aeneid* is centrally concerned with Aeneas' visit to the underworld, and in this respect functions largely as a reflection of the poet's deathly surroundings. It also, however, describes renewed contact with a dead father, and offers the potent images of Daedalean flight and the fleet poised on the brink of departure from harbour, as well as reference to the inspired multivocal-ism of the Cumaean Sybil. Most importantly perhaps, it's through the very act of engagement with literature (explicitly as reader, implicitly as writer) that the poet transcends his oppressive environment; the metrical freedom of the line, unique in the poem, tellingly reinforces the guarded intima-tions of release from stifling domestic constraints.

Focusing on the connection in Harrison's thought between linguistic and domestic structures may help us to arrive at a fuller understanding of the complex and even contradictory attitudes which inform the poetry. Recognition of the recurrent suggestions that the poet's childhood home was in some sense inhibitory needs to be balanced by acknowledgement of Harrison's insistence on the idea of home as a source of nurture and protection: speaking of his parents in an interview with Richard Hoggart, he referred to the 'very loving formation I had', adding that this was 'as important as anything I'd got from the literature I also devoured.'[7] The two forms of nour-ishment are in fact intimately linked. In 'Jumper' we see the poet's mother knitting through an air raid, the click of her needles a 'sort of human metronome | to beat calm celebration out of fear'[8]—and the connection of this with Harrison's later statement that the rhythmical aspect of verse is 'like a life-support system'[9] is both clear and significant. Just as the patterns of sound set up by his mother's clicking needles provide a fragile bulwark against the terrifying bombs which send 'shivers through the walls' of the cellar in which she sits,[10] so the rhythmic patterns of Harrison's own poetry provide a partial protection against the tremors he experiences as he deliberately brings himself to confront 'the fire [. . .] the darkness' of human existence.[11]

This doesn't, of course, negate the equally insistent suggestions of constraint: much of the best of Harrison's poetry seems in one way or another to grapple with the disturbing knowledge that the very structures which offer definition, protection, and sustenance may simultaneously constitute a form of confinement. Harrison's negotiations on this front are peculiarly and productively complex; and I want to come back now to the question of conclusions, drawing attention to two sonnets in particular in which the effect of structural containment is perhaps rather less obviously compromised than in either 'Pain-Killers II' or 'Study'. In 'A Good Read' Harrison picks up on the discrepancy between his own reading habits and those of his father, highlighting the arrogance with which he once dismissed the latter, and closing with one of those punchline endings which he handles with such apparent assurance:

> These poems about you, dad, should make good reads
> for the bus you took from Beeston into town
> for people with no time like you in Leeds—
>
> once I'm writing I can't put you down![12]

Harrison has spoken of his admiration for the technique of the stand-up comedian, linking this with an acute sense of structure—with being 'almost aggressively aware of line-endings and the rhythmical entity of each line',[13] and the final line here seems to wrap up the sonnet with a kind of jocular finality. But he also regards stand-up comedy as subversive of its own constructs ('that technique of setting something up and then taking it away'); and the full effect of this conclusion depends upon our both recognizing the cliché and understanding the challenge to it. The poet's attempts to sum up his father are radically compromised not only by the explicit and significantly equivocal acknowledgement of the dubiousness of his own earlier judgements ('I've come round to your position on "the Arts" | but put it down in poems'[14]), but also by the suggestions that verbal structures, including the sonnet in hand, are inadequate to contain his subject. The substitution of 'writing' for the expected 'reading', defining the father as an uncompleted text rather than a finished publication, prefigures and reinforces the rich ambiguity of the final phrase: dealing with the memory of a figure who can neither be laid aside nor captured in words (and this subsidiary reading has been sign-posted by the earlier 'put it down in poems') the poet is forced to register the inevitable inconclusiveness of his negotiations.

The poem's final phrase permits a third reading, according to which the act of writing provides access to a more compassionate state of mind: attuned to his father's life in ways previously unavailable to him, the mature poet no longer finds appropriate the contemptuous disparagement which characterized his earlier judgements. There's a similar hint of emotional enlargement in 'Illuminations I', in which the poet recalls his childhood obsession with the penny machines on Brighton's Central Pier, and the resulting tension in the relationship with his father, rounding off the recollection with a trio of well-worn phrases:

> I see now all the piled old pence turn green,
> enough to hang the murderer all year
> and stare at millions of ghosts in the machine—
> The penny dropped in time! Wish you were here![15]

Much of the impact of the punchline here depends upon our recognizing that the phrases are, like the piled pre-decimal pence, old currency, while simultaneously registering the extent to which they have been invested with new life. The play on 'ghosts in the machine' and 'the penny dropped' creates an edgy vibrancy which gives place to something more profound with the introduction of the postcard cliché; breezily reticent, worn smooth by overuse, it nevertheless resonates in this context with a poignant sense of grief and loss.

More explicit in this respect than either of these two sonnets, 'Bye-Byes' takes further the ideas of emotional reticence or containment and the breach effected by the act of writing.

Recalling a childhood visit to a museum, the poet describes his mother's attempts to get him to leave the stuffed exhibits ('Say bye-bye . . . sanderling, bye-bye . . . ruff'), and his own refusal ('I won't say anything') to articulate the farewells which he now identifies as presages of deeper loss.[16] The mother's stemming of her four-year-old's incipient tears is a manifestation of her protective and nurturing love, but it also makes her an accomplice in an act of repression which the poem itself must now redeem:

> 43 years on this filial sonnet
> lets the tears she staunched then out: Bye-bye!

The finality of that farewell is only apparent: articulating the word he refused to utter as a child, the poet creates a parallel to the revitalizing 'judder of energy' which his antics once transmitted to the stuffed titmouse in its glass case; and the poem seems ultimately to open out, offering access to previously unexplored emotional territory.

Harrison's poetry has in fact been informed throughout by a fundamentally expansive territorial awareness. In 'The Railroad Heroides', the black man who 'sweeps | cartons and papers into tidy heaps'[17] in Leeds City Station stands at the end of a line which in effect reaches back, via London, Paris, and Bordeaux, to Africa; the suggestions of contraction implicit in the traveller's return from regions of dangerous unruliness represent only one aspect of a more ambiguous dynamic, neatly summarized in the first of 'The Zeg-Zeg Postcards': 'Africa—London—Africa'.[18] In *Newcastle*, the 'cluttered room' opens out onto African, East European, and South America vistas, geographical and other boundaries dissolving as the poet presses vertiginously outward to establish a vision of unity at once liberating and terrifying in its intimations of effacement.[19] More recently, Harrison has focused on the boundary between the supposedly civilized and the wild round his Florida home, most notably in *Fire-Gap*, where he describes himself traversing the swathe of cleared ground 'between the wild land and the tilled',[20] alert to the disturbing presence of a rattlesnake 'whose length can bridge them both'.[21] Spanning the fire-gap, the snake enforces awareness of a world of darkness and disorder at the margins of the cultivated plot; and the poet's refusal to accept the bulldozed line of demarcation as an

absolute limitation finds structural reflection in a double conclusion. If we isolate the first of the two 'tails' (or tales) to
which Harrison pointedly draws attention in the subtitle, the
poem ends on a decidedly deathly note, with a reference to the
murderous purpose of the Cruise missile 'blessed and bap-
tized' by a perverse Church.[22] However, he sets literally alongside this a muted celebration of the 'real eternity' conferred by
words and emblematized by the snake with its tail in its
mouth. It's not a question of choosing between these alternatives, but of acknowledging both; as so often in Harrison's
work, it's the poem's resistance to unequivocal closure which
to a large extent accounts for the complex energies still in play
at its conclusion.

'I believe', wrote Harrison in 'Long Distance II', 'life ends
with death and that is all'.[23] Well, yes—and, of course, no. That
is patently not all, for there are three further lines to the sonnet,
lines which significantly qualify the blank finality of that negative credo:

> I believe life ends with death, and that is all.
> You haven't both gone shopping; just the same,
> in my new black leather phone book there's your name
> and the disconnected number I still call.

There are no easy consolations here; but the phrase 'just the
same', delicately sustained by its positioning, opens up a space
beyond the apparently definitive statement of the preceding
line. It's not merely the patterning of ingrained habit which
keeps the poet trying his dead parents' number; the attempt to
communicate, endlessly baulked and repeatedly renewed (and
this is as apt a description of the sequence in which the sonnet
appears as of the phone-calls themselves), is a form of engagement which subtly counterbalances his avowed 'blight of dis-
belief' and his acknowledgement of the twin spectres of death
and silence. Those spectres have shadowed his work more and
more persistently in recent years, but there's no hint of capitu-
lation on the poet's part. 'Gaze and create', advises Heine in
Gorgon, offering an alternative to submission and petrifac-
tion,[24] and there's no doubting the firmness of Harrison's own
gaze, or the vigour with which his poetry continues to promote
and embody the claims of life and art.

6

Culture and Debate

CHRISTOPHER BUTLER

THE work of Tony Harrison confronts a number of problems concerning culture, and it finds a distinctive way of opening up a debate about it. Harrison treats culture in all his writing as something that people can know a good deal more or less about, and even think they possess, and which can make real and imaginary worlds which interact, and which we can inhabit, more or less separately, as Harrison and his father and mother did. His work also brings the 'high culture' as an educational ideal (or at least as the result of a grammar school education) into a confrontation with the 'way of life' culture of those whom it seems to exclude. This is not without a great price in terms of tension, violence, and self-division.

All these themes seem to me to lead to important and enduring literary work, in so far as it is true that one of the main values of art is that it helps us to explore ideas in their most problematic and so debatable form. Underlying Harrison's best works are some basic philosophical concerns which are to be found in many periods and under different social conditions. It is not surprising that he is a great translator of Greek tragedy, and found a way of presenting mystery plays to a predominantly secular age.

Harrison himself is aware that he has this relationship to perennial problems. In looking back at his formation before the publication of *Loiners*, he says:

The forms I taught myself, through use and an enormous amount of translation, none of which I kept, are now enactments of unresolved existential problems, of personal energies in ambiguous conflict with the stereotype, sexual, racial, political, national. Their themes, like

Zarate's *History of Peru*, are about discovery and conquest; celebration and defeat.[1]

These are thought of as 'existential problems' I think because Harrison sees the external debate brought about by poetry as related to his own internal self-divisions, his 'personal energies in ambiguous conflict with the stereotype'. These arise through his ambivalent relationship to a working-class upbringing, which is for many of his later readers inevitably surrounded by its own stereotypical, quasi-literary myth (bits of Orwell, the memoirs of Hoggart or Williams so often cited by critics, and so on). This myth is perpetuated in his own work, which, however authentic it may be, will be made part of a stereotyped myth for his predominantly middle-class readers, as in the poems about his father, such as 'Book Ends', 'Long Distance', and 'Flood'.[2]

The main division in him thus notoriously arises in the pull between a meritocratic education and a warm and supportive and loving but culturally less 'sophisticated' home (which didn't prevent Harrison's father from telling him to read popular verse in Yorkshire dialect *'to remind yer 'ow us gaffers used to talk'*, in 'The Queen's English'.[3] This gives rise to an emotional tension which feels most acute 'when the hawser of the blood-tie's hacked, or frays'.[4] As Richard Eyre comments, this is 'as characteristic a Harrison line as one could find: rhythmic, memorable, muscled, alliterative, dramatic and impenitently English'.[5] The last phrase suggests another myth which haunts his poetry, the belief that Harrison may have a class-transcending national cultural characteristic, a sense of 'real English' which, in a 'Yorkshire' kind of way, may yet come to unify his divergent impulses and enable him to write 'state of the nation' poetry. But these various cultural and political loyalties will always be in some kind of conflict with a deeper, more 'universal' philosophical thought; and I agree with Terry Eagleton at least in this, that Harrison approached 'a cross roads within himself in middle life between angry proletarian and bruised metaphysician'.[6] It is this type of internal conflict which seems most likely to guarantee the endurance of his major poetry.

The word 'unite' often collocates with 'with'. In *v.* it collocates with 'versus'. These words also help to refer us to the two conflicting linguistic registers of the poem, that of a resisting skinhead, and that of the poet, who is trying to pull it all together, and—as the successor to the Gray of the *Elegy*—putatively shares the accent but not the register of his opponent. In *v.* then, one major problem for the poet is 'Who am I?', as the poet-descendant, at beginning and end of the poem, of a butcher, publican, and baker. For this is a memorial poem, in which the identity of the dead may seem to be fixed, but in which that of the poet is peculiarly open: he has no memorial yet. This is accompanied by the political and cultural worry: 'Could I be like or identified with a skinhead?' As I will show, to this end all sorts of linguistic indicators of identity are put at issue in the poem, from the occupations recorded in graveyard memorials (who of that class would trouble now?), to the question of the poet's own genealogical descent as recorded in the conclusion to an elegiac poem, to the contrast between the callings of poet and graffiti writer, which are all dramatized by the conflict of accent, register, and swearing in the poem. As Harrison joins in the swearing in *v.*, he's 'trying it on for fit', though to 'quote' a swear word is going to be, for some of his audience, tantamount to using it anyway. The speech act seems expressive enough—this is a case in which language enacts its content.

I have called these problems of language and identity 'philosophical', not just because they are part of the traditional disciplines of philosophy, and not because they come to be expressed in philosophical form in Harrison's work, but because the puzzles and mysteries which such ideas evoke are not at all likely to be brought to a final solution. For in *v.* (which will be the centre of my concern in this essay), there is a sustained exposition and analysis of the very idea of conflict itself—in the speculation in the poem about what V itself can mean beyond 'versus' and 'verses'. It always seems to be accompanied in the poem by a contradictory and ghostly '[LEEDS] UNITED', if only because when you are against, your need is to unite with others. The historical background to the poem, the miners' strike of 1984, is also of great importance as providing a penumbral shadow of political solidarity, and this is reinforced in the photographs of incidents of the strike in the book editions of the poem. V therefore stands for an implied tribal solidarity, as well as being a symbol; for conflict, for the ambiguity of the V-sign (Churchillian and obscene), and, once it is itself aggressively attacked, as sign for the cunt—in its ambiguous appearance here as an insulting description of men—deeply misogynistic. When Harrison comes across the [LEEDS] V, along with CUNT, PISS, SHIT, and FUCK, used by skinheads to desecrate the graves on Beeston Hill, including that of his own parents (though the very sense in which this can be a desecration is in dispute in the poem), he reflects that

> These Vs are all the versuses of life
> from LEEDS v. DERBY, Black/White
> and (as I've known to my cost) man v. wife,
> Communist v. Fascist, Left v. Right,
>
>   class v. class as bitter as before,
> the unending violence of US and THEM[7]

This is a big set of themes, grouped round just such a common-denominator concept as the philosopher may grasp at, in the underlying 'them' and 'us' or '[uz]' which Harrison so often pursues in his poems, including one of that title.[8] As a counterweight to all this division in *v.*, there is the ironically diminished UNITED of a football team, of his parents' marriage, and of his own love for his wife, which seems to take its place outside the social context of the poem, in the safety of home. But it is the language, or more particularly the register, of the expression of these feelings of conflict which is at issue in the poem. Harrison deepens the analysis when he asks: 'What is it that these crude words are revealing?'[9] It is a question of interpretation, only partly to be answered by the convincing evidence of the poem.

This leads to some knockabout comedy. Swearing is, *prima facie*, a pretty obvious form of expression, and it can seem beside the point to attempt to get much beneath its surface, with expressions like *'prima facie'*, or by seeing it as somehow a skinhead's *'cri-de-coeur'*. When the poet does this he gets a rough reply, which depends on a self-conscious irony. The skinhead thinks that French is Greek, so unwittingly catching Harrison at the weak point of his classical education:

> *Can't you speak*
> *The language that yer mam spoke. Think of 'er!*
> *Can yer only get yer tongue round fucking Greek?*
> *Go and fuck yerself with* cri-de-coeur![10]

But there is a good point here: if you don't use the 'right' (register of) language your claim to identify with others' modes of thought and feeling may be diminished. You merely interpret them. It is even worse if you pretend to speak for them. So Harrison works a beautiful double bluff with language here, and one typical of much of his poetry.[11] He draws attention to the nature of his own intervention, and to its shortcomings, as he invents another flyting riposte:

> 'Listen, cunt!' I said, 'before you start your jeering
> the reason why I want this in a book
> 's to give ungrateful cunts like you a hearing!'
> *A book, yer stupid cunt, 's not worth a fuck!* [12]

Of course the whole strategy of *v.* is indeed, as Harrison then retorts: 'to give some higher meaning to your scrawl!' by provoking an interpretation of it. This is an approach to the poem which is conspicuously absent in the public discussion of it: see below. It's a poem which reflects seriously on its own possible meanings, and passes these reflections on to an audience which is not likely to contain many skinheads. But the ventriloquial invention of the skinhead's riposte here (*'Don't fucking bother, cunt! Don't waste your breath!'*) puts the very identity of the poet at issue, as it leads on to another comic interchange, about Rimbaud's famously Modernist claim for the poet, as abandoning his usual personality—*'je est un autre'*:

> 'You piss-artist skinhead cunt, you wouldn't know
> and it doesn't fucking matter if you do,
> the skin and poet united fucking Rimbaud
> but the *autre* that *je est* is fucking you.'

The theme receives its final twist, or completion of the circle that Rimbaud started, in the poet's final admission that it is the skinhead in him who signs Harrison's own name on his 'work'. But how can the poet in any disguise, or indeed the critic of the poet, claim to represent groups whose very mode of self-expression is alien to that of poetry?

> *Don't talk to me of representing*
> *the class yer were born into anymore.*
> *Yer going to get 'urt and start resenting*
> *it's not poetry we need in this class war.*[13]

This debate between skinhead and poet has a good deal to do with the left-wing anguish of much recent critical theory, with its ambiguous and witty attribution to the skinhead of resenting/*ressentiment*. For what is the status of poetry—as a representation of the voice of others—in any such 'class war'? Or more decorously, how can the conceptual deconstruction or recasting of art actually contest any kind of Gramscian hegemony in society at large? Does not 'class war' here seem a crude, superseded skinhead way of seeing things? Or does it call us back to the realities of conflict, with a man who doesn't so much resent the dead past as feel anger at his own lack of employment in the present?

> *folk on t'fucking dole*
> *'ave about as much scope to aspire*
> *above the shit they're dumped in, cunt, as coal*
> *aspires to be chucked on t'fucking fire.*[14]

Can the poet in any way transcend these stereotypical versuses? Harrison is clearly worried by the problems of what I am calling ventriloquism, and that is why he is internalizing the debate about it. For he is caught in a dilemma which arises for him as the child of his parents, as loyal to a class, as inheriting political loyalties from his formative years, and as educated into a culture powerful enough to give a skinhead a 'hearing'. These bring him back to that internalization of division and of conceptual conflict which we saw him admit to earlier.

For there is no doubt that the skinheads have a flourishing form of self-expression, quite independent of Harrison's view. This skin has his words all over Leeds '*like this UNITED 'ere on some sod's stone*',[15] and the force of the poem partly depends on the audience's knowledge and fear of this. There is also, I think, a suppressed joke here—much postmodernist art has been based on graffiti, and the skinhead's 'work' could be seen as a contemporary visual art-form, indeed as a peculiarly authentic form of protest, in a world in which the polite conventions for speech demand to be challenged by swearing, and in which graffito-as-political-protest is seen by some as a self-authenticating (because so obviously sincere) form of artistic expressivity. After all, both poet and skinhead write on grave-stones, but which of them has the authority to write? With what? Why? To what effect? And who for?

But then Harrison insists on internalizing the skin's voice: so that another underlying problem of the poem becomes the nature of his own imaginative identity. As the skinhead rises to Harrison's challenge to aerosol his name, and sign his work, the internality of the ventriloquized debate is revealed. Of course the skinhead wasn't really there. Only the extraordinary difference of his linguistic register made him seem to be. And so: 'He aerosolled his name. And it was mine.' On a tombstone too, which is there precisely to commemorate the past experience and social identity of the dead: there is an irony in the skinhead's superimposing self-commemoration. The conflict within the poem is therefore internalized in a manner that is positively Arnoldian as the working-class poet and the libidinal skinhead succeed to the 'divided self' and Hebrew and Hellene:

> Half versus half, the enemies within
> the heart that can't be whole till they unite.

It is a rather vague wholeness of *heart* that Harrison romantically inclines after, much as we shall see him yearning after the 'wholeness' of a Greek culture that included satyr plays. Nor does the rather Yeatsian ending to the poem seem likely to solve its major conflicts, once Harrison moves off:

> Home, home, home, to my woman, home to bed
> where opposites seem sometimes unified[16]

and where political conflict is watched on TV.[17] The domestic is allowed to overcome the political in Harrison's conclusion, as

> Turning to love, and sleep's oblivion, I know
> what the UNITED that the skin sprayed *has* to mean.

And yet an aggressive debasement of the act of making love also fuels the force of the original conflict, with its adversarial 'cunt' and 'fucking' vocabulary. The poem seems to be trying to move towards some kind of definitional conclusion, towards a unified conceptual scheme, but it remains open to challenge from a satirical voice which sees such thoughts as a pretty crude form of self-gratification:

> The ones we choose to love become our anchor
> when the hawser of the blood-tie's hacked, or frays.
> But a voice that scorns chorales is yelling: *Wanker!*
> It's the aerosolling skin I met today's.

As George Steiner has shown, the debate between Antigone and Cleon will never come to an end.[18] Nor will that between Harrison and the skinheads (or, as we shall see, between gods and scholars and satyrs). Nor can it be assumed that 'educated speech', or any kind of speech, *should* win in such a battle of identities, even if it does win out in the history of literary tradition. The great commonplace being tested here is that you discover your identity as you experiment in language, as you find out what you are willing to say. And what you are able, or allowed to say. (Hence the terrible story of Marsyas which ends *Trackers*.) Harrison gives the impression that his father and mother had a clear sense of their willed limitations in this respect. And of course they don't need to explore or discover as poets do. But his use of language had to be fought for, out of a conflict intimately related to a sense of tradition and the individual talent, which easily arises between teachers and their pupils:

> Poetry's the speech of kings. You're one of those
> Shakespeare gave the comic bits to: prose![19]

This insulting teacher's retort in Leeds Grammar School is frequently quoted, and it is quite rightly seen in the context of class and exclusion. Harrison's vocation was all the same for poetry rather than prose, but he also accepted (and exemplified in this very poem) an implicit challenge, to make a comic response to injustice. Although the grim humour of a poem like *v.* is obvious, I wish to emphasize his use of a comic mode, which is not enough noticed in writing about him. It is so often comedy, which is popular and oppositional, but also beguiling to a (middle-class) audience, which Harrison uses to cajole and joke his audience into an understanding, even a painful one, as in 'Turns'.[20] Once you laugh, you *ipso facto* agree: the joke is a great revealer of prejudice. Harrison's work is, as Romana Huk notes, 'comic, subversive, heteroglossic',[21] and Harrison himself draws our attention to Werner Jaeger's remark that the Greeks 'placed laughter on the same plane with thought and speech as an expression of intellectual freedom'.[22]

The scene of much of his poetry (and of his plays) isn't that of a mere battle of ideas, for even at its most violent, as in *v.*, there is comedy, which allows Harrison's audience to infer a good deal more than his characters can say, as in the joke about French and Greek above. Even if the past history of culture doesn't show that those on the oppressed side of political or class conflict have tended to do well in the battle for articulacy, or for authoritative modes of discourse, they have nevertheless been able to assert their own, as for example in the wonderfully comic Browningesque monologues of the PWD Man.[23] Even the skinhead, the phallic 'sprayer master of his flourished tool', may be working so fast that he

> get[s] short-armed on the left like that red tick
> they never marked his work much with at school.[24]

But his work still challenges the poet, and us.

It's an ironized battle between ways of life and their articulations that Harrison presents. In *v.*, he'd like the skinhead's 'UNITED' to mean 'in Heaven' for his parents' sake. And yet this rereading of the word sprayed on their grave is

> an accident of meaning to redeem
> an act intended as mere desecration[25]

This comic mediation has the basic benevolence of comedy, even when satirical, for comedy accepts the inevitability of cross-purposes, and of conflicting values. Even when recording his mother's cremation, Harrison can say that

> The undertaker would've thought me odd
> or I'd've put my book in your stiff hand.
> You'd've been embarrassed though to meet your God
> clutching those poems of mine that you'd like banned.
>
> I thought you could hold my *Loiners*, and both burn![26]

Such a technique respects the sense of identity of the self-proclaiming individual (as in Dickens, from whom Harrison says he has learnt a good deal). But these cross-purposes are only perceivable as comic to those with a conflicting or flexible sense of their own identity. Hence Harrison's self-consciously ironic and ambiguous approach to the incidents of poetry. He makes us see that the most protesting or indignant of classes or subcultures is held together, as a way of life, and will confer upon its members some kind of dignity or status within that mode of existence, at least for the means of self-expression which goes with it—as in his moving evocation of his father's changing way of life in *v*.

When the cultural elements of such 'dignified and meaningful ways of life' are brought to our attention in this way they become arguable, as culture and status go together. Indeed, '[i]t is at this point that culture is transformed into ideology', says Berger, and I agree. By 'ideology' he simply means ideas which are 'deployable for rational intellectual combat in promoting and defending the legitimacy of group interests and practices', so that ideology is 'what replaces taken-for-granted culture when the latter is subjected to critical scrutiny, and hence must be defended with argument'.[27]

Trackers brilliantly centres around such thoughts. It is the intensely contemporary re-presentation of a primary myth, about the way in which the 'divided and divisive categories' of 'high' and 'low' in culture come about. Compared to the theorizing of an Adorno or a Horkheimer, it is unnervingly direct: but it raises the same questions: 'Does high art build on low?' 'Is low art just high art degenerated?' And it does so in a way which is accessible to precisely the kind of potentially tolerant audience, a bit guilty about these cultures' interrelationships, that Harrison wants to warn, that:

The loss of satyr plays is both a symptom and a consequence of the division. What is lost is a clue to the wholeness of the Greek imagination and its deep compulsion to unite sufferer and celebrant in the same space and light. In the end those who feel excluded from 'high' art and relegated to 'low' will sooner or later want to destroy what they are not allowed to inhabit.[28]

All this presupposes a deep cultural analysis: what is it in the post-Greek, Christian tradition that concentrated on the 'serious' relation of men to the gods, and suppressed all this comic questioning of them? *Trackers* revives this questioning by following the Greeks and Shakespeare in admiring and re-creating literary work which is meant to appeal to the 'great amalgam' of an audience containing both 'learned and unlearned'.[29] The play is written 'in honour of that ancient wholeness'.[30]

In *Trackers*, past and present merge and interact, so that we have to interpret on a number of levels, as ancient Greek gods and satyrs, two Oxford dons of the 1920s and the football hooligans of the present day, metamorphose into one another, not without a good deal of contemporary allusion (all this to comic effects which are rather in the traditions of Offenbach's operas based on myth). The Queen's College dons, Grenfell (who thinks he is being pursued by, and is to become, Apollo) and Hunt (who is to become Silenus), are hoping to find literary papyri in the desert with the help of Egyptian fellaheen (who become satyrs). They dig up many legal petitions (which reveal an anguished social life) but these don't communicate to them on the 'right' cultural level: 'It's tragic poetry, not this petition in prose, | that makes the woes of ancient sufferers seem woes', says Grenfell.[31] As they discover the papyrus of Sophocles' lost satyr play *The Ichneutae*, *Trackers* brilliantly mutates into a re-enactment of the Greek play (even more so in the first, Delphi version), which is a version of the myth of the satyrs' search for the lost cattle of Apollo. This is brought up to date by Harrison, for example when the satyrs are rewarded for their efforts with gold-foil-wrapped ghetto blasters, and finally metamorphose (in the National Theatre version) into those who are most thoroughly and literally excluded from 'high' cultural institutions—the homeless in their cardboard boxes on the South Bank. (Even these props are metamorphosed, from those used by the fellaheen in the desert to pack up the two dons' discoveries, which then become a stage for clog dancing.)

This play between past and present is often very funny, as we are pushed towards a perpetual ironic comparison of the changing situation of the protagonists—for once Harrison has set up his historical parallels, he can easily combine an imagined Greek past, Grenfell's time of discovery, and a style of thought which puts into question our present attitudes. For example, when Grenfell-as-Apollo marks the transition from the scene of discovery of Sophocles' play to its re-enactment:

> half the things I say
> time or the desert mites have gnawn away.
> But I'm Apollo and my role's to inspire us
> so no more pauses for gaps in the papyrus.[32]

They'll be filled in by Harrison the interpreter. Or the moment when Hunt-as-Silenus encourages the audience in the theatre to sing an invocation (in Greek (!)) which of course they can't manage (the National Curriculum is topically blamed) to the Yorkshire, clog-dancing satyrs, as if they had come to a pantomime.

> He [Apollo] gets that vicious when he's vexed,
> so you'd better 'elp out and get lads from 'text.
>
> Perhaps there's a doctor [. . .] some don from Queen's
> who can tell the less educated what this means [. . . .]
>
> Come on, you'll be the first to have a go
> since about BC 450![33]

Once the satyrs are on the job of tracking the cattle, the sound of (Hermes') newly invented lyre terrifies them.[34] For clog dancing and the music of the lyre are in competition, particularly once a snooty Kyllene appears to rebuke the satyrs for their most un-hymnlike 'coarse racket', their 'crazed folly', and 'utter cacophony'.[35] There follows Kyllene's comic explanation of the evolution of the lyre to the rudely dismissive satyrs,[36] who in the end tell Apollo that

> Of all your prize bullocks there's nowt left to show
> but a dribbling baby [Hermes] with a homemade banjo.
>   [. . .] that little lad
> 's squeezed all your steers into t'prototype Strad.[37]

But since Apollo has appropriated the lyre to himself, 'high' art is born:

> Simply by plucking these magical strings
> I can raise my soul and man's to higher things.
> Deserts, a papyrus torn to tatters,
> theft, a trail of turds, and sniffing satyrs.
> From that unpromising, unlikely start
> from barrenness and shit we have brought ART![38]

whereas

> Your 'music', and I put that firmly in quotes,
> is suitable only for brutish men/goats.
> The point of my music is to put a stop
> to your type of prancing and clippety-clop.
>
> .   .   .   .
>
> satyrs, half beasts, must never aspire
> to mastering my, and I mean *my*, lyre.[39]

As Harrison makes clear in his account of satyrs, and as his play suggests, we come here to a tremendous divide—and one which has been perpetually traded upon by right-wing cultural commentators of the school of Allan Bloom—this is the idea that those who remain within or pay attention to certain types of 'Dionysian' popular culture (most notoriously rock music) are somehow degenerate, disnatured, and less than human.[40] But the Greek seems to say, why not let the animal out? Why not admit to our divided nature? (Closer to Darwin than original sin, this.) The conservative post-Christian shudders at the 'lower' impulses let loose by popular art; and Harrison cleverly equivocates on this in his presentation of the satyrs' dancing. It is at once Dionysian, and a 'folk' art, that is of a kind which even the most disapproving of cultural commentators (such as T. S. Eliot) have prized (though often for its conveniently subordinating, keep-in-your-place qualities). Harrison even allows himself to comment on this categorization of human psychology by art in a stage direction: as they receive their ghetto blasters in reward, the satyrs become 'aware for the first time of the division between their animal and human selves'.[41] We are told by Apollo that his temples, palaces, and sanctum were

> Never intended
> for creatures with dicks so grossly distended.
>
> .   .   .   .
>
> There'll be in the future an unbridgeable split
> between the spirit of music and mere mention of shit.
> No clues should remain I had any connections
> with clog-footed satyrs with gruesome erections.[42]

His lyre-playing then metamorphoses into the 'string music of the future' with its opera houses and theatres as the play comes to a climax with the narration of the most threatening of all past myths about art—Silenus' horrified account of the contest between Apollo and Marsyas.[43] After this, Harrison enacts the threat of his introduction, about the reaction of those who are excluded from high art. The satyrs, now thoroughly anti-Apollonian, work a variation on the themes of *v.*, as they meta-morphose into graffiti-aerosolling 'hooligans',[44] angrily rejecting 'Apollonian art' in favour of a 'Dionysian piss up in which Hermes' harp becomes Harp lager',[45] then into glue-sniffers who beat up their own leader, Silenus, and finally become the homeless.[46]

The last image of the play is of Silenus' face, frozen into the 'silent scream' of Marsyas confronting his flayers in a Crucifixion which (I hope Harrison is inviting us to think) records at least as significant a fall as that involved in the Christian myth. For yet another thrust in Harrison's work derives from that long post-Nietzschean tradition amongst classicists, which runs through much Modernist art, and is recorded also in the work of Freud and Jung (and E. R. Dodds)—the attempt to get us really to think our way back past Christianity and the moral and social arrangements it has presupposed. That is another form of radicalism, and perhaps the most dangerously transformative that an artist can imag-ine. It may well follow from this that Harrison in *Blasphemers' Banquet* proposes a toast in the name of Omar Khayyam to Salman Rushdie, 'and all those, then or now, damned by some priest'.[47]

These tensions between the freely expressive individual and the conforming community, between the assertion of reasoned as well as violent difference, and the reminder of the need for cultural solidarity, are central themes in Harrison's work. They should earn it a place within any serious canon of contempo-rary literature,[48] for its deep intellectual engagement as sug-gested above, and for another reason, which stems from Harrison's sense of the drama. His work in all genres both con-tains and promotes *dialogue*. And comedy wins here again, because a serious thesis without irony or ambiguity can be sim-ply opposed and dismissed, whereas comedy forces a more participatory awareness of different sides of the question, since its life-blood is the exploration of the consequences of just such discrepancies of awareness as I have explored above. Such work also helps its audience to sustain a conversational response to conceptual and social problems, as it opens itself to interpretation. All this is something that Harrison well knows as a man of the contemporary theatre.

In these ways poetry can open up a mediating space for politics, through the particular province of the poet, which is the peculiarly metaphorical language he or she uses. Harrison is in a tradition descending from Yeats and Auden and Lowell of social diagnosis and existential commitment, and of the willingness to let public events be reflected within the personality of the poet. He confronts political divisions in which he attempts to speak to both sides. In this he is very much like Seamus Heaney, who in his *The Redress of Poetry* attempts to analyse the room for manœuvre of the creative individual (who is under pressure to conform to historical, political, and cultural forces).[49] He asks what a poet can do to open up the right kind of conceptual space for thinking about such pressures, and for imagining possibilities that may be redressing or redeeming of them, and so actually in the end, as I think he believes, help to lead to states of affairs which are more just. He praises 'poems about the way consciousness can be alive to two different and contradictory dimensions of reality and still find a way of negotiating between them'.[50] Such poems have a 'redressing effect' which 'comes from being a glimpsed alternative, a revelation of potential that is denied or constantly threatened by circumstances'.[51] Indeed, Heaney goes on to assert that

poetry [. . .] has to be a working model of inconclusive consciousness [. . .] when a poem rhymes, when a form generates itself, when a metre provokes consciousness into new postures, it is already on the side of life. When a rhyme surprises and extends the fixed relations between words, that in itself protests against necessity.[52]

These are brave thoughts, but they usefully point to the fact that a poet like Harrison doesn't typically just offer a new or a different political view. That would run the risk of falling back into or merely confronting older positions (a job well left to politicians, who are paid to be one-sided), and it would not make a distinctly creative contribution. What the writer can do is open up the room for manœuvre *between* positions, and the chief means for this are the metaphor (think of the immensely complex metaphorical interrelations in 'The skin's UNITED underwrites the poet | the measures carved below the ones above'[53]), the humour,[54] the irony, and the ambiguity typical of the work of both these poets.

Of course it would be absurd to pretend that the work of a left-wing poet like Harrison is using these techniques just to mediate or split the difference. His work is oppositional. As Blake Morrison points out, his role, 'rather like Heaney's is that of an avenger speaking for the silent or dispossessed'.[55] Poetry liberates as a mode of opposition since in 'any movement towards liberation, it will be necessary to deny the normative authority of the dominant language or literary tradition'.[56] This does not necessarily involve literature in performing a simply left-wing critical function, of opposition to a dominant ideology, and of opposing it with an alternative. As I have argued above, it can best dig below historical political conflict, to concentrating on the comedy and irony of its underlying philosophical problematic.

Liberals say that the political issues raised by competing artistic traditions, nationalist and other pressures, multiculturalism, and subcultural differences should all be part of a debate, in which free expression should be protected, and dissident groups positively encouraged to develop ideas about new ways of life. Debate about works of art may seem quite likely to be moved by this ideal, because cultural institutions seem to be ultimately about the entertaining of new ideas in our enjoying works of art and our engaging in debate by interpreting them.

If we remember also that liberals insist on value pluralism and upon the value of a critical self-examination on the part of the individual, then we can see that they will prize the artistic culture as having just the kind of critical function aimed at by Harrison. The text may be a forum within which different ways of life and cultural traditions may more or less peaceably confront and even learn from one another. Any ideologically restricted political culture (e.g. strictly nationalist, or strictly theological, or totalitarian Marxist) will be inimical to this process. The artistic culture can challenge and put into per-

spective such commitments by enabling a comparative function, so that within works of art the ideas within different cultural formations can confront one another, as in *Trackers*.

For even if works of art may be constituted by and appeal to
our most deeply embedded convictions (those we invest in the
group or even in the self), they can, ideally, still be compatible
with an anti-monist liberal criticism. The relationship of any
particular work of art to the production of such a critical attitude is, however, immensely complicated, as Brecht for one
found out. Critical stimulation of this kind is perhaps most
obviously to be found in Harrison's *Blasphemers' Banquet*, in
which he opens up a multi-level debate between himself (inviting the absent Salman Rushdie to dine with him in a Bradford
restaurant), Omar Khayyam (as his *alter ego* who provides him
with some significantly anti-Muslim values and his verse
form), Byron, Voltaire, Molière (for whom he also ventrilo-
quizes, as writers persecuted by priests). These heroes and
many bigots (quoting themselves in film clips) appear in the
TV film. (Ayatollah Khomeini, for example, is cited as saying,
'*There is no humour . . . in Islam*'.[57]) The central political issue, of
the *fatwa* and of censorship, should hardly be a difficult one for
most of Harrison's audience.[58] But once more what counts is
the internally subversive voice: of Khayyam, praising wine
and despising the paradise 'promised to Moslem *men* by the
Koran';[59] of the auctioneer's voice as a sly tester of the 'fear of
loving what's fleeting for itself'[60] as he exemplifies for us the
'transience that makes the life-warmed ring | dangle for buy-
ers from a numbered string'. Harrison attributes the cause of
much of the conflict between priests and writers to fear of
death and delusory hope of heaven. But his aim is also against
those monistic, simple explanations which turn people away
from a love of 'this fleeting life' (a significant chorus to the film,
sung by Teresa Stratas). As I have tried to show throughout, his
cultural position is one which is entirely in favour of those
'thorny whys and wherefores, awkward whences', and of
'things that seduce or shame or shock the senses' of Rushdie's
book, and indeed of his own work.[61] He at the same time recognizes that they can 'panic the one-book creeds into erecting
| a fence against all filth and all offences'. Harrison seems to
see fear as the prime source of all such intolerant evils, and he

combats them, as the (comic) writers he admires did, by pointing to the sheer incongruity and illogicality of our behaviour,
in this case in Bradford, where demonstrators burnt Rushdie's
Satanic Verses, and so contributed in their evil way to the defeat
of Harrison's simple, hedonistic invitation to him, to dine there
in a restaurant, named after Omar Khayyam, and in his
spirit.

Cultural ideology within the poem and debate outside it go
together. There is not just an internal dialogue within
Harrison's work, but a varying challenge to an implied audience. Harrison makes an important assumption here: 'I prefer
the idea of men speaking to men to a man speaking to a god, or
even worse to Oxford's anointed.'[62] This is even more confrontational than its Wordsworthian (or Tolstoyan?) demo-
cratic allusion suggests. In *v.* the swear-word language of the
poem (justified as being within the actual register of the two
antagonists) has a shock effect. But what the skins have done to
him, Harrison in turn does through his poem to the TV audience, to the literati, and to 'Oxford's anointed' (who are yet
another tribe gathered outside that circle of his supporters represented in the film as gathered together in a wine bar or pub).

So far, the liberal ideal: but the confrontations brought about
by *v.* exemplify the actual modes of diffusion of ideas within
our society. They offer us an unusual opportunity to see how a
poem was interpreted in the public forum, and with the additional irony that its ideas began to circulate in the parodic sum-
mary of its detractors, most of whom had not read it.

I am not so much concerned in what follows with the row
about the swearing in the poem as with the way in which it
stimulated contradictory interpretations. For these I rely on the
second edition of *v.*, which contains an extended selection of
photographically reproduced newspaper and other reactions
to the poem. Astley points out in his introduction to all this
material that *v.* is concerned with the Heaneyesque theme of
'frustrated human potential', and that the nihilistic and alienated skinhead is what Harrison might have been but for his
education. The poem thus raised the embarrassing topic of
class, in a society in which many 'believe (or pretend) that class
no longer matters'.[63] Hence Astley's amusing citation of the
view of the Conservative MP Sir Gilbert Longden: 'once you

admit Jackson Pollock to the ranks of great painters, anybody can paint; once junk can be sculpture, anybody can be a sculptor . . . the riff-raff takes over'. Like so many, Longden just doesn't like Jackson Pollock or much else, but when a supposedly intelligent person uses the 'anyone can be' argument, he doesn't show any actual understanding of art, or of the institutional world in which it operates.

Such reactions for and against the poem might seem to be interesting test cases for the hidden presence of current right- or left-wing agendas, as it is so often argued that critical ideas are secretly motivated by the social situations created by government. Astley even suggests that government cuts, threats of censorship, political appointments, cutbacks in arts funding, and so on may lie behind much of the hostile response to the poem. Despite over twenty years of Marxist and cultural materialist criticism, the attacks on Harrison as reported here are very far from clearly related to such wider political conditions. This despite the *Daily Mail*'s claim that the controversy would involve a 'clash' with the 'political establishment', which was no doubt partly brought about by this newspaper's false belief that the poem was 'dedicated to Arthur Scargill'.[64] Scargill's words are actually the epigraph to the poem (as the *Guardian* correctly pointed out later).[65]

This is not to say that the specifics of the poem are allowed to count for much, either. Metre, form, and style of address get lost for a start.[66] The description of *v.* as 'a torrent of four letter filth', and 'a cascade of expletives' in which 'the crudest, most offensive word is used 17 times', doesn't show much awareness of the careful measured relationship of Harrison's quatrains to those of Gray's *Elegy*. Indeed newspaper judgements about the prominence of 'football hooligan language' in the poem typically involved phrases like 'packed with', 'a string of', 'a cascade of', 'piled up',[67] and in a parliamentary motion, the poem was described as an 'offensive stream of obscenities'.[68] *v.* was treated as if it had been vomited rather than written. This is a very significant metaphor-schema for the detractors of the poem. It assimilates the writing of a poem to the hangover of a skinhead, and so conveniently bypasses just those challenging mental processes which make up its argument.

Of course such cheap moral indignation skates by an appreciation of the problematic of serious art, which can only be approached by a form of participation of which reading is the most simple, hearing the poem performed less so, and thinking about how the poem may be presented (or indeed what its relationship is to the photographs which accompany it) very complex. One has to think with a poem like this. It doesn't just pour over us.

A few of the newspaper commentators did attempt a more complex response. The *Guardian* reported that 'it is a poem about the use of language, the anger of being inarticulate'.[69] For this writer the poem was 'too sentimental and masochistic', but 'deeply felt', and on important themes such as 'industrial decline' and 'post-industrial despair [. . . .] it even has a few good jokes'. *Guardian* readers were therefore offered some real literary criticism. Bernard Levin (strongly in favour, in a long essay in *The Times*, 19 October 1987) saw *v.* as 'a meticulously controlled yell of rage and hope combined'.[70] (It is interesting that even intelligent critics think that Harrison had to shout to make himself heard.) But Levin is one of the few who actually quote the poem, and concerning the swear words he quotes, he satirizes the British tendency to think that publishing or broadcasting them 'will have the effect of undermining all moral standards and restraints'.[71] This silly reaction seems indeed to have come from Ronald Butt, who replied to Levin in *The Times* on 22 October, denying that what he had quoted could even be 'construed as poetry, if poetry has anything to do with heightened awareness', and concluded that the poem was 'not fit to be heard' in 'people's homes'.[72] He thought the bits cited by Levin to be the doggerel of 'a politically minded youth who had well absorbed the sociological platitudes of the age about conflict', and no more than 'versified reportage' (and from the polytechnic classes, no doubt).

Harrison of course pointed out that 'the offensive words have been taken out of context',[73] thus stating a basic intellectual criterion for any kind of worthwhile understanding. But the whole point of the statements I am reporting is that like all interpretations they are to some extent deliberately decontextualized for the purposes of controversy. Harrison was also aware that the threat of censorship lay ahead of *v.* He is defending his right to a performance of the complete poem in which not only would the context be fully displayed, but a basic *mimesis* achieved. For he goes on:

If we want to debate some of the obscenities in our culture, including the way graveyards have been outrageously graffitied by four-letter words and swastikas, we must represent them.

Martyn Green in the *Telegraph* attempted what might seem a more critical approach, but produces as subtly insulting an *ad hominem* argument as that against the 'politically minded youth' cited above. Only this time the youth has found his way to the pub: 'Harrison is the kind of pedant who will never let an image unfold in the reader's mind, will never make a point once if he can make it three times, and like a pub bore will never let you go until he is *quite sure* you have got the joke'.[74] He is 'humourlessly didactic', like 'a kind of politicised Pam Ayres. Not that this is an argument for banning V'.

Of course it is easy for those who may have accepted an analysis of the poem like that offered in this essay to find such crude judgements ridiculous, but they are, all the same, as well-entrenched features of a conceptual world driven by stereotypes as anything to be found in the poem. Indeed they extend it, by showing that political debate in the newspaper medium may have as little grasp of detailed actuality as that depicted between Harrison and the skinhead in the poem, and be equally exploitative of cliché. Geoff Dyer seemed to be aware of this:

The headlines in the gutter press were, for me, as depressingly mindless as were the original graffiti to Harrison. Poetry and grave were defiled by aerosol and print alike. I expect little enough from the media, but it seems, as with graffiti, there's no getting away from them.[75]

So is cultural or political debate served in this case? The answer seems to be 'not much', for although there were one or two notable exceptions no serious engagement with the argument of Harrison's poem took place, and certainly none in papers which would have diffused his ideas beyond the charmed circle of educated readers of the 'quality' press. The poem was not seen as an opportunity to reflect by its detractors, or by more than a few of its praisers. Its effects were in the end relegated to private reading, and to the thoughts and feelings of the millions attracted to the TV broadcast by scandalous publicity. Channel 4 and Richard Eyre, who had interpreted the poem very seriously, came out by far the best. Maybe one has to console oneself with the thought that one of the strengths of art, if you pay sustained attention to it (as the film so magnificently did), is that it can be relied upon to create its own effects in the hearer. Once that had happened, all of Harrison's audience were left with something to reflect on. What then counts after that is the poem's survival—but how? In some educational process, perhaps; in some claim to be on the syllabus or in the canon. Hence the row reported in January of the following year over the use of Harrison's works as A-level texts has considerable importance. And beyond the literati or 'Oxford's anointed', the hope for continued thought about Harrison's themes is indeed likely to lie with a generation not hindered by the shocked responses so typical of the old, and maybe also, in the shorter term, within some kind of collective consciousness of those original viewers for whom *v.* may be some kind of canonic reference point.

It was a visual artist, Tom Phillips, who, in a rare reflection on the nature of the implied social structure that the poem tries to create around itself, seems to have offered the wisest remarks to be published in a newspaper on the *v.* affair:

Tony Harrison's elegy in an urban churchyard is a vision of Charity broader and higher than Mrs Whitehouse's narrow obsessions would allow.

In it, the communion of souls seeks to embrace the mindless vandal even in terms of his own verbal poverty.

Congratulations on publishing this eloquent, witty and passionate sermon, such unfashionably high-toned family breakfast reading.[76]

The political voice of poetry readers is not a very conspicuous one, but the arguments in favour of as many people as possible coming to the point of view sketched above remain as strong as ever.

7

Book Ends: Public and Private in Tony Harrison's Poetry

N. S. THOMPSON

> I would say that my head faces human history, and has a very bleak and pessimistic view of the possibilities for mankind, while at the same time I am very conscious of having a very sensual, celebratory nature: much of my work seems to be a confrontation of the two.[1]

It seems to me that English poetry today would be infinitely poorer without the work of Tony Harrison and the witness it so readily affords us of the life and times of the poet and the nations he has experienced. If Harrison is a poet of his times, it is because of the wide-ranging public landscape his work inhabits—both physical and intellectual, local and international. But equally, it is because of the private nature of the changes he has witnessed in those landscapes and has so meticulously charted. Where other modern poets have a reputation for a private hell inside their public personae (Eliot, Berryman, Lowell, Larkin), Harrison—although plagued by pessimism—shows us private celebration inside public hell:

> Bad weather and the public mess
> drive us to private tenderness[2]

but what he celebrates most of all between the book ends of public and private is his vibrant art.

As a poet his concerns are far from aesthetic: they are about life, about concrete reality, political and class consciousness, the decisions and indecisions which leave us floundering as our reality changes. But a question which I wish to raise in this appreciation of his work is about the kind of aesthetic which he has evolved in the course of his poetry to deal with the polarities of public and private and how they might be brought together. What is it based upon? How might it be validated? If one might prematurely say that it is an aesthetic validated simply by the man himself, and the way he bears witness, then at least we have arrived at a rather singular aesthetic judgement. As with many other considerations in the work of Tony Harrison, aesthetics and autobiography meet.

Indeed, it is my argument here that the articulate energy of Harrison's work exudes from the interstices of a dissociation of sensibility (see below). One book end holding up his work is classical and learned; the other is romantic and full of feeling. This dissociation is the more acute in that, in both cases, the persona of either book end has taken him away from his roots. As the 'learned' grammar school boy he has transcended the usual horizon promised by his background; but as the free romantic soul looking for his own fulfilment (especially sexual) in life, he comes up against the respectability (of his mother), which complained of his 'mucky books'.[3] As a grammar school boy Harrison has also achieved a public reputation way above his roots, but as a private searcher for his own true nature (or identity), he enters and entertains areas that are far from the respectability of public concerns. Like the poet himself, we are left wondering what might exist *between* the book ends.

As poet and man Harrison both celebrates and deprecates his public success, whereas the private in his work reveals 'a man of doubt';[4] the man who, while ardently faithful to his calling of poet, is also privy to things he would prefer not to witness or experience. It is these tensions which give Harrison's work its bite. But how does he marry the various aspects—public and private—into a continuous poetic flow? The answer suggested here is the poet's arresting style. It is my contention that what is best in Harrison's work can be summarized by a description of a poet he mentions, but whose Cavalier sympathies are entirely alien to the modern poet, namely John Cleveland,[5] whose 'Epithetes were pregnant with Metaphors, carrying in them a *difficult plainness*, *difficult* at the *hearing*, *plain* at the *considering* thereof.'[6]

Tony Harrison has often been described as a defiantly

working-class poet, or one who, if he has transcended that class himself, still celebrates its warmth and humanity or mourns its loss under the greater strains of a world of late capitalism. Whether a traditional, historical working class still exists is a question that cannot be entertained here. What is important is that Harrison saw his parents, extended family, and childhood friends as working class, and wrote about them as such. What can be called into question in the wider scope of his poetry is whether Harrison is celebrating the working class or his own hard-won escape from it; furthermore, does he mourn its alienation from the benefits of a learned culture, or his own alienation from the culture of his roots? It is often difficult to locate the poet's true sympathies because the strictly personal confines of his family were actually very nourishing (despite class oppression),[7] and because the wider public poems on working-class oppression are often objectively historical ('The Rhubarbarians I', 'National Trust', 'Working'[8]). The problem of personal identity links up with the aesthetic problem posed above. What means can one use to talk about the disadvantaged if one has been exposed to advantage? And how can one talk about one's own advantage without mentioning disadvantage?[9]

The solution Harrison found was to talk about the inarticulate in an articulate way. He adopted the form(s) of high art for the purpose of hymning the *sermo humilis* (humble [lowly] speech). It is in this way that his work is articulated around a dissociation of sensibility.[10] It was by this term that T. S. Eliot (though he later repudiated what he said as historical theory)[11] defined the disunion of thought and feeling he felt obtained in the work of Dryden and Milton from what had gone before. I wish to reinstate the term aesthetically and try to develop it.

According to Eliot, the poets of the seventeenth century 'possessed a mechanism of sensibility which could devour any kind of experience. They are simple, artificial, difficult, or fantastic, as their predecessors were', and, as he famously said, 'A thought to Donne was an experience; it modified his sensibility'.[12] The 'dissociation of sensibility' of the seventeenth century was 'aggravated' by the influence of Milton and Dryden, so that first, 'while the language became more refined, the feeling became more crude', and secondly, 'they reflected',[13] and thought and feeling—according to Eliot—were never the same again.

As ever, turning the contents of an essay to support his own aesthetics, Eliot inserts a note on the modern poet:

We can only say that it appears likely that poets in our civilization, as it exists at present, must be *difficult*. Our civilization comprehends great variety and complexity, and this variety and complexity, playing upon a refined sensibility, must produce various and complex results. The poet must become more and more comprehensive, more allusive, more indirect, in order to force, to dislocate if necessary, language into his meaning.[14]

One never really knows if Eliot's 'must' is prescriptive or descriptive, but Harrison would fulfil these conditions of the 'difficult' poet. If there are traces of Donne and Cleveland in his poetry, then he also exhibits the latter's 'plainness'. There is a directness to the polemic in a good deal of Harrison's work which sits uneasily with the complexity and wit of expression. If the social and political injustices of which his poetry speaks are undeniable, there is also the question of whether or not the polemic makes good poetry. Furthermore, the conceits of the metaphysicals, no matter how far-fetched, were always current and consonant with the Renaissance world-view, whereas Harrison's public *world*-view is—I suggest—a reflective, pessimistic one, while his emotional response is reserved more for his private world. Thus Harrison's barbs may be crude, although—as we will see—he is nevertheless adept at appropriating metaphysical techniques.

Furthermore, in opting for formal poetic procedures in order precisely to occupy high culture's 'lousy leasehold Poetry',[15] Harrison has appropriated the expressive means of the public works of classical poets such as Pindar and Virgil, and English neo-classicism (including Eliot's) in order to investigate not so much the condition of the working classes as the private worlds of Tony Harrison. But where Eliot hid his classicism and conservatism under the fracture and collage of a modernist subversive aesthetics, the fracture in Harrison's work lies in the dissociation between form and feeling. He has appropriated the formal techniques which once assumed the eighteenth-century's 'gentleman's agreement about taste' in order to purvey the uncomfortable facts of the lack of justice and equal opportunity for those who are not born gentlemen or ladies in a class-based society. In the 'School of Eloquence' there can be no Horatian *concordia* in his *discors*:[16] the work seeks to remind the reader of the working-class struggle during the centuries of underprivilege which have bred an inarticulacy which has in turn further marginalized the class from the centres of culture and excellence, especially in education.

This is the essence of the aesthetic problem. The fact of high culture is assumed, and also assumed to be excellent. It is unquestioned, almost unexamined: a good opera is a good opera, but in Harrison's work, high culture is never given the privilege of expressing what, in Horatian terms, it should, namely human(e) values.[17] Instead, high art is used against itself: it is used against the holders of culture. The poet cleverly adopts the means of high art in order to protest against the inhumanity of a class and a culture which will happily consume that art but not let its heart be moved by it. Indeed, Harrison reacts against an impersonally classical art and obviously distrusts the possibility of a transparent reception: his poetry is filtered through the voice of Tony Harrison, literally and figuratively. In his private moments, he is the humane (albeit troubled) centre in an inhumane public world, although, as we will see, his language exhibits the inevitable strain.

Under Harrison the poet, words are manipulated, distorted, and fractured, as if he were frustrated by them and, like the Luddites, wanted to break those threatening 'posh' words, as the industrial rebels wanted to break the revolutionary machines which threatened them. And Harrison wields a wonderful rhetorical hammer in his use of the metaphysical conceit, in as much as this is a distortion of the normal analogical relationships of a metaphor. This fracture is conceptualized in one of the poems from the 'School of Eloquence' sequence, 'Me Tarzan':

> *Off laikin', then to t'fish 'oil* all the boys,
> *off tartin, off to t'flicks* but on, on, on,
> the foldaway card table, the green baize,
> *De Bello Gallico* and lexicon.[18]

The working-class scholar is forced to participate in the middle-class cult of deferred gratification, forgoing the present consumption permitted to his peers. The boys enjoy the hedonistic freedoms expressed in local and class slang of *'laikin'*, *'fish 'oil'*, and *'t'flicks'*, all of which still look aggressively subversive in the formal sonnet. The poet is left with the plain percussive scansion of 'on, on, on,' in his Julius Caesar laid out on the ludic surface of the 'card table', but is able to express his own frustration in the delightful distortion of his hate for the 'Cissy-bleeding-ro' author who keeps him at his desk. Here we have all the violence of a working-class boy's hatred of a culture perceived as effeminate and here fractured by the expletive 'bleeding'. There is, however, a clever play here, in that the head which the juvenile poet pokes out of the window to his mates is seen without the body, as if held up for show after a decapitation.

Harrison further exploits his 'difficult plainness' in the public and private concerns of an early sonnet sequence. After the quatrains and couplets which make up the bulk of *SP* before the 'Curtain Sonnets', with the one foray into *terza rima* ('Travesties'), Harrison produces a sequence of five Petrarchan sonnets which describe a gift of guavas in Cuban rum, scenes from a love affair, and two scenes of public culture (a people's palace in Leningrad and a gargoyle on a Prague cathedral). Public and private are gathered together here in the manner that Johnson attributed to the metaphysicals, in which 'the most heterogeneous ideas are yoked by violence together',[19] but are further linked by Harrison's use of wit. The internationalism of reference and association overlays the private in the way that the Communist regime at the time was overlaying the European culture of Leningrad and Prague: the first sonnet carries a public dedication to Jane Fonda, the last gives the private knowledge of the poet's birthday.

'Guava Libre'[20] yokes together images of sex, violence, and disease in a series of fantastic conceits in order to thank the donor for the gift of guavas in rum, at the same time as reaffirming the poet's traditional identity as an Orphic figure. In this case the slices of guava are depicted as vulval or bucal lips pickled in formaldehyde, either those from 'Gold Coast clitoridectomies' or the 'screen cult kiss' (or vulvae) of Marilyn

Monroe. The next quatrain of the octave then suggests that the
fruit may be the lips 'cropped off a poet', an image this poet
prefers because it is 'almost the sort of poet I think I am'. What
kind of poet is this: flawed? muted? mutilated? The poem does
not specify beyond the usual Orphic associations, but this association ties in with the aspects of flaw and muteness he sees as
part of his family tradition. One only has to think of the personal epigram 'Heredity' used as the epigraph to the still
unfinished sonnet sequence:

> *How you became a poet's a mystery!*
> *Wherever did you get your talent from?*
> *I say: I had two uncles, Joe and Harry—*
> *one was a stammerer, the other dumb.*[21]

Curiously, however, these lips/guavas receive a classical fate:

> The lips of Orpheus fished up by a dyke
> singing 'Women of Cuba Libre and Vietnam!'—

which is presumably a reference to the Maenads' terrifying
final mutilation of the mythic poet. Is the poet here muted by
the feminist lesbian, or simply by the singing? The question is
forgotten as we are brought to another classic association, food
and sex, in the transformation of Orpheus as a crop-lipped poet
to a sexual performer 'going down' ('again') on the guavas
which are now 'the honeyed yoni of Eurydice'.

The poem is an adventurous variation on the eighteenth-
century theme of addressing relics and meditating on their cultural value, and is a highly witty 'thank-you' note where the
image of a mutilated and mute poet is eloquently belied by the
extravagant conceits in which the poem is couched. The grammar school boy is showing he can strut his rhetoric on the international stage while not, here, offering any commitment to the
cultural and political issues which appear as a backdrop to the
poet's private expression of gratitude.

Where 'Guava Libre' harks back to a traditional poetic motif,
as well as traditional views of the poet (Ovidian as well as
Orphic), the sonnet which follows it, 'The Viewless Wings',[22]
has an overtly Romantic association in its title and its allusion
to both Keats and nightingales. The sonnet is an *aubade*, a song
of the announcement of dawn (traditionally, a musical, even

choric, event), which cheerful phenomenon also brings sadness when lovers have to part. In Monkwood, England's 'northern edge for nightingales', the poet listens to the poetic bird and longs for the nights he has passed with his lover. He remembers the last night with her when he wanted to watch the dawn, whose Latin appellation also happens to be the name of a battleship which sends off the military chorus of a 'sudden salvo'. The beauty of a dawn chorus is rudely shattered in a military round of fire, which echoes the fracture of the lovers as one reluctantly leaves the other.

The private event in 'The Viewless Wings' is framed not only by the salvo from the battleship 'AURORA', but by the opening lines' reference to the 'EEC' and its decree which turns 'Worcester orchards into fields of sage'. Harrison has developed the theme of the coercion of public authority from the beginning of his work, and it is seen again where public and private again conflict in the next poem, 'Summer Garden'.[23] In the 'false dawns' of a Leningrad winter, poet and lover wake to the chorus of babushkas chipping ice off the roads. Harrison imagines the chorus of condemnation at this relationship (the woman still possibly the INTEL courier of 'The Curtain Catullus' and 'The Bedbug'[24]), and notes that the statues the lovers walk past in the garden include Psyche:

> whom strong passion made forget
> conditions of darkness and the gods' taboo.

The yoking together of myth and actuality is further adumbrated in the next sonnet in the statues of 'IUSTITIA and POMONA',[25] mythic archetypes which the Communist curators allow to be seen by the public even less than when the palace belonged to the tsar. The sequence concludes with another series of conceits which imagine a Prague gargoyle muted with his 'stone-locked lute' as

> The last snow of this year's late slow thaw
> dribbles as spring saliva down his jaw.[26]

The title of 'Prague Spring', pointing to the Soviet muting of the attempted Czech independence movement and uprising of 1968, is not fully exploited for its public concerns. The poet prefers to show his private perspective (on his birthday) from the 'finest vantage point in all Prague' of the stone gargoyle.

If Harrison's early poems show their protagonists' sexuality or sexual curiosity oppressed by parental or societal authority ('Ginger's Friday', 'The Pocket Wars of Peanuts Joe', 'Allotments', 'The White Queen'), the theme of lovers oppressed by the world and its discontents is developed to the full in *Newcastle* and 'Durham', two longer poems where Harrison creates a vivid picture of various circling movements of life all captured within one moving frame. Public and private are mercilessly yoked together, and almost always opposed, but we see the strain in the fracture of words.

Newcastle tells of the poet's return to England after Nigeria and Prague, and his self-induced ('nine or ten *Newcastle Brown*'[27]) disorientation at the event. The poet sets the scene and the state of mind:

> I lay down, dizzy, drunk, alone,
> life circling life like the Eddystone
> dark sea, but lighting nothing; sense
> nor centre, nor circumference.[28]—

and the reader is taken on a remembered catalogue of dizzying fairground and pleasure-beach rides, mingled with a sexual initiation. Already we have a fracture of words which cannot, as it were, take the strain: Harrison divides words and runs them over in an enjambment which both splits and yokes the syllables together, recalling his earlier fracturing of the adverb 'FORTIT- | ER'[29] of Newcastle's royalist motto: 'Pop- | eye', 'Chair- | o-planes';[30] it is almost like the children's game where the last on the end of a line of children is swung off!

From the memory of dizzy circles on popular rides, the poet then remembers his home town of Leeds: the statues of Venus, Vulcan, and Cupid; the Grammar School's chapel and its stained-glass windows dedicated to *Mercator* and *Miles*, both related by a chiasmus to the 'blood' and 'brass' of the following line. As the language of power and authority, Latin also appears symbolically above a bank: *Deus iuvat impigros* (God helps the industrious), as well as in the Newcastle motto. As the poet says, these scenes create a sense of rotating confusion:

> Leeds landmarks blur
> to something dark and circular.

Introducing the poem at a reading in May 1968,[31] Harrison said that the drunken circles of the poet's mind seem to be concentric, a figure he relates to that figure of confusion, the labyrinth, specifically the labyrinth of Juan de Mena's eponymous poem, which has 'three concentric circles'.[32] In Harrison's case these are Nigeria, Prague, and, latterly, Newcastle, where he looks out and says:

> I look out over life and praise
> from my unsteady, sea-view plinth
> each dark turn of the labyrinth

The winding of these circles leads to the epiphany of:

> Newcastle is Newcastle is New-
> castle is Peru![33]—

the fracture of the word in this case leading to the 'new' insight of the conceit that the north-east seaport and mining area is the seafaring and mining country of Peru. Again in his introduction to the poem, Harrison says:

I am interested in the point where one can say 'Newcastle is Peru' and the point where a man like John Donne can suddenly brood over his woman and say:

> O my America! my new-found-land

Donne's conceit in 'Going to Bed' is embedded in a range of geographical and exploration imagery fully developed in 'Love's Progress' ('The *Sestos* and *Abydos* of her breasts')[34] and 'The Sunne Rising' ('She's all States'[35]), and continues in 'Going to Bed', leading up to the famous last lines:

> My kingdome, safeliest when with one man man'd,
> My Myne of precious stones, My Emperie,
> How blest am I in this discovering thee![36]

After a Donnish glance at beauty's imperfections ('Some Island moles may scattered there descry'[37]), in *Newcastle*, Harrison develops his rediscovered geographical conceit to include his lover.

> Discovery! wart, mole, spot
> like outcrops in a snowfield, dot
> these slopes of flesh my fingers ski.
> ·   ·   ·   ·   ·
> O you; you also are Peru.[38]

Although the conceit is less novel to Harrison's readers than to Donne's, who were living at the time of real discovery, it is still vibrant. If the image smacks too much of male domination in Donne, it nevertheless empowers the lady with a good many raw and refined materials, and treasures her as a rich subject of witty poetic dominion. In Harrison, we have the more doubtful image of his lover's body 'like an endless maze', connecting her to the 'labyrinth' of his concentric circles, but offering no epiphany. Rather, like Peru, she is 'distant', although apparently only upstairs,[39] and the poet's mind wanders off to Africa.

For Harrison, the world is not a fresh, exciting place for love; rather it is love which offers a refuge from a troubled world. Donne used the conceit that lovers were a world unto themselves ('The Good-Morrow', 'The Sunne Rising'), where they are all the world, the whole world, eclipsing all else: 'Nothing else is'.[40] Although concerned to state the centrality of love to experience, and to give it a centring quality, Harrison sees it in direct contrast to the world. His internationalism here is hardly a world where he can say 'I look out over life and praise', because the evidence of *this* work gives little support. His reminder of Nigeria is one of

> mortar bombs
> smashing down Onitsha homes[41]—

and the beauty of Prague becomes

> slides. Bloodless mementoes, all
> Time-Life International.[42]

Perhaps more disturbing than the violence is the imagery of disease which burrows through the poem. It pervades Harrison's early poetry like a cancer. As he makes a fire to warm his house, the 'urgent prose' of the newspaper

> like flies across a carcass, spreads
> and fattens on the voiceless dead.[43]

The catalogue of fairground rides is undercut by the references to 'sick sixpennyworth' and 'vertigo'. In the later catalogue of eminent Victorians (and others), we learn of William Hey:

> the first to show
> syphilis *in utero*.[44]

The description of knotted condoms floating on the Tyne with their freight of 'unborn semen' which will never be discovered (or become seamen) leads on to the image of Peru, where

> Slaves, now trains,
> like *spirochetes* through dark brains
> tunnel the Andes[45]

But ultimately it is violence which draws the plain statement of private love. The iron railings sawn off for the 'victorious artillery' of the 'last World War'

> are enough reminder that we brave
> harsh opposition when we love.

And so, like Newcastle in the Civil War, the poet's house is an 'embattled fortress', a 'strong- | hold of love [. . .] against the world's bold cannonade | of loveless warfare and cold trade'.

It is difficult to see these things impinging directly on the poet's love when we know these activities produce more direct sufferings, but there is a direct link back to the grammar school which produced *Miles* and *Mercator* and their union in imperialism. Perhaps, like Donne, the poet is a sexual adventurer who wishes to

> celebrate
> as panic screws up each charged nerve
> to cornering the next sharp swerve,
> Earth, people, planets as they move
> with all the gravity of love.[46]

If so, then the centre he calls his 'Shangri-la, Pankshin'[47] is not one with the pre-seventeenth-century 'fair chain of love', nor the idealistic pattern of ascending love of Neoplatonism. The poem concludes with

> I'm left gazing at the full-page spread
> of aggressively fine bosoms, nude
> and tanned almost to *négritude*
> in the Colour Supplement's *Test*
> *Yourself for Cancer of the Breast*.[48]—

where sexual attraction is collocated with disease, and at the same time—as with 'The White Queen'—an exotic Africanism.

If Harrison is here recording his own move to Newcastle as the setting up of a new empire, a new world, a new castle (or 'stronghold') with his new partner, with Neptune and Venus guarding him along the way, it seems to be a private mythology of Aeneas that will help him survive the world's empty maze of *miles* and *mercator*, not lead him beyond to found or refound a bravely new civilization as Aeneas did.[49]

Newcastle is a slippery poem. It sets domestic love at its centre, but—as we find elsewhere—at the centre of the poet and his world there is a 'nothingness'. In the end, we are given a strange simultaneity in which a wash of images is presented apparently consecutively, but each one adds to the other to create not a hierarchy of ordered, subordinated, and reasoned conceits, as in a true metaphysical poem (despite its wordplay and conceits), but rather the deconstruction of one, as those conceits are seen to contradict or not explain each other.

It seems unlikely that Harrison deliberately set out to undermine the Renaissance stance (historically, it had already been done, as Eliot noted, see above) but use it as a reference point around which to base the lovers' centre *and* his own lack of it. Nevertheless, wit and allusion and wordplay point back to a traditional poetic without making that poetic one which assumes a traditionally conservative outlook or consensus about taste.

Harrison's work exhibits the craft of cultural tradition and is not antagonistic to any previous movement. Although the Sixties with its 'NOW' aesthetic was awash with free verse and universal collage techniques adapted from the Simultaneist poets of World War I, Harrison has kept fairly rigorously to formal techniques. In this his work enjoys a clarity which is not shared by other poets of that decade. If his work is crammed with the cultural references which sometimes make it difficult, he is trying to encompass the complexity of the world, and here successfully eschews ratiocination by imbibing nine or ten Newcastle Browns. The sensibility may seem crude, but the poetic means is not; the meaning is plain, but the delivery ornamental. It is a 'difficult plainness', and one which could be exemplified time and again in the poet's work.

In the poem which follows *Newcastle* in *SP*, Harrison manages to convey an even more overt disaffection for the authority of civilization. 'Durham' is reduced to an unholy trinity of 'University, Cathedral, Goal', where the students get high smoking pot, the Cathedral reminds the poet of his own 'moral turpitude' (sexual freedom), and the Goal of the state and its police,

> a power-driven mill
> weltering in overkill.[50]

Church and State appear to blend in the poet's mind as two 'church- | high prison helicopters' search for escapees and seem to him to be after the lovers. His simple response is

> Bad weather and the public mess
> drive us to private tenderness,

followed by the observation

> though I wonder if together we,
> alone two hours, can ever be
> love's anti-bodies in the sick,
> sick body politic.

Unlike Donne's conceit of two lovers being a model for all, a 'pattern of love' ('The Canonization'), these two lovers are simply up against it, and are represented as

> just excrescences that kiss,
> cathedral gargoyles that obtrude
> their acts of 'moral turpitude'.

But if Harrison yokes together strange images in an arresting way, it is without the resonance of a new world-view enjoyed by the one which was embodied in the vision of the poets of Donne's school.

What lies between Harrison's public and private worlds is exactly that which he found between himself and his father. In lieu of any spiritual centre or larger vision to his life than his personal (and family) love(s), in his early poems it is 'books, books, books' ('Book Ends I') which provide Harrison with a quasi-metaphysical means with which to apprehend that life in the best way he can, and with it enliven his witness. It makes him a 'Wit' in the seventeenth-century meaning of the word.

Many critics have said that Harrison's most moving poetry comes from the record of his family in the 'School of Eloquence' sonnets. If his status as poet and 'Wit' demarcate him from that family, his emotions are fiercely protective of them, even where he is in disagreement with them over matters as deep as religion or as trivial as fashion. The sonnets are also a fascinating anthropological record, as they chart the end of an era for the British northern working-class life that he and his parents knew. The changes experienced by Mr Harrison senior in his old age add to the pathos we feel. If we take his extinction metonymically for a whole class, this is further adumbrated in the sonnets dealing with the extinction of species in nature, 'Art & Extinction'.[51]

After the fierce vitality of Harrison's reaction to the 'Nothingness' he perceives in the poems leading up to and including *Newcastle*, 'Durham', and 'Ghosts: Some Words Before Breakfast', the sonnets turn back the clock from such life on the edge, and allow us to see how the poet arrived at the persona of those poems and their aesthetic of the present. Although they contain the theme of public and private, they do not allow the poet to achieve a search for identity in his roots, because again he is exploring contradictions and his own differences from the world of his parents. His being a difficult poet puts paid to any desire to be the poet that his father would read.[52]

The poem which most successfully encapsulates Harrison's private approach to life, and most successfully negotiates the problem of his aesthetic of difficulty, is *Kumquat*. The poem portrays the poet as a 'man of doubt at life's mid-way'. The possible analogy with Dante is not developed, although there are images which could correspond to an infernal landscape,[53] and the fruit farm is a kind of earthly paradise where the poet's beloved benignly picking fruit 'with one deft movement of a sunburnt wrist' is more reminiscent of Matilda than Eve.[54] Instead, the persona Harrison creates here is not the 'lad who gets the alphas', 'scholar', or 'Northern bard', but simply that of a man of 42. However, there is still a little sexual swagger apparent in the mention of the noise the couple's bedsprings make at night.[55]

The poem is richly bedded in literature, an interesting reworking of the opposed *mel* and *sal* of life so beloved of Renaissance writers.[56] Harrison uses not so much a metaphysical conceit to yoke these oppositions together as a precise (and natural) objective correlative: the bitter-sweet fruit of the kumquat unites the opposites in one 'citrus scarcely cherry size'. And Harrison wishes to offer this fruit for his approval to that most sensuously sweet of melancholy poets, John Keats. He suggests that Keats would have been able to make metaphorical use of the kumquat in developing his suggestion that 'Melancholy' (bitterness) dwells in 'Delight' (sweetness):

> Ay, in the very temple of delight
>   Veil'd Melancholy has her sovran shrine
>   Though seen of none save him whose strenuous tongue
>   Can burst Joy's grape against his palate fine;
> His soul shall taste the sadness of her might,
>   And be among her cloudy trophies hung.[57]

Harrison's choice of dedicatee is acute. Keats struggled with his love of the sensuous apprehension of things and his darker forebodings, and he famously loved to yoke separate sensuous things together in the trope of synaesthesia. He would indeed have been captivated by nature creating the same thing in one exotic fruit. As the poet of 'negative capability', he would also have been able to cope with the doubt of not knowing which part of the fruit was sweet and which sour, a question Harrison poses for him:

> You'll find that one part's sweet and one part's tart:
> *say where the sweetness or the sourness start.*[58]

Keats would have taken it all in his sensuous stride, according to his theory that: 'man is capable of being in uncertainties, Mysteries, doubts, without any irritable reaching after fact and reason'.[59]

As 'a man of doubt', Harrison is gnawed at by the negative aspects of life: 'Flora asphyxiated', 'dehydrated Naiads, Dryad amputees', children in a 'shirt of Nessus fire',[60] which he imagines in classical images in horrid metamorphoses—a technique

echoing the great creative stroke which Dante employed to
lend some Ovidian pathos to his citizens of hell and purga-
tory.[61] Some lines later he gives a more denuded presentation
of the hell within, when he recalls

> days, when the very sunlight made me weep,
> days spent like the nights in deep, drugged sleep,
> days in Newcastle by my daughter's bed,
> wondering if she, or I, weren't better dead.[62]

Despite the bitter recollections, in this poem it is the fulsome
descriptions of fruit and light and the connections between the
two which one feels the poet has been striving to achieve all
through his life of 'grey days' and the languages he has 'slaved
to speak or read',[63] and which Africa was perhaps too extreme
and exotic to supply. As a celebration of man and woman in a
locus amoenus[64] it is a private celebration all too rare in
Harrison's work, and aptly, sensuously, and wittily suggests
the zest that the poet still feels despite his infusions of melancholy at the grip of Nothingness. The pun on 'zest' itself is an
excellent one: 'life has a skin of death that keeps its zest',
despite the fact that, like an unnatural fruit, 'Man's Being [is]
ripened by his Nothingness'.[65] Thus the apprehension of death
and the void beyond is turned into a learning experience,
where the negatives of life and its negation become a means
whereby the positive is appreciated all the more. *Carpe diem*, as
Horace said.

If Tony Harrison finds the celebration of life difficult,[66] and a
great deal of his concerns are with the depradations man com-
mits on nature and on man, he is all the braver when he does
so because he is not shored up by any wider consolatory view.
He is not synthesizing a world-picture as the metaphysicals
did, nor even as twentieth-century poets such as Yeats, Eliot,
Seamus Heaney, or Geoffrey Hill have done. If he has
eschewed the consolation of religion, then he has also avoided
the patrician mode of certainties. What gives his work its vitality is that he adopts the mechanisms of a learned poet as a defiant stance against pessimism and despair. Between his own
positive and negative, his own sweetness and sourness, is a
poet greedy for words, for 'books, books, books'. One can only
surmise that it is in the same ironically hopeful spirit that

Chaucer wrote at the end of the *Parliament of Fowls* when he wakes out of his dream vision of birds:

> I wok, and othere bokes tok me to,
> To reede upon, and yit I rede alwey.
> I hope, ywis, to rede som day
> That I shal mete som thyng for to fare
> The bet, and thus to rede I nyl nat spare.[67]

8

Tony Harrison and the *Guardian*

ALAN RUSBRIDGER

MODERN wars do not often inspire great journalism. In the post-infantry age much war reporting takes place from the safety of the briefing room, where five-star generals provide jokey commentaries to video clips of smart bombs popping down chimney stacks.

In the post-Vietnam, CNN age, few politicians are willing to commit ground troops to a foreign soil unless in overwhelming numbers—and with the media at a closely shepherded distance. Even the Falklands War—with its minute control over every word filed by an increasingly frustrated corps of constantly shadowed war correspondents—saw individual flashes of brilliant reporting. By the time the Gulf War came along in 1991, the Military had the supply of information pretty well taped. Just one western print journalist, Alfonso Rojo of *El Mundo* (filing also for the *Guardian*), remained in Baghdad to add any depth and context to the pictures beamed out around the clock by CNN. Overwhelmingly, the war was filtered through the reports and transmissions of the daily press briefings held by the coalition top brass, with General Norman Schwarzkopf topping the bill. In particular, the massacre of retreating Iraqi troops on the road from Kuwait was an event viewed only from the air—a turkey shoot through laser-sights, with a sound-track of whooping Top Guns.

Back in Fleet Street, the war was not a terribly edifying experience. The consensus was that this was a just and necessary war against an overweening tyrant. The tabloids by and large tried to rekindle the jingoistic flame of the Falklands, stumbling over each other to be the most vocal in supporting 'our boys'. There were few voices of dissent, even in the broadsheets, with Edward Pearce, then of the *Guardian*, an honourable exception. There were even fewer images to disturb the peace of the British newspaper-reading public. It was not until a day or two after the 'turkey shoot' on the retreat from Kuwait City that any images of Iraqi victims started filtering back to London. One picture in particular—an AP photograph of a hideously charred Iraqi soldier: half flesh, half bone—was considered too disturbing for use by all but one newspaper, the *Observer*. It remains one of the most shocking images of war I have ever seen.

At the time I was Features Editor of the *Guardian*, and struggling to think of novel ways of covering this long-drawn-out, distant, anaesthetized war. We had reporters in the briefing rooms, reporters on the ground and on the seas. We had diplomatic specialists, defence specialists, and knowledgeable correspondents in all the relevant places. We commissioned commentaries from leading Jewish writers, leading Arab writers; from American hawks, Turkish doves, and a retired Vice Air Chief Marshal who would come on the blower every 48 hours or so with a new piece of enthralling analysis about the capabilities of the Tomahawk missile. It was, frankly, difficult to think of new things to say about this war, or ways of saying them.

And then I thought of Tony Harrison. I remembered reading *v.* the previous year, and seeing *Trackers*. I had been particularly impressed by the latter, and its ability to find vigorous and accessible contemporary resonances in classical legend. Through the good offices of Peter Lennon, a *Guardian* writer who had recently profiled him, I made contact with Harrison. The result was two poems about the Gulf War—'Initial Illumination' and *A Cold Coming*—the latter of which will surely deserve a place in any future anthology of twentieth-century war poetry. We carried the poems on the main editorial page since it seemed to us important that they be seen as a commentary upon current events and not as a piece of contemporary Eng. Lit., which would undoubtedly have been the case had they been consigned to the arts or features pages.

A Cold Coming was inspired by the photograph no one except the *Observer* had thought appropriate to print. Much of the poem consisted of the words of the charred figure in the picture—a rhetorical device which harked back to Thomas Hardy's pre-First World War *Satires of Circumstance*, in which voices from the grave are often used ironically with similarly telling effect.

> That night your great guns, unawares,
> Shook all our coffins as we lay,
> And broke the chancel window-squares,
> We thought it was the Judgement-day
> And sat upright.[1]

Harrison's poem is an elaborate conceit: in turn, poignant, witty, ingenious, knowing—and unutterably powerful. It cannot be much more than 1,500 words in all, but in that space it managed to say more than scores of conventional commentaries, whether by Jew, Arab, strategic observer, or armchair wing commander. It cut through all the phoney euphemisms and cold, strange unreality of this war-by-video, and forced the reader starkly face-to-incinerated-face with the unwilling soldiers of Saddam who were at the receiving end of the most awesome array of military hardware the world has ever seen.

The experiment was such a success that we asked Tony Harrison to accept a regular retainer in return for a few poems a year on contemporary themes; in effect, to be the *Guardian*'s Poet Laureate. He eagerly agreed, and has remained in this strange unofficial role ever since, writing poems on subjects as diverse as the royal family and the war in Bosnia. He has posted poems from his home, and filed them to copytakers via satellite phone from war zones. His work has appeared on the news pages, the commentary page, and the front page. He is not there to replace a Maggie O'Kane, a Hugo Young, a Martin Woollacott, or an Ed Vulliamy, each of whom can brilliantly reflect the different truths and aspects of war and peace. But you know the moment a new Tony Harrison poem arrives that it will have a depth and texture quite apart from the work of any journalist or commentator.

Paul Fussell, who has written so acutely about the literature of war, once wondered whether the paucity of Vietnam war poetry was attributable to the 'unpleasant' fact that 'we are now inescapably mired in a post-verbal age, where neither writer nor reader possesses the layers of allusion arising from wide literary experience that make significant writing and reading possible'.[2] For five years now I've been meaning to send him Tony Harrison's work from Iraq and Bosnia by way of reassurance.

9

Doomsongs: Tony Harrison and War

RICK RYLANCE

'ONE of my very earliest memories', Tony Harrison wrote in an introduction to an early selection of poems in 1971:

is of bombs falling, the windows shaking, myself and my mother crouching in the cellar listening, me begging to be allowed to rush out into the lit-up streets, the whistlings sounded so festive [. . . .] Another is of a street party with a bonfire and such joy, celebration and general fraternity as I have never seen since. As I grew up the image stayed but I came to realise that the cause of the celebration was Hiroshima. Another is the dazed feeling of being led by the hand from a cinema into the sunlit City Square after seeing films of Belsen in 1945, when I was eight. Around all these too is a general atmosphere of the inarticulate and unmentionable, a silence compounded of the hand-me-down Victorian adage, 'children should be seen and not heard' and the mock Yorkshire taciturnity of 'hear all, see all, say nowt'. Even now, when I have finished a poem I have bouts of speechlessness in which that fireside atmosphere casts dark shadows in my skull.[1]

I am intrigued by the tangled assembly of Harrison's memories in this early piece. He introduces them by way of a Pablo Neruda story in which two boys, unknown to each other, communicate silently by passing toys through a hole in a fence. What drove him to poetry, he writes, was a similar compound of silence, exchange, and blessing: 'I can find nothing quite so significantly beautiful, but there are things which brought to me, early but obscurely, the same precious idea "that affection that comes from those unknown to us who are watching over our sleep and solitude . . . widens out the boundaries of our being and unites all living things!" My images are all to do with the War'.[2] I am intrigued by the sudden transition from the Wordsworthian register, which cradles the quotation from Neruda, to the abrupt sentence which announces memories of war, by the inexplicit focus of those unknown carers who remain invisible beside the atrocity of what follows, and by the moral ecology of the unity of living things which is levelled beside the air-raid and the concentration camp. In the family portrait that follows, ordinary reticence seems easily to introject war and genocide which, thus internalized, finds its form in the shadows cast in the poet's skull beside his fireside. The passage thus brings uneasily together three subjects which have dominated Harrison's work: family and community, art, and war.

As Harrison's work develops, the fireside skulls and shadows become a familiar iconography in his war poetry. Shadow San in *Shadow*, and the scorched Iraqi soldier, whose crumbling skull, 'like someone made of Plasticine', engages the poet in interview in *Coming*, both contend with nullifying ordinariness, with failures of memory or representation, and the smooth incorporation of their disappearance. The former resents his heedless, consumerist counterpart in contemporary Hiroshima, the ironically named Mitsufuji San:

> The A-Bomb Dome and all the rest
> make Mitsufuji San depressed.
> He wouldn't mind if it was made
> into a vast pinball arcade,
> a game that millions will play
> even tomorrow, A-Bomb Day.[3]

—while the dead Iraqi contests the 'ordinary reality' of the media screen and makes demands of the poet's vocation:

> Isn't it your sort of poet's task
> to find words for this frightening mask?[4]

In both cases, what is at stake is a series of issues about the memory of war and its relationship to the survivor community.

What Harrison's childhood recollections entwine is, in one sense, a series of familiar ambiguities about his own background. His career is often pictured as a rupture from home and community imposed by his re-culturation as a 'scholarship boy' and passage to different kinds of class and cultural experience. Harrison himself encourages this view:

I had a very loving upbringing; without question, a very loving, rooted upbringing. Education came in to disrupt that loving group, and I've been trying to create new wholes out of that disruption ever since. They're not reconcilable, it seems, in the kind of class system we have in England.[5]

There can be, of course, no question of gainsaying the importance of this. It is a powerful, established fact of post-war society which has shaped the experience of many (including myself, as it happens). But there are problems in the account, not least because it can portray working-class communities as somewhat inert. Significant change, when it comes, is represented as arriving from without as, for Harrison, in the case of educational opportunity. Partly as a result, the evocation of rootedness co-exists with stories of sad failure, passive suffering, and cultural narrowness. The community that nurtures also inhibits. Shy of its place in the world, it is coated with silence where the skulls and shadows grow.

One particular anxiety for the poet therefore concerns his imagined audience. Famously, he would like to be the poet his father reads,[6] but this cannot be. So the image he takes from Neruda for his own poetic motives—a transaction between unseen strangers either side of a fence—seems doubly important. At one level it has an alluring neighbourliness. It is close and familiar, and it is easy to see in it the residues of working-class intimacy. But at another level it is also strange and alienated. The boys are outsiders, not known neighbours at all, and never meet face to face. And though they connect briefly, Harrison's version of the story subverts their blessedness by cutting abruptly away to war and extermination.

So several themes are knit together: the ambiguities of family and community, the pressures of conflict's relentless presence, and the need to speak beyond the fence. Harrison pits the creativity and communication of art against the absence of community and the presence of war, and that boy behind the fence, whose benign surveillance Neruda's story celebrates, turns, as Harrison's work develops, into a community of lost and angry souls who represent, in turn, the betrayed and misused working-class community of his parents' generation, and the war dead whose disappearance from memory allows societies to organize further atrocious vanishings. Neruda writes

of 'those unknown' whose solicitude 'widens out the boundaries of our being and unites all living things'. In Harrison's
work, those unseen communicators give way to hostile dop-
pelgangers (the skinhead *alter ego* in *v.*, for instance), or dia-
logues with Virgilian companions in the hell of modern
warfare: Shadow San in *Shadow*, Heine in *Gorgon*, or the
charred Iraqi in *Coming*. This is one way of imagining an audience, as a lonely boy behind a fence who turns out to have an
unfleshed face like Plasticine. But these are also figures of reparation, and this structure of feeling is a compound of unstable
parts: loss, guilt, anger, and a sense of powerlessness before
history's violence. They issue, however, in an equal desire to
give voice to the unhappy dead who may then speak from their
obliteration for posterity's benefit. It is a tragic knowledge that,
in the end, the positives of life are contaminated by social fates.

In the verse, one form this takes is a relentless use of juxtaposition and superimposition, and of multiple word-play to
release diverse perspectives. This ignites the moral and emotional energies of the poems to face up to the appalled fascination provoked by their subjects. In a poem from 'School of
Eloquence', Harrison revisits his air-raid experience. He
stresses the caring proximity of his mother and the fond array
of objects shared:

> Our cellar 'refuge room' made anti-gas.
> Damp sand that smelled of graves not Morecambe Bay.
> Air Raid Precautions out of *Kensitas*.
> A Victory jig-saw on Fry's Cocoa tray.
> Sandwiches. Snakes & Ladders. Thermos flask.[7]

This poem uses these techniques of superimposition and juxtaposition because the violence of history is always intrusive.
Just as Belsen and Hiroshima are internalized by the Leeds fireside, so, in these lines, the air-raid and the seaside visit are held
together in the boy's mind and the war decorates the picnic in
the euphemistic 'refuge room'. But the poem performs another
superimposition devised in the title. 'A Close One' refers to
both the near-miss of the bombs and to the mother herself who,
at the time of writing, is recently dead. Death avoided in the
Blitz is held in poignant proximity to his 'Day old bereavement'.

The poem draws no moral from this. Like Harrison's other elegies for his parents, it speaks its loss tenderly and directly. However, his mother disappears from the poem in several ways. She vanishes in her death, of course, but she is also physically absent in the childhood memory. Her voice is never heard in response to his questions ('which one was Jerry, which our own'), and she is not physically described. Instead, she is displaced on to objects, searchlights, sandwiches, and cigarette cards, whose details are vivid as if to specify the absence. The poem's syntactical organization is curious too. Each line is fiercely end-stopped, and many carry a blunt, drumming staccato created by mere listed items as in, for example, the first: 'Hawsers. Dirigibles. Searchlights. *Messerschmidts*.' These tense rhythms convey locked emotions and the fragmentariness of memory. But their cumulative effect is also to impede onward development, as though the motion of sentences toward sense or conclusion is resisted. So a contrary effect is achieved. The poem both summons up memory and, as it develops, blocks its passage to the future. The syntax inhibits completion and thus emotionally postpones the time which brings the actual death. The same effect is also gained in the spacing of the last four lines, which are separated from each other as the feelings and memories, the poet's relation with his close one, and the sonnet itself, with its integrative formal organization, disassemble. The only line in the poem which doesn't close with a full stop is the penultimate:

> These lines to hold the still too living dead—
>
> my Redhill container, my long-handled hoe.[8]

All that remains is objects.

This registers the grief and mourning, but in the effort to push away the present, and recover what is lost, what happens is an embedding of memory, and his mother's existence, in an ambiguous place of both danger and security—the air-raid shelter. The analogy made in the title's play on words between mother and bomb is uncomfortable and is reinforced in the second line:

> Half let go. Half rake dark nowt to find . . .[9]

Here the searchlights raking the dark for the bombers crossing the city are like the poet's feelings for his mother after his bereavement. She too is 'Half let go', and there's 'nowt to find'. Violence and destruction, on the one hand, and love and intimacy, on the other, are inseparably allied, and loss and love are chained together. The family is valued at the point where its existence is most under threat; the community is created most vividly at the point of its destruction; and a memory of ministration becomes a source of lifelong moral revulsion against war.

Other poems maintain and explore these ambiguous juxtapositions. In 'Jumper', what is remembered from the air-raid is the reassuring 'human metronome' of Harrison's mother's knitting as the bombs fall:

> the click of needles steady though walls shake.
> The stitches, plain or purl, were never dropped.[10]

In later life, their clicking returns 'to beat calm celebration out of fear', an oddly violent way of expressing a positive, as the poem balances her stoic creativity against the bombardment. There is, in fact, no separating the two, and the poem plays eerily with the image of Madame Defarge knitting below the guillotine in *A Tale of Two Cities*. Likewise, Harrison returns to his memory of VJ Day in a later sequence of poems sometimes grouped as 'Sonnets for August 1945'. 'The Morning After' describes a VJ Day street-party in which Harrison recalls

> that, now clouded, sense of public joy
> with war-torn adults wild in their loud fling
> has never come again since as a boy
> I saw Leeds people dance and heard them sing.[11]

The unique celebration of this community emerges from war, and 'for me it still means joy though banked by grief'. The puns on 'bank' are, as usual, multiple: as a fire is banked to keep it going, as we speak of a memory bank (in which, note, it is grief that deposits memory's joy), and as a plane banks to commence its bombing run. The second 'Morning After' poem again deploys Harrison's technique of juxtaposition, superimposing the nuclear blasts in Hiroshima and Nagasaki on the celebratory bonfire in Leeds. The structure of such images is elaborate, and their effects are complex and disconcerting as they shift from the local to historical catastrophe, and eventually to a bleak prophecy of a dead universe in which the military archer (Sagittarius) and the scales of balance and justice (Libra) are destroyed alike.

> That circle of scorched cobbles scarred with tar' s,
> a night-sky globe nerve-wrackingly all black,
> both hemispheres entire but with no stars,
> an Archerless zilch, a Scaleless zodiac.[12]

The perspective is morally chastening, and the pressure on the poetic personality perceiving such things is considerable. But the artistry of their construction is also disconcertingly fine. Art is being made to bear the paradoxical weight of guilty complicity, awful knowledge, *and* the creative opposition to it. It must become an imaginative reparation for a dwarfed community and an appalling history.

Harrison's poetry moves easily between the local and the global, intimacy and rank alienation, and it dramatizes the adjacency of festivity and violence. Its key motif is commemoration of, simultaneously, things good and awful. The celebratory, impressively rich *Kumquat* which, in performance, Harrison reads with an extraordinarily exquisite tenderness, resumes Keats's preoccupation with the proximity of joy and pain. But its celebration of love and maturity emerges from a 'bigger crop of terrors, hopes and fears' from the century of history 'between John Keats's death and my own birth':

> years like an open crater, gory, grim,
> with bloody bubbles leering at the rim;
> a thing no bigger than an urn explodes
> and ravishes all silence, and all odes,
> Flora asphyxiated by foul air
> unknown to either Keats or Lemprière,
> dehydrated Naiads, Dryad amputees
> dragging themselves through slagheaps with no trees,
> a shirt of Nessus fire that gnaws and eats
> children half the age of dying Keats . . .[13]

The effect of lines like these does not rely on the mere reversal of beauty into ugly deformation characteristic of 'modern' poetry since *The Waste Land*. Though it plays in a shocking way with Keats's famous phrases and motifs, and mutilates his urn into a bomb, the shape and movement of the whole, delicate poem is not represented by this quotation. What it achieves across its meditative length—its verse, like that of many of the 'American' poems, hauntingly following the rhythms of thought and speech—is a multiple celebration in the face of atrocious prospects: of the gifts of natural resilience, beauty, and abundance, of erotic love, and, in its own creation as much as its homage to Keats, of art.

This aspect of Harrison's work has come under attack. The Glasgow writer Tom Leonard, for instance, a poet sometimes leagued with Harrison in his use of demotic language and attention to working-class life,[14] argues that art as a category is evasive and socially discriminatory. Because of its class associations, art is always a reserved realm, a 'Magic Thing', as he puts it. It 'clears the streets' of the bulk of the population and, having done so, purports to reconcile social alienations and problems which in fact it perpetuates by containing its treasures in a closed value-system. Leonard writes (it is worth quoting at length):

Part of the verification of the closed value-system must consist in indicating that the lower orders don't have access to it. Classical music, literature, philosophy; a narrator couldn't casually mention, without comment about conflict, that a working-class person happened to be listening to Beethoven. That is one of the things that the working class 'don't do'. The narrator would have to bring in some Magic Thing to cure the supposed conflict within the work, or more likely, let the Beethoven stand as the Magic Thing that showed why the narrator couldn't go back to his poignant old roots. (I think some of Tony Harrison's work does this very clearly.) The truth is that having nodded through the value-system, it's almost impossible for the narrator not to sound either patronising (being functionally superior to his personae in the first place) or sentimental. But the profits paid out by the Magic Thing in this area show the imposed, restricted nature of the behaviour from which they are derived: bathos, nostalgia, a kind of 'baffled poignancy'—or laughter at the expense of the described.[15]

These points carry weight, and it is easy to recognize in them an argument familiar in recent criticism. It is a distinctive contemporary structure of response which is aggressively, and in many respects rightly, scornful of the historical monopoly of art by certain social classes and groups. It is hostile to the ideological agendas which follow from this confiscation and suspicious of (while remaining thoroughly absorbed in) the privilege art still enjoys in cultural debate as a standard of value.

Such arguments are clearly germane because Harrison invests so much in, and thinks so widely about, the role of the poet. The issues take a number of forms in his work. They include the peccancy of abandoning the culture in which he was raised (a theme of many of the 'School of Eloquence' sonnets), his anger at the derision and mistreatment of this culture and its values at the hands of 'high' refinement, and the anxiety that an escape into art means that poetry loses purchase on the world's material issues. This is the accusation levelled by the skinhead in *v.* in relation to working-class life, and the dead Iraqi in *Coming* in relation to modern warfare. It is repeated in a different form in the militarist Commodus' taunt to Orpheus before the lions' and tigers' cage in *Kaisers of Carnuntum*:

> Art will have to acknowledge that it's truly beaten
> when he plays his magic lyre but still gets eaten.[16]

And by Heine in *Gorgon*:

> Gaze and create. If art can't cope
> It's just another form of dope,
> and leaves the Gorgon in control
> of all the freedoms of the soul.[17]

Art's way of 'coping' in drastic social contexts—an equivalent of human survival—is the theme of much of Harrison's work, and a specific concern of *Gorgon*.

One of the arguments in this film, as in other Harrison poems, is that any consolatory or reconciling functions art may have are merely residual. *Gorgon* attacks artistic patronage, from the aristocratic liberalism of Elizabeth of Austria to the corporate sponsorship of opera in contemporary 'Bankfurt':

> Music is so civilising
> for the place with new banks rising.[18]

The film/poem traces the wanderings of Heine's statue across this warrior century from the beginnings of the First World War to the smart culture of plutocratic 'ECU-land' which leaves its underclass and racial victims strewn below its glass towers. (There are connections here, by the way, with Tom

Leonard's and James Kelman's attacks on the City Council's enthusiastic promotion of Glasgow as 'European City of Culture' in 1990.) The Jewish Heine's homeless statue stands for the pariah quality of art, adopted by the patronizing classes, and dumped as quickly when the high-cultural liberal enclave of Elizabeth turned to militaristic racialism after her assassination. From thence it was a short step to the First World War. Heine's is a restless, displaced voice (the film/poem is a dramatic monologue spoken by Harrison). It represents one side of the poem's symbolic binary and stands for intelligent, clear-sighted, non-violent (but, in a sense, thereby powerless) creativity. The other side is the Gorgon, which, excavated by the Kaiser at Elizabeth's culture-palace in Corfu, symbolizes a principle of dehumanizing, destructive militarism surfacing through the ages.

Art and war are clearly opposed. But not war and patronage. The Kaiser banishes the Jewish lyrical ironist and installs his self-glorifying version of Homeric warmongering in which heroes like Achilles are made to represent a self-advancing and, crucially, self-defeating Kaiserian destructiveness. *Gorgon* is therefore a meditation on art's power to resist the Gorgon, but also its fate to be manipulated before it:

> you'd think this Opera House foyer's
> a long way from the Gorgon's gaze.
> Escape, they're thinking, but alas
> that's the Gorgon in the glass.[19]

So art does not quite stand to the community as an ideologically reconciling 'Magic Thing' in Tom Leonard's sense. It is a much more awkwardly situated, always-compromised, but still persisting value.

The argument, however, has problems. Its virtues include the attack on cultures of heedless patronage, its recognition that art lives on contaminated and contaminating ground, and its insistence that militaristic culture is not just destructive but self-destructive. Its weakness stems, however, from the abstraction of its symbols on both sides of the binary. In Heine, Harrison has chosen a representative for art who is, like himself, a cultural in-between, unrooted, peregrinatory, and thereby condemned (the film suggests) to ineffectual marginality. It is in the nature of the symbolization of Heine in *Gorgon* that art should become spectatorial and passive, except in so far as it embodies, in and for itself, the oppositional value of creativity and non-destructive passion. However, in some of Harrison's subsequent work which resumes these themes, like *Labourers of Herakles*, such ideas can turn to frail wishes and hopes:

> To honour Phrynichos, who gave theatre a start
> in redeeming destruction through the power of art,
> and, witnessing male warfare, gave the task
> of mourning and redemption to the female mask,
> to honour such a poet, all modern actors need
> to celebrate his genius, and get their spirits freed
> from Europe's impasse, where art cannot redeem
> the cry from Krajina or the Srbrenica scream.[20]

This speech, spoken in performance by Harrison himself, and maybe to a degree conceived ironically (after his exit, a Labourer asks 'who the fuck was that?'), seems, apart from anything else, to be internally contradictory. Its opening suggests that art is able to redeem destruction, but by the close of the quotation it seems to be saying the opposite.

Meanwhile, in *Gorgon*, the other side of the symbolic binary is problematic too, for this is a poem about stoniness in the complementary forms of statue and Gorgon's stare. The Gorgon represents a human drive to destruction, and the film/poem opens with a 'once upon a time':

> From long ago the Gorgon's Gaze
> stares through time into our days.
> Under seas, as slow as oil
> the Gorgon's snaky tresses coil.
> The Gorgon under the golden tide
> brings ghettos, gulags, genocide.[21]

The Gorgon comes under the 'golden tide', which is a neat point about the economics of aggressive cultures, but it represents an abstracted Thanatos, a death-drive of prejudice, cruelty, and extermination whose twin is expansionist wars. There may be a pertinent truth in this at a somewhat abstract level, and Harrison is careful to relate it to a specific gender politics (as in the quotation from *Labourers of Herakles* above). But as an account of the origins of war it tilts the explanation towards the extra-social, even the mythological, towards, indeed, a kind of 'Magic Thing' in a different sense from Tom Leonard's. This 'Magic Thing', the Gorgon, is not generated from within and between societies, but arrives, like bombers, from afar. Though it gestures towards an endemic destructiveness at the roots of the human constitution, by symbolizing the Gorgon as an external agent in human history the impact of the point is blunted. This in turn creates a turbulence in other parts of the work. In *Labourers of Herakles*,

> The spirit of Phrynichos cries out, 'Cast aside
> mythology and fables and look at genocide!
> Cast aside mythology and turn your fearful gaze
> to blazing Miletos, yesterday's today's.'[22]

This argument urges a turn from myth to historical fact, but *Gorgon*'s Thanatic symbolism in no way casts mythology aside. Indeed it rests on ancient myths given a post-Freudian authority.

Harrison begins from a powerfully realized, and morally and historically persuasive, revulsion from war as *the* driving fact of twentieth-century history. This is rooted in his own experience of a community damaged in visible and invisible, immediate and long-term ways by the Second World War. But, in generalizing the position, he puts it under some strain. Art bears that strain, for it has to present the war record, gain a perspective on it, speak for communities hitherto lost to it, and embody alternative values in its creative moment. These things can disjoin, however, and the values of art can diverge from the values of the community which the poetry summons up and for which it offers to speak. That community, in Leeds, manifests the contradictions which the symbolic opposition of art to war in *Gorgon* prises apart. In poems like 'The Morning After', Leeds people (including Harrison) 'gloried in our blaze' on VJ Day, but also shared the guilty fact that the end-of-war festivities were engineered by the nuclear bomb. Victimhood and aggression are terribly mixed in ordinary experience. I have no idea what Harrison's family's attitudes were to the Second World War. His mother's voice is silent on these and other issues in poems like 'A Close One', and it is therefore hard to unpick what is implied in the witting or unwitting superimposition of mother and bomber in that poem. Especially if one remembers that the Nagasaki bomb was horribly nicknamed 'Little Boy'.

Large-scale issues bear upon this problem. One of these is the characteristic situation of dissident, literary intellectuals who, committed to artistry rather than social activism as their primary role, use realized creativity as the best measure of positive values. This is the situation of Heine in *Gorgon*, and, in a much more troubled, self-questioning way, of Harrison himself in *v*. It is also the case that independent intellectuals and writers from working-class backgrounds, like Harrison, are in a particularly exposed situation in this respect. In moving from their culture of origin, but resisting incorporation by the dominant forms and institutions, their portable craft, and the values which it embodies, can often become the beleaguered 'refuge room' for an unhoused, dissident talent. This was certainly the case with D. H. Lawrence, whose career is, of course, a touchstone in this respect for many writers of working-class origin in this century. In fact, Lawrence and Harrison can be interestingly compared in more ways than the obvious facts of northern, Protestant, industrial upbringing, and a globe-trotting life. 'Lassy-lads' (in Harrison's phrase) in their native culture, they both become preoccupied with the adjacency of sexuality to destructiveness and an apocalyptic vision of war. Both also articulate a vision of the natural world which is unhomely but ambiguously enticing. (This last seems the area of Lawrence's most obvious influence on Harrison in his 'American' poems.) Both writers, too, share an appetite for the twisting oxymoron, for the description which settles to neither unambiguous pleasure nor pain, and both foreground an often ironic play with their own literary personalities.

A murderous view of history, an uneasy relationship to art's social presence, and a radical unsettlement from community are three reasons, perhaps, why Harrison's poems look so steadily at death as a subject, and why, in the middle of celebratory poems like *Kumquat*, Grecian urns turn into bombs, and modernity is pictured as an open crater. War poems, of course, pose problems about values in an exceptionally acute state, as they deal continually in matters of heightened crisis.

As a result they generate contradictions. One form of this is put by Wilfred Owen's famous poem 'Futility', in which the death of a comrade provokes Owen to ask:

> Was it for this the clay grew tall?
> —O what made fatuous sunbeams toil
> To break earth's sleep at all?[23]

Part of the answer to Owen's question is contained in the fact of the poem itself. The metaphysical futility is gainsaid by the act of writing the fine poem in which it is proposed.

Harrison has an interesting variant of this argument. In his conversation with Richard Hoggart, he comments on the importance of strong rhythm to his work:

Those rhythms mean to me that appetite for life I was talking about. My brain can tell me life isn't worth living, I would like to die; but my heart beats on. For me, it's the struggle and tension between what the head is saying and what the heart is feeling which is how I make my poetry.

That rhythmical thing is like a life-support system. It means I feel I can go closer to the fire, deeper into the darkness, because I think we have to experience that darkness [. . . .]

The metre itself is like the pulse. That's what it's about. I don't have the heart to confront some experience unless I know I have this rhythm to carry me to the other side. It's an existential need, the metrical form, for me.[24]

These existential arguments are, in a sense, familiar ones in post-war writing, and testify to the particular vocation of art to speak about modernity's pain.[25] Though their articulation is sometimes defensive—as Harrison here describes strong metre as a protection against personal crisis—they none the less make a strong assertion of the value of human creativity as a response to the destructive instincts in human culture and being. In Harrison, these arguments are backed by an equally tenacious defence of art as having an historical and not a transcendental value, and he is preoccupied by the answerable relation between his own late-twentieth-century articulacy and his forebears' speechlessness. This is represented by his dumb and stammering uncles, and his father's defeats. His angry rebuttal of the way 'low', marginal, or powerless cultures are lost to posterity's high-brow condescension is one of his most vigorous and impressive themes.

Harrison rehearses these issues widely. They often find focus in arguments about social class and cultural division, but they also extend to his thinking on issues of war and ecological survival, where assertions of value in the face of extinction are, of course, most sharply put. A writer, in the late twentieth century, he remarks in an interview, cannot bank on posterity for his or her recognition. Values have to be found in the present: 'we are faced with the very real idea of extinction, not only of personal extinction but of the work and of memory'.[26]

The theme of living with the prospect of extinction—glimpsed also in the syntactical staccato, fierce end-stopping, and possible third meaning of 'A Close One' discussed above—has become a leading thread in Harrison's most recent work. In his *Chorus*, a hybrid of Aristophanes' *Lysistrata* and Euripides' tragedy *The Trojan Women* set outside the wire of Greenham Common, Lysistrata warns the audience:

> So if occasionally some names are new
> Just think of the ground that's under you.
> If we're destroyed then we
> take with us Athens 411 BC.
> The world till now up to the last minute
> and every creature who ever was in it
> go when we go, everything men did or thought
> never to be remembered, absolutely nought.
> . . . .
> Since 1945 past and present are the same.
> And it doesn't matter if it's 'real' or a 'play'—
> imagination and reality both go the same way.[27]

Lysistrata argues that, in destroying ourselves, we also destroy history, for which we are as responsible as we are for our children's future. Though this definition of the contemporary as an eternal present shares something with a glib postmodernism, its existential urgency and historical commitments are of a different character. This burden of responsibility for history, of living in daily proximity to catastrophe, reinforces for Harrison the presence of those stubborn values invested in human creativity and agency, and found in historical memory. Because not anything, but everything, goes, such values cannot be relativized beyond conviction.

In 'Facing up to the Muses', Harrison argues powerfully against one established response to the existential burden of 'the dark catastrophes of our century that undermine creativity at its very roots'.[28] He will have nothing to do with what 'George Steiner has characterized as a "retreat from the word"'[29] which was sloganized by Adorno as 'There can be no poetry after Auschwitz'.[30] He rejects the 'self-indulgences of obscurity and some of the audience-dodging evasions of much modernism',[31] and makes a plea for a literature which faces carnage directly. His model is derived from Greek tragedy. Greek theatre, he argues, was a daylight theatre, exposing the audience and the players fully. It did not, as modern theatres do, segregate its audience 'by arm-rests and darkness into individual pockets of anxiety'.[32] The function of the mask, too, was to keep the human carriage erect, to keep faces uplifted and eyes open. The whole demeanour of Greek theatre was to look disaster in the face. It is a drama of 'existential survival', and represents a tough, unblinking humanism which is exemplary because of our necessity to look straight at the nuclear 'theatre of war', which is 'probably the worst thing that our imagination can, and I'm afraid must conceive'.[33]

Harrison's is, in a sense, an ambiguously historicized imagination. Vividly alive to the specific depredations of recent history, and fiercely conscious of his own historical situation as a writer, he is nonetheless committed to the rewriting of ancient myth as a mode of articulation for these predicaments. To go back to the Greeks is, for him, a way out of the traps of language, form, and sensibility which maroon contemporary responses to events in literary self-absorption, modernist obscurantism, or the partial abandonment of moral and articulatory effort. While the pursuit of ancient symbols in *Gorgon* and other works can abstract history to repetition, the value of the tactic is also clear. The purchase on the contemporary gained by Harrison's translation of *The Oresteia* is a case in point.

The Oresteia plays start many themes which have exercised Harrison throughout his career: the dominion of destruction, the effects of trauma, the emotional, moral, and political confusions of war, the common vulnerability and enforced passivity of victims, the impact of partial knowledge and, then again, catastrophic illumination, and the relation of violence to corrupted politics and to masculinity. Much of this focuses on the role of the chorus. Folding in and out of events, becoming sometimes agents and then mere spectators, understanding and not understanding, the chorus embodies the pliant, impure responsiveness which characterizes Harrison's account of warfare.

The Oresteia is obviously a war play. It deals, like Harrison's poems about the end of the Second World War, with the contaminated world which follows a putative success. However, like Harrison's reading of post-war history, the plays present no victories. Instead there is a catastrophic, onward spiral of violence driven by an inexplicit 'Necessity':

> Bloodflow for bloodflow the doomsong goes—
> blood shrieks for the Fury as it flows
>
> The Fury forges the long bloodchain—
> the slain that link the slain that link the slain . . .[34]

Harrison's *Oresteia* was written over a ten-year period during the 1970s, and was first performed in November 1981.[35] Its composition thus coincides with the re-escalation of the Cold War in its sharp new phase at the end of the seventies. This period marked the end of *détente* and the dwindling away and rubbishing of the Strategic Arms Limitations Talks (SALT), perceived as defeatist by hawkish, newly elected administrations in both the UK and USA.[36] It saw the decision, taken in December 1979, to 'modernize' NATO's nuclear systems (including the 'Trident' programme and the decision to install nuclear-armed Cruise missiles at USAF bases in the UK) and, in the same month, Soviet forces began their ten-year occupation of Afghanistan. It also saw the resurgence of CND and the creation of END (European CND), and other energetic and morally charged protest movements. In May 1982, a few months after the first night of *The Oresteia* and a month before the Falklands War, E. P. Thompson memorably described the mood of the times for dissident intellectuals whose views—like Harrison's—were shaped during the endgame of World War Two:

my generation, which had witnessed the first annunciation of exterminist technology at Hiroshima, its perfection in the hydrogen bomb, and the inconceivable-absolute ideological fracture of the first Cold War [. . .] had become, at a deep place in our consciousness, habituated to the expectation that the very continuation of civilization was problematic.[37]

Thompson labelled this condition 'Exterminism' and struck a chord with many. I would like to suggest that Thompson's experience is very close to that of Tony Harrison, and, further, that in some major respects *The Oresteia* is a response to the reinvigorated Cold War whose psychological fibre had been in place for thirty years. *The Oresteia*, that is, is 'about' Exterminism.

Harrison's trilogy describes the after-effects of a period of geopolitical collision between the Greeks, identified with Europe and the West, and Troy, which is identified with Asia and the East. (These identifications, by the way, are in neither of the other translations of *Agamemnon* I have consulted, though Harrison points out that a US plan to obliterate seventy Soviet cities was called 'War Plan Trojan'.[38]) On Agamemnon's return to Argos, Harrison stresses the General's triumphalism as Agamemnon depicts a city blasted in a very modern way:

> Troy! you can almost see it smoking from Argos!
> The rubble and debris still breathe out destruction,
> the ashes of surfeited Asia still sighing.[39]

The modernity is palpable, and not just in the language. This is a work written when new classical deities—Poseidon, Titan, Vulcan, Trident—populated the silos and airbases. The rest of *The Oresteia* is preoccupied, as Agamemnon makes clear later in this speech, with social dissension and civic emergency, including a period of autocratic despotism under Clytemnestra and Aegisthus with its spreading Cold War tactics of surveillance and fear. It is a culture of—in a neat Bergman joke—'whispers with spies'.[40]

But what drives the plays is 'the grudge', and for the bulk of the trilogy *The Oresteia* presents a world without reconciliation, forgiveness, charity, blamelessness, or a ground for dialogue. 'The grudge' is much compounded in the text, both in the action and in the poetry—mangrudge, godgrudge, bloodgrudge—but each changed prefix merely sows the idea more widely, leaving its essential state undefined. It is a principle of motivation which squeezes individual experience into repetitive grooves and is barely understood beyond the exigency of its compulsions. Its qualities are legion, contradictory, and invasive. Its drives percolate the consciousnesses of individuals and families, swashing through the plays with its obsessive demands. Now gangrenous or demonic, now a clean principle of justice or religion, now a family covenant or psychological drive, the grudge shape-changes through the text before, in the end, becoming personified in the Furies, and inhabiting the voice and bodies of the chorus itself, from whence it is brought off and buried in the theatrical optimism of the *Eumenides'* closing tribunal.

In essays of the early 1980s, E. P. Thompson described Exterminism in its ideological form of 'deterrence theory' as a condition close to that of addiction:

Deterrence theory, by accelerating R & D and by summoning new weapons forward, is the ideological drive of addiction. In this ideological role it is indeed an operative force. Like an addictive drug, it induces euphoria, inhibits the perception of manifest consequences, and excuses the inexcusable.[41]

Its nature overrides everything, and gathers everything to it. Its nurture accelerates political emergency, and the surveillant machinery of the repressive state,[42] and it creates an unresolvable cycle of violence between matching powers:

Exterminism simply confronts itself. It does not exploit a victim: it confronts an equal. With each effort to dominate the other, it calls into being an equivalent counter-force. It is a non-dialectal contradiction, a state of absolute antagonism, in which both powers grow through confrontation, and which can only be resolved by mutual extermination.[43]

'Bloodflow for bloodflow the doomsong goes— | blood shrieks for the Fury as it flows'. The analogy is not, of course, exact, but the structure of feeling is a close one.

The theory of Exterminism was criticized for its determinism, and Raymond Williams's comments remain cogent and powerful:

[Exterminism] steers us away from originating and continuing causes, and promotes (ironically, in the same mode as the ideologies which the weapons systems now support) a sense of helplessness beneath a vast, impersonal and uncontrollable force. For there is nothing then left but the subordinated responses of passivity or protest, cynical resignation or prophecy. That the latter response in each pairing is infinitely better, morally and politically, should go without saying. But that the character of resistance to the threat of massacre can be radically affected by the initial assumption of so absolute and overpowering a system is already evident.[44]

This is trenchant, for it points to the way the ideological hall-of-mirrors of the Cold War can accommodate a further room. The Soviet and NATO blocs reflect each other, and the dissenting analysis replicates the structures of assumption posited by its opponent. Williams's picture of 'helplessness beneath a vast, impersonal and uncontrollable force' describes the grudge in *The Oresteia* as it describes Exterminism, and both reflect the problems in the abstraction of war as a self-present, extra-human agency encountered in Harrison's depiction of war as the Gorgon in his film/poem of a decade later. *The Oresteia* follows Aeschylus and, in its final tribute, the trilogy ends with a change in the polity towards a version of rational democracy, a relinquishing of the grudge and a ceremonial procession of the Furies to an undisruptive reservation. This, however, is an imposed settlement, by Athena and Apollo, and there is plenty of evidence that Harrison sees its reconciliations as incidental. In a weird way, in fact, it is prescient of the settlements brokered for some international conflicts since the end of the Cold War by the authority of American money and arms.[45]

In his introduction to *Chorus*, set outside the wire of Greenham Common, Harrison writes that:

The American psychologist Robert Jay Lifton, who studied the survivors of Hiroshima, showed that when our sense of 'symbolic immortality' is undermined and threatened, as it was in the Cold War after 1945, then, 'our confidence in the overall continuity of life gives way to widespread death imagery'.[46]

Harrison's work is saturated with such imagery—the language of The Oresteia presents a gangrenous human body to the audience throughout, and in 'The Ballad of the Geldshark', broken human bodies become the currency of war:

> Geldshark Ares god of War
> broker of men's bodies
> usurer of living flesh
> corpse-trafficker that god is—
>
> give to war your men's fleshgold
> and what are your returns?
> kilos of cold clinker packed
> in army-issue urns.[47]

A way of accounting for this should not be by reference to a gloomy temperament, or millennial pessimism, or, still less, the misery of being a northerner and working class. A more appropriate point of reference lies in the times, and one way of understanding the several components of Harrison's response to war is in relation to the developing structure of Cold War feeling which shaped literary responses to both domestic and world events over the past half-century.

Palladas: Poems articulates the lineaments of some of these structures very clearly. Harrison's preface situates the Greek poet within the epochal death-throes of the transition from Hellenism to Christianity. Palladas is caught between two hegemonic blocs, one in decline, the other in the ascendant. Neither commands his conviction, though their zealotries shape his life.

His are the last hopeless blasts of the old Hellenistic world, giving way reluctantly, but without much resistance, before the cataclysm of Christianity. It is difficult if not impossible at this time of sectarian violence, Pagan hopelessness and Christian barbarity, to characterise Hellenism as world sanity, or Christianity as sweetness and light. Poor Palladas seems to be in the predicament of his murderer in that rather nasty poem 'The Murderer & Sarapis'[. . . .] There seems to have been little or no moral sustenance or sense of identity left in the one, and little sense of hope in the other. The choice was between a crumbled past and a future of specious regeneration.[48]

The parallel with Cold War feeling is telling. In the poem to which Harrison refers, a murderer is warned in a dream that a wall will fall on him, and he escapes death. The next night his dream-visitor tells him that he has been saved from a quick death for the slower one of crucifixion. It is a Beckettian world without escape, and without innocence. Palladas' advice to his reader is a vicious *carpe diem*: to live for 'wine and company and all-night bars'.[49] His vision of the self is of cynical factitiousness: 'Life's a performance. Either join in | light-heartedly, or thole the pain'.[50] It reminds me of another recent anatomy of the millennial sensibility of nuclear Exterminism, Martin Amis's *London Fields*.[51] Harrison describes *Palladas: Poems* as a 'siphoning-off' of the deep pessimism of his intellect,[52] and, because the poems lack the rich dialectical interactions of pessimism and celebration which energize his best work, this is to a degree true. But Palladas' situation is historically indicative.

Harrison's is a world of schisms, divisions, conflict, 'all the versuses of life' accounted in *v*.[53] These include 'East/West' with its Iron Curtain of punctuation which recapitulates the fence through which Harrison imagines the two boys making reparative contact in Neruda's fable. His use of that story introduced six poems from his first full volume, *Loiners*, which has the Cold War as one of its principal subjects. The collection, indeed, can be read as an excursion through post-war history using loosely autobiographical scenes and dramatic monologues. From the bombsites, concentration-camp memories, and 'Dig for Victory' allotments of a Leeds adolescence in part 1, through the dramatic monologues of representatives of the colonial twilight in part 2, the same tone of edgy, half-comic desperation is sustained. In turn, several poems in part 3 cockily manipulate popular Cold War scenarios taken from spy films and thrillers: assignations on trans-European sleepers, microphones in bedrooms, the suspicion of spies, 'tails', and sexual 'honey traps' familiar from John le Carré. The tone, and the varying perspectives introduced by the dramatic monologues, give the collection a dizzying, feverish feel, and create some fundamental uncertainties about identity which are typical of the period in work by many writers. In a radio programme in 1988, and in *Chorus*, Harrison speaks of the way that, in the post-nuclear world, 'the imaginary and the real become dependent on the same facts',[54] and many of the Cold War poems in *Loiners* situate the self at the violent intersection of supposition, fear, prejudice, illusion, and desire where what 'happens' and what is fantasy inveigle each other as in the political perceptions of the period. The squib 'The Bedbug' is a neat example:

> Comrade, with your finger on the playback switch,
> Listen carefully to each love-moan,
> And enter in the file which cry is real, and which
> A mere performance for your microphone.[55]

Acting and being are here inseparable. The speaker thinks he revenges himself on the surveillance, but actually the surveillance has struck inauthenticity, duplicity, pretence, and the awareness of living for others and not yourself into the heart of his acts and the centre of his being. Other poems display the same features. The 'Curtain' poems—'The Curtain Catullus' in *Loiners*, and the 'Curtain Sonnets' grouped with them in *SP*—clearly refer at one level to the Iron Curtain (they are set in Eastern Europe), and express a yearning for sex to overcome political division ('We're human, young, and lustful, sick of wars'[56]). But such experiences are hardly triumphs, and it is even unclear in 'The Curtain Catullus' whether the sexual encounter takes place or is mere desperate, randy delirium.

What is true, however, is that the consciousnesses of these speakers are saturated by the full set of male, Cold War assumptions that vitiate their desire for a neutral, separate peace. These speakers, for all their aspirations to transcend conflict, remain part of the problem. In 'The Curtain Catullus', erotic voyeurism plays with and against Cold War contexts: the woman's calves 'bulge left, right, left' like soldiers marching, and the man glances around for 'my tail', thus adroitly super-imposing surveillance by the secret police on to a smutty pun. In 'The Chopin Express', the naive American dissident desires:

> Breasts and thighs
> the colour of clear neutral skies
> like Africa's . . .
> Neutrality! Brave cocks and cunts
> belong to no barbed continents.[57]

It is clear, especially after the African poems in part 2 of the volume, that Africa's imperialist condition is not one of 'Neutrality'. This speaker understands geopolitics in the same way he understands bodies, as an assembly of parts, some of them fantastically desirable.

The psychology of Cold War communities is the subject of *Loiners*. From another version of a 'VD Day' celebration in 'The

Pocket Wars of Peanuts Joe', in which the community has drawn tight around patriotic ceremony,[58] to the sexual psychology of colonial and Soviet-bloc adventurers in parts 2 and 3, the collection diagnoses the selfhoods of its cast of characters as profoundly lost. In this, *Loiners* is similar to classic Cold War texts like Doris Lessing's *The Golden Notebook*,[59] which also portrays incapacitated selves in disarray under the pressure of political events. Like Harrison's various Cold War Loiners, the characters of *The Golden Notebook* are unable to negotiate or discriminate between love and hostility, or existence and hallucination. In these poems, as in many others written by Harrison later, there is no abstract, stony opposition of Eros to Thanatos; the parts mingle like blood under the pressure of events. Like other English male poets of the period—Gunn, Hill, Larkin, Hughes—Harrison writes of the contaminations of innocence and its complicity with, and adjacency to, violence.[60] 'Black and White' and 'Snap', two of Harrison's 'Sonnets for August 1945', deal particularly with similar themes of the contexts and uses of innocence in a violent world.[61] Harrison's speakers in *Loiners* are isolated and solitary, desperately introjecting public experience as a fearful, anxious inwardness. Like Lessing's Cold War dissidents, like Harrison's characterization of the modern theatre-goer as 'segregated by arm-rests into individual pockets of anxiety', these are lineaments of the Cold War condition, and they are as powerful as factors in the perception of community as those of Harrison's other great themes, the segregations of culture and class.

10

The Drunken Porter Does Poetry: Metre and Voice in the Poems of Tony Harrison

MARTYN CRUCEFIX

1

HARRISON'S first full collection, entitled *The Loiners* after the inhabitants of his native Leeds, was published in 1970 and contained this limerick:

> There was a young man of Leeds
> Who swallowed a packet of seeds.
> A pure white rose grew out of his nose
> And his arse was covered in weeds.[1]

Without losing sight of the essential comedy of this snatch, it can be seen as suggestive of aspects of Harrison's career. For example, the comic inappropriateness of the Leeds boy swallowing some seeds becomes the poet's own ironic image of his classical grammar school education. As a result of this, in a deliberately grotesque image, arose the growth of the white rose of poetry—from the boy's nose, of course, since Harrison in the same volume gave credence to the idea that the true poet is born without a mouth.[2] The bizarrely contrasting weed-covered arse owes less to the intake of seeds (rose seeds wherever transplanted will never yield weeds) than to the harsh conditions Harrison premises in the Loiner's life, as indicated in an early introduction to his work, where he defines the term as referring to 'citizens of Leeds, *citizens* who bear their loins through the terrors of life, "loners" '.[3]

Harrison's now legendary seed-master on the staff of Leeds Grammar School was the one who humiliated him for reciting Keats in a Yorkshire accent, who felt it more appropriate if the boy played the garrulous, drunken Porter in *MacBeth*.[4] The truth is that the master's attitudes determined the kind of poetic rose that grew, in particular its technical facility, which Harrison worked at to show his 'betters' that Loiners could do as well as (better than?) they could. Yet this was no sterile technical exercise, and Harrison's success lies in the integrity with which he has remained true to those regions 'covered with weeds', and in the fact that his work has always struggled to find ways to unite the weed and the rose. Perhaps the most important of these, as the limerick's anatomical geography already predicted in 1970, is via the rhythms of his own body.

Harrison has declared his commitment to metrical verse because 'it's associated with the heartbeat, with the sexual instinct, with all those physical rhythms which go on despite the moments when you feel suicidal'.[5] In conversation with Richard Hoggart, he explains that without the rhythmical formality of poetry he would be less able to confront, without losing hope, the unweeded gardens of death, time, and social injustice which form his main concerns. 'That rhythmical thing is like a life-support system. It means I feel I can go closer to the fire, deeper into the darkness [. . . .] I know I have this rhythm to carry me to the other side'.[6] There are few of Harrison's poems that go closer to the fire than the second of his Gulf War poems, *A Cold Coming*. Its initial stimulus, reproduced on the cover of the Bloodaxe pamphlet, was a photograph by Kenneth Jarecke in the *Observer*. The picture graphically showed the charred head of an Iraqi soldier leaning through the windscreen of his burned-out truck, which had been hit by Allied forces in the infamous 'turkey-shoot' as Saddam's forces retreated from Kuwait City. In the poem, Harrison makes the Iraqi himself speak both with a brutal self-recognition ('a skull half roast, half bone')[7] and a scornful envy of three American soldiers who were reported to have banked their sperm for posterity before the war began (hence, with a scatological nod to Eliot, the title of the poem). There are undoubtedly echoes in the Iraqi's speech of the hooligan *alter ego* in *v.*, yet Harrison worries little over any narrow authenticity of voice in this case, and he does triumphantly pull off the balancing act between the reader's emotional engagement with the fierce personal voice and a more universalizing portrayal of a victim of modern warfare. Furthermore, it is Harrison's establishment and then variation of the poem's metrical 'life-support system' that enables him to achieve this balance, to complete a poem which weighs in against Adorno's view that lyric poetry has become an impossibility in the shadow of this century's brutality.

The poem's form—rhymed iambic tetrameter couplets—seems in itself chosen with restraint in mind, as if the photographic evidence of the horror lying in front of him led Harrison to opt for a particularly firm rhythmical base 'to carry [him] to the other side'. Indeed, the opening five stanzas are remarkable in their regularity with only a brief reversed foot in the fourth line foreshadowing the more erratic energies soon to be released by the Iraqi soldier's speech:

> I saw the charred Iraqi lean
> towards me from the bomb-blasted screen,
>
> his windscreen wiper like a pen
> ready to write down thoughts for men.[8]

The instant the Iraqi's voice breaks in, the metre is under threat. Each of his first four stanzas opens with trochaic imperatives or questions, and at one point he asks if the 'gadget' Harrison has (apparently a tape-recorder, but a transparent image of poetry itself) has the power to record 'words from such scorched vocal chords'. Apart from the drumming of stresses in lines such as this, Harrison deploys sibilance, the alliteration of 'g's and 'd's followed by an horrific mumbling of 'm's to suggest the charred figure's effortful speech in the first moments of the encounter. Regularity is re-established the moment the tape-recorder's mike is held 'closer to the crumbling bone', and there is a strong sense of release from the dead man's initial aggressive buttonholing as his voice (and the verse) now speeds away:

> 'I read the news of three wise men
> who left their sperm in nitrogen,
>
> three foes of ours, three wise Marines,
> with sample flasks and magazines [. . . .]'

In the stanzas that follow, the dead man's angry, envious sarcasm is controlled within the bounds of the form, and it is rather Harrison's rhymes which provide much of the kick:

God/wad, Kuwait/procreate, fate/ejaculate, high tech's/sex.
It is only when the man demands that Harrison/the reader
imagines him in a sexual embrace with his wife back home in
Baghdad that the metrical propulsion again begins to fail. It is
in moments such as this that the difficult emotional work in the
poem is to be done. This is our identification with these ghastly
remains, with the enemy, and it is as if the difficulty of it brings
the verse juddering and gasping to an incomplete line with
'the image of me beside my wife | closely clasped creating
life . . .'9

The difficulty of this moment is further attested to by the
way the whole poem turns its back upon it. Harrison inserts a
parenthetical section, preoccupied not with the empathic effort
the dead Iraqi has asked for, but with chilly, ironic delibera-
tions on 'the sperm in one ejaculation'. Yet all is not well, since
this section stumbles and hesitates metrically as if Harrison
himself (or rather the persona he has adopted in the poem) is
half-conscious of retreating into safe, calculative, and ratioci-
native processes. Eventually, a conclusion yields itself up, but
it is once again the metrical change of gear into smooth regularity that suggests this is a false, defensive, even cynical avoidance of the difficult issues raised by the charred body in the
photograph:

> Whichever way Death seems outflanked
> by one tube of cold bloblings banked.
>
> Poor bloblings, maybe you've been blessed
> with, of all fates possible, the best
>
> according to Sophocles, i.e.
> 'the best of all fates is not to be'
>
> a philosophy that's maybe bleak
> for any but an ancient Greek.10

That this is the way to read this passage is confirmed by the
renewed aggression of the Iraqi soldier who hears these
thoughts and stops the recorder with a thundering of alliterative stresses:

> 'I never thought life futile, fool!
> Though all Hell began to drop
> I never wanted life to stop.'

What follows is the Iraqi soldier's longest and most impassioned speech, by turns a plea for attention and a sarcastic commentary on the collusion of the media, whose behaviour will not 'help peace in future ages'.[11] Particular mention is given to the 'true to bold-type-setting SUN'[12] and, as can be seen from such a phrase, Harrison once more allows particular moments of anger and high emotion to burst through the fluid metrical surfaces like jagged rocks. There is also a sudden increase in feminine line-endings in this section which serves to give a barely caged impression, as if the voice is trembling on the verge of bursting its metrical limits and racing across the page. The impression is further reinforced in the series of imperatives—again in the form of snapping trochees at the opening of several stanzas—that form the climax to this section of the poem:

> Lie that you saw me and I smiled
> to see the soldier hug his child.
>
> Lie and pretend that I excuse
> my bombing by B52s.[13]

The final ten stanzas culminate in a fine example of the way in which Harrison manipulates metrical form to good effect. In a kind of atheistic religious insight, the 'cold spunk' so carefully preserved becomes a promise, or perhaps an eternal teasing reminder, of the moment when 'the World renounces War'.[14] However, emphasis falls far more heavily on the seemingly insatiable hunger of the present for destruction because of the way Harrison rhythmically clogs the penultimate stanza, bringing it almost to a complete halt. The frozen semen is

> a bottled Bethlehem of this come-
> curdling Cruise/Scud-cursed millennium.

Yet, as we have seen, Harrison understands the need to come through 'to the other side' of such horrors, and the final stanza does shakily re-establish the form (though the final line opens with two weak stresses and does not close). Any naive understanding of the poet's comments about coming through fire can, however, be firmly dismissed. This is not the place for any sentimental or rational synthetic solution. Simply, we are returned to the charred face whose painful, personal testament

this poem has managed to encompass and movingly drama-
tize without losing its form, thus ensuring a simultaneous
sense of the universality of its art and its message.

> I went. I pressed REWIND and PLAY
> and I heard the charred man say:

2

It was Wordsworth whose sense of physical rhythm in his
verse was so powerful that he is reported to have often composed at a walk. It should come as no surprise that Harrison
has been known to do the same. Though it was Keats's 'Ode to
a Nightingale' which Harrison 'mispronounced' at school,
Wordsworth is in some ways more important to him, because
they both share a belief in poetry as the voice of men speaking
to men.[15] This conception of poetry as speech is a powerful
constituent in Harrison's work, and perhaps one not clearly
understood. John Lucas finds some lapses in Harrison's customary metrical exactness in *v*.[16] But, to reverse Harrison's
comment that all his writing (theatrical or otherwise) is poetry,
all his poetry needs to be read as essentially dramatic, and
deserves to be tested in the spoken voice as much as in the
study. On occasions, Harrison, only half-humorously, draws
attention to the fact that two uncles—one a stammerer, the
other dumb—had considerable influence on his becoming a
poet, and it is the struggling into and with voice that such a
claim highlights.[17] I have already mentioned Harrison's interest in the curious idea that the true poet is born without a
mouth. This, too, implies the difficult battle for a voice or
voices which can be found everywhere in his work, and it is in
this clamour that I find its dramatic quality. In a public poem
like 'A Cold Coming', Harrison makes use of the contrasting
and conflicting voices by playing them off against a regular
form. This is almost always the case, but in what follows I prefer to concentrate less on metrical effects than on the way
voices interweave, in this case in more personal work from the
'School of Eloquence' sequence.

　　The very title of the pair of sonnets 'Them & [uz]' seems to
promise conflict, at best dialogue, and it opens with what could
be taken as the howl of inarticulacy. Each pair of these opening
syllables gestures towards crucial worlds in Harrison's uni-

verse. The αι αι of classical dramatic lament is echoed by the 'ay, ay!' of the music-hall comedian cheekily working up an audience. Immediately, the reader is plunged into the unresolved drama of two differing voices, instantly implying the two cultures of the sonnets' title. The line and a half which follows, sketching Demosthenes practising eloquence on the beach, is intriguing in that its locus as speech is hard to pin down. It is perhaps intended at this stage (apart from introducing the poems' central issue) to hover in an Olympian fashion above the ruck of dialogue that follows, implying the heroic stance which will be taken up in the second sonnet.

Line 3 opens again into a dramatic situation with the voice of the narrator (the adult Harrison) repeating his own interrupted recital of Keats in the classroom, while the master's scornful comments appear fresh, unreported, as if still raw and present, in speech marks. The narratorial comment on this—'*He* was nicely spoken'—confirms the poem's tendency to switch voices for its effects, this time its brief sarcasm barely obscuring the unironic comment likely to be made by an aspiring Loiner, or by an ambitious parent. The example of nice speaking (again in direct quotes) in the following line is the master's claim to possession, to authority in matters of language and culture, and the separated-off reply of the narrator—'I played the Drunken Porter in *MacBeth*'—with its full rhyme and sudden regular iambic pentameter, implies a causal link between the two lines, painting Harrison as dispossessed specifically by the master's attitudes, as well as conveying the tone of resignation in the young schoolboy.

It will be clear that much of the tension and success of the poem has already risen from the dramatic interchange of voices, and the master's voice asserts itself again in line 7, ironically claiming a kind of monolithic, aristocratic purity for poetry which this poem has already attempted to subvert:

> 'Poetry's the speech of kings. You're one of those
> Shakespeare gives the comic bits to: prose!'[18]

The following lines contain a curious wavering in the clear interplay of dramatic voices, only part of which is resolved as the poem proceeds. Evidently, the intrusive, even hectoring, parenthesis (at line 9) is the narrator's questioning of what appears to be the master's voice's continuing argument that 'All poetry' belongs to Received Pronunciation. Yet the aggression of this attack, with its harsh alliteration and sarcastic question mark, is out of key with other narratorial comments in part I, though the tone is re-established in part II. In addition, I have some difficulty in accepting the master's words as appropriate to the situation which—with no break—continues the speech made to the young Harrison. For example, the word 'dubbed', with its implication of the deliberate laying of a second voice over an 'original', already hands victory to Harrison's claim for the authenticity of dialect, and as such would not be used by the believer in 'the speech of kings'. Equally, the apparent plea, 'please believe [ʌs] | your speech is in the hands of the Receivers', does not accord with the voice that summarily dismissed the pupil as a 'barbarian' seven lines earlier. In this case, Harrison's desire for the dramatic has foundered momentarily on that old dramatist's rock, the necessity for exposition which compromises the integrity of the speaking voice.

The true note of the master returns—interestingly, following one of Harrison's movable stanza breaks, as if confirming a shift in voice though the speech actually continues across the break—with ' "We say [ʌs] not [uz], T. W.!" ' The tone of the responding voice, after the suggestion of a more spirited response in the Keats comment, has returned to the resignation of the browbeaten pupil. This is reinforced by the more distant comparison of the boy to the ancient Greek of the opening lines, heroically 'outshouting seas', while the young Harrison's mouth is 'all stuffed with glottals, great | lumps to hawk up and spit out'. The first sonnet draws to a close with this tone of frustrated defeat for the boy, yet the drama has one final twist, as the voice of the master, sneering, precise, and italicized, has the last word: '*E-nun-ci-ate!*' There can be little doubt that the boy must have felt as his father is reported to have done in another sonnet from the 'School of Eloquence', 'like some dull oaf'.[19]

The second part of 'Them & [uz]' contrasts dramatically with the first, though the seeds of it lie in the image of heroic Demosthenes and the accusatory tone of the reference to Keats which seemed a little out of place in part I. This second sonnet's opening expletive aggression strikes a new tone of voice altogether.

> So right, yer buggers, then! We'll occupy
> your lousy leasehold Poetry.[20]

The poem's premise is that it will redress the defeat suffered in part I in an assertive, unopposed manner. Neither the master, nor any other spokesman for RP is allowed a direct voice, yet the interchange of speech and implied situation can still be found to ensure a dramatic quality to the verse.

The passionate and confrontational situation of the opening challenge is clear enough, yet it's striking how it has taken the autobiographical incident in part I and multiplied it ('yer buggers [. . .] We'll occupy') to present the wider political and cultural context as a future battlefield. Even so, there is no let-up in the clamour of voices raised in the poem. Immediately, the narratorial voice shifts to a more reflective past tense (at line 3), as the rebel reports action already taken—and with some success, judging from the tone of pride and defiance: '[I] used my *name* and own voice: [uz] [uz] [uz]'. Even within this one line, the final three syllables are spat out in a vivid re-enactment of Harrison's defiantly spoken self-assertion. It is this slippery elision of voice and situation which creates the excitement of these and many of Harrison's poems as they try to draw the rapidity and shorthand nature of real speech, its miniature dramas and dramatizations, into lyric poetry. A further shift can be found in lines 9 and 10, in that the voice now turns to address a different subject. The addressee is not immediately obvious as the staccato initials in the line are blurted out in what looks like a return to the situation and voice with which this sonnet opened. Only at the end of line 10 does it become clear that the addressee is the poet's younger self, or the self created as the 'dull oaf' by the kind of cultural repression practiced by the schoolmaster. The reader is further drawn into the drama of the situation by this momentary uncertainty:

> RIP RP, RIP T. W.
> I'm *Tony* Harrison no longer you!

The remaining six lines are, as a speech act, more difficult to locate. There is an initial ambiguity in that they may continue to address 'T. W.', though the stanza break suggests a change and, anyway, this makes little sense, as T. W. is now 'dead'. These lines use the second person pronoun in the impersonal sense of 'one', addressing non-RP speakers in general, and it is the generalized nature of these lines which disarms the effectiveness of the passage. This is particularly important in line 14, '[uz] can be loving as well as funny', the tone of which commentators such as Haffenden have questioned.[21] The difficulty here is that if Harrison is addressing those who might use [uz] anyway, though there may be many amongst them for whom the fact that 'Wordsworth's *matter/water* are full rhymes' is useful ammunition and reassurance, the same cannot be said of the 'loving as well as funny' line, which might be variously construed as patronizing, sentimental, or just plain unnecessary. Nevertheless, the poem regains a surer touch in the final lines in its use of the reported 'voice' of *The Times* in renaming the poet 'Anthony'. The effect here is both humorous (this, after all the poet's passionate efforts!) and yet ominous in that the bastions of cultural and linguistic power are recognized as stubborn, conservative forces, still intent on redefining the poet according to their own agenda, imposing their own voice where there are many.

Harrison's use of both metre and voice reflect the struggle in much of his work between the passion for articulation, especially of experiences capable of overwhelming verse of less conviction, and the demands of control which preserve the poet's utterance as art. Harrison's more recent work—especially that written in America—is more relaxed, meditative, less inhabited by differing and different voices, more easily contained in its forms. There are undoubtedly great successes amongst these (*Kumquat*, 'The Mother of the Muses', part III of 'Following Pine'), but it is likely that Harrison's legacy will eventually be seen as a reassessment of the uses of formal verse and an exploration of the dramatic potential of lyric verse. These elements are rooted ultimately in his attempts to unite the rose of poetry with the weeds of truth and (often painful) experience, by trusting to the measures of his own body, and to a language he returns to the mouth.

11

The Chorus of Mams

OLIVER TAPLIN

TONY Harrison's creativity is like a giant oyster irritated by numerous grains of sand. Some of the resultant pearls grow and grow. A prize example of this process is the poetry that has accreted round his ambivalent attitude to his classical education. This crops up not only in the 'Leeds Grammar School Sonnets', but, for example, in the behaviour of the satyrs at the end of the Delphi version of *Trackers*. They become a whole chorus of the 'hooligan' figure who is Harrison's *alter ego* in *v*. In revenge for Marsyas, the satyr who was flayed by the elitist Apollo, they graffiti his name in inflammable fuel on the papyrus backcloth, and then set fire to it. Their old dad Silenus pleads:

> Don't burn the papyrus. We're all inside.
> Don't burn the papyrus. It's satyricide![1]

Their response is:

> Either fuck off, old feller, or give us a hand,

and when he does not join in:

> Then fuck off, old feller, back to fairyland.

Harrison is a natural-born researcher, who loves following up leads in specialist publications. Yet this kind of book-learning, the bibliothecal burrowing, the footnoteophilia, that leads the poet to the papyrus fragments of Sophocles and Pindar's *Paeans*, is the route to 'fairyland'. At the same time, if he reneges on this undiscovered territory—a world of imaginative and imaginary connections (where men may not always be 'real men')—then there will be no poetry, no *Trackers*. 'We're all inside'.

One of the main sources irrigating Harrison's 'fairyland' has been Greek drama; and the most influential of its formal features has surely been the chorus. It is there right back in *Bow Down* (1977), and doubled into the two flocks of sheep (black-faced Cheviot and horned Wiltshire) in *Yan Tan Tethera* (1983). And there is the very title of *The Common Chorus*.[2] The chorus, especially the chorus of women, is to be the subject of this exploratory celebration of the theatre works.[3] I hope to bring out how Harrison's use of the chorus, constantly refreshed by thinking about ancient Greek drama, has developed a nexus of themes and motifs, which, with each various occurrence, accumulate more depth and complexity.

In his unlocking of the choral potential, Harrison has been a step ahead of the vanguard of classical scholarship—as he has in other ways, for example realizing the importance of the satyr play for the understanding of tragedy. For most of this century most scholars (and theatre directors) have seen the Greek chorus as a difficulty, a problem that has to be explained and even excused. Set off on the wrong track by Aristotle's assertion that the chorus 'should take the part of one of the actors',[4] they have wasted ink trying to apply over-pragmatic notions of 'relevance' to the choral contribution to the play. Another fruitless approach has been to try to tune into the dramatist's personal voice through the chorus, or to try to distil timeless lessonettes from its moralizing. The chorus cannot be extricated from the play as a whole: on the contrary, for the Greeks it was so much of the essence that drama, both tragedy and comedy, was spoken of in phrases about the chorus. Above all, the playwright did not write the script, he *taught* the chorus; similarly, the wealthy sponsor, the *choregos*, 'managed' the chorus.[5]

Some excellent recent work has turned perceptions of the chorus from an encumbrance into a core strength of Athenian tragedy.[6] This has explored two particularly relevant aspects. First, the chorus is a group, a collective, and so supplies a dimension fundamentally different from that of the individual actors. This connects with Harrison's continual preoccupation with the relationship between the lone individual and the group. John Gould writes of 'the sense that the human condition embraces both the individual and the group, that all experience, even the ultimate, all-consuming experience of "the tragic", is to be lived through, perceived and recollected collectively as well as individually':[7] he rightly sees this combination as essential to the Greek tragic theatre. This same buried insight has, I think, been put into living theatrical practice by Tony Harrison. The second fresh development is the emphasis that, just as the chorus's primary form of movement is dance, so its primary form of vocal delivery is song: 'a group that dance-sings'—that is what the Greek χορός means. And by turning from the spoken word and moving into song, the theatre can face things that would be inexpressible in 'real life': Harrison's often inspired handling of this level of expression owes much to the Greek masters. I hope to show all this at work—or at play.

There is another crucial characteristic of the chorus that Harrison has been alive to, in advance of the heavy tramp of scholarship: its resilience. On the one hand, the chorus is involved in what is going on, it can feel deeply for the terrible things it witnesses: on the other hand, it never goes under along with the individual tragic protagonists. However disturbed by the events of the play, it always survives.[8] The great ones fall, are killed, or have their lives irremediably shattered: the anonymous group lives on to see another day and to tell the story. Through the chorus the tragedy is collectively 'lived through, perceived and *recollected*' (to emphasize Gould's words). Harrison has been obsessed in his poetry with surviving the darkness and despair and horror, with not going under, with ploughing on.[9] And in the theatre this experience is passed on to the audience also. Like the chorus, the audience lives through the tragedy, suffers with it, and survives. For Harrison, the audience is not invited to be blandly entertained, but should expect to be put through the emotional and mental mangle, and to come out the other side.

Harrison had occupied yet another prominent height of Greek drama before the main scholarly bandwagon arrived: gender. In step with the larger social, political, and cultural move towards gender awareness, and particularly of inequity in the treatment of women, this aspect of Greek tragedy has come in for special attention—indeed it has been cited by Women's Studies from the start.[10] The point is, of course, that Athenian men minimized the importance of women, and yet made them central to their most prestigious art-form, tragedy (and to a lesser extent comedy). Generally speaking, the ancient Greeks treated their women repressively and patronizingly, regarding their chief functions as rearing legitimate children and minding the house—this is, ethnographically speaking, the case with most human societies past and present. It is, at first sight, paradoxical that the classical Athenians, who achieved in many ways the most liberal and emancipated culture of ancient times, treated their women even more repressively than most other Greeks.[11] But if the all-powerful citizen (the adult free-born male) is to be put on the highest pedestal, then everyone else, including his wife, let alone his slave-woman, has to be accordingly devalued.[12]

Hence the question which has understandably so preoccupied recent studies:[13] given this dismissive attitude to women, why are they so important in tragedy? Not only are they important, but—variously—articulate, brave, determined, intelligent, powerful, vindictive, virtuous . . . Clytemnestra, Deianeira, Antigone, Electra, Alcestis, Medea, Iphigineia, Andromache, Hecuba . . . They must make between them as strong and fascinating a collection of *femmes*, more or less *fatales*, as any comparable team in the history of human story-telling. And as well as these daunting protagonists, many of the *choruses* are female also. If tragedy is to retell heroic myth, then it is inevitable that some of the main roles had to be female; but there is no reason, in theory, why the chorus, which was performed by fifteen citizens selected annually, should not have always been given a male identity. In fact, on the contrary, about two-thirds of our surviving tragedies have a chorus of women, sometimes free, sometimes slaves; and in Euripides, where the chorus is often in close sympathy with a female protagonist, the figure is fourteen out of seventeen.[14] Moreover, there seem to have been female choruses from the start. The earliest to survive is in *Seven Against Thebes* of 467 BCE, but there are a dozen others indicated by the titles of lost plays of Aeschylus, and yet more by the titles of Pratinas and Phrynichus, the most famous of Aeschylus' older contemporaries. Phrynichus' entry in the *Suda* says that he was first to bring a female role (literally 'mask') onto the stage.[15] More about this later.

So why? This is the 64-talent question. I have reached the view that this cannot be answered until a decision has been made on another notorious question: whether or not women were present in the audience at the original performances. When I was asked this question by Harrison himself back in 1981 (he wanted to divide the audience of the *Oresteia* in the Olivier Theatre into two gendered blocks), I retreated into the respectable indecision of the standard discussion: there seems to be good evidence both for and against.[16] Since then I have made up my mind they were *not* there. Very briefly: (1) I find the absence in comedy of any allusion to their presence inexplicable if they were there, while (2) the chief witness *for* their presence, Plato, is, I think, talking polemically about the dangers of theatre throughout the Greek world, not particularly at the Athenian festival.

Now, assuming that women were *not* there, it makes sense to see tragedy's fascination with women, especially with powerful and dangerous specimens, as the Athenian men taking the opportunity to explore their worst anxieties in the 'security' of an exclusive gathering. Rather as it was possible to confront the horrors of unnatural death in the theatre, because there was no actual carnage,[17] so the potency of women, especially the dangers of their resentment and defiance, could be explored when there were no *real* women present. As with the other nightmares of tragedy, it does not really happen, and yet it is 'lived through'. Athenian citizens took this opportunity to explore what it was like to be non-free, to be women and/or slaves, to 'play the other', in Froma Zeitlin's phrase.[18]

This notion may, I suggest, give some wider insight into the place of women and the female in Harrison's theatre works. It is not a matter of a feminist programme; it is, rather, playing the other, but without the Athenian assumption that other means inferior. Harrison has sometimes been criticized for being an imperfect feminist—and that might well be true. This very male poet has no interest in being PC; and he acknowledges the impossibility of *being* the other. What happens is that men, and the world that males have made, are shown up, and often denounced, through the process of playing the female.

To resume the topic of women choruses: they have a special

sympathy with women characters; but it is of the essence that, unlike most protagonists, male or female, they survive—they sympathize, witness, grieve, live lives of slavery, but they plough on. This complex of characteristics can be traced again and again in Harrison's work, usually implicit, occasionally explicit, especially in his (as I write) latest theatre work *The Labourers of Herakles* (1995). I shall follow—with deviations— the chronological sequence of composition.

In the highly wrought and rather difficult script of *Medea: A Sex-war Opera* (1985) there is a Chorus of Men and a Chorus of Women, both of which go through multiple transformations. The Chorus of Men begin the work with multilingual misogynist denunciation of Medea's infanticide, and go on to dispute with the Chorus of Women who defend Medea's case.[19] Eventually, following a non-Euripidean version of the myth, a chorus of Corinthian Men stone the sons of Medea (who have become fourteen in number). There is then a stage direction, which is an instance, as I hope to trace, of the early stages of a Harrisonian pearl: '*the* Chorus of Women *enter and "bury" the* Sons of Medea *in the Pit'*.[20] The male chorus does not figure any more after this, but at the end, the Chorus of Women enters wearing '*their own clothes, no stage make-up'* as '*members of an opera chorus dressed for going home after work'*.[21] Yet they sing the ancient Greek of Euripides' *Medea* (lines 410–30), setting straight the misogynist traditions of mythology, interleaved with neo-Latin and French versions. One woman addresses the audience:

> These words from a woman's chorus
> at least 2000 years before us
> weren't much heeded,
> but since what they sung then
> should be listened to by men
> a translation's needed . . .[22]

The archetype for two opposed choruses of men and women is, in fact, a comedy, Aristophanes' *Lysistrata*. In *Chorus* the Chorus of Men is mostly replaced by the three British guards inside the Greenham fence. There is one scene which recalls the Aristophanic structure, however, and which accretes one of the pearls I am stringing. The three men become jingoistic First

World War veterans; and in response the women of the chorus become the mothers of sons killed in the Great War, with a series of couplets such as:

> Why is my baby in bright red bath water?
> I didn't wash him for this World War slaughter.[23]

Had the part of *Chorus* based on *Trojan Women* ever been finished (see note 2), then some of these motifs of the Chorus of Mothers would no doubt have been further developed. And they definitely would have been combined with another related Harrison obsession: the ambivalence of fire.[24] There is the fire which destroys—and the sack of Troy is its archetype—and the creative fire which sustains life. In the draft there is a sequence of choral stanzas on this theme, such as:

> The nightlight flames, the wedding brands,
> the flame of oven and kiln creates.
> The same element in other hands
> chokes, burns, asphyxiates.

Square Rounds (1992) has its chorus of women—and all but two of the individual roles are played by actresses who emerge from and return to it, melting into and out of the division between the individual and the collective. They begin as Funeral Directors and as Nurses, but are soon metamorphosed into Munitionettes. In the second shorter 'half' they are 'Women in Mourning Veils'. Yet they never really sing out for the themes of the bereaved chorus that I am picking up (the best lines are reserved for Clara Haber, who usurps some of the choral function). They do not even end the play as women, but are transformed finally into magician Chinamen.

Although an ensemble play, *Square Rounds* never seems to become fully choral. The chorus, as chorus, is arguably more integrated in *The Kaisers of Carnuntum*, although its lines are fewer. This is the second of three plays composed, after the Londinian tribulations of *Square Rounds*, for performance at special, resonant sites, and published as *Plays 3*. No one who saw one of the performances at Carnuntum on 2 and 3 June 1995 will forget the scene when, after Commodus (the brutal Emperor son of the saintly Marcus Aurelius) has finally been spitted on the spike of Orpheus' cello, the whole chorus—well over a hundred men and women, Austrian, Hungarian, Slovakian, all dressed in their ordinary clothes—gathered, hesitantly at first, round the monster, hardly able to believe that the tyrant was dead. Suddenly, as they broke into jubilant (Latin) song, ordinary people were drawn into the heart of this fantastical, grotesque reincarnation of the Roman Empire; and it was, in John Gould's formulation, 'lived through, perceived and recollected collectively as well as individually'.[25]

And earlier in the play, there was a Chorus of Mothers. The scene needs to be set visually. The floor of the Roman Amphitheatre was painted with a huge map of the Roman Empire, and in the centre at the site of Rome was a miniature Colosseum.[26] The play emphasizes that in Roman amphitheatres the point of killing exotic animals from distant parts of the Empire was to signify Rome's domination over their far-flung habitats. Commodus has a sack of bloody chunks of meat in his Colosseum, and he deposits them one by one at the appropriate locations on the map: bear in Britain, croc in Egypt, lion in Syria, ostrich in Libya, and so forth.[27] As he completes this grisly distribution, the ethereal voice of Marcus Aurelius rings out in Greek: μή, τέκνον· πρὸς ἄλλο πεφύκαμεν· ἐγὼ μὲν οὐ μὴ βλαβῶ, σὺ δὲ βλάπτηι, τέκνον.[28] In the text, there is then this stage direction:

With the same text as their song, **Women**—*representing the conquered countries—pick up the pieces of meat from each circle and wrap them in their national flags and begin to process towards the Colosseum, which they circle, cradling their butchered children. The subjugated women form a circle round the Colosseum facing the audience, to whom they display their pitiful lumps of meat, as if they were showing to the world a recently slaughtered child.* [29]

In performance the solemn choreography, the familiar 'anachronistic' flags, the tenderness with which the women cradled carrion, and the hauntingly beautiful music, as they sang Marcus Aurelius' words, translated into German and English,[30] showed at its best Harrison's ability to incarnate major themes and to arouse pathos.

This scene is recalled with redoubled power in Faustina's speech, perhaps one of the finest passages of poetry in all Harrison's theatre works:

Sometimes when I imagine that I hold
my Commodus again a one-year-old,
I cradle carcasses whose eyes can't close,
to whom no gentle rocking brings repose.
I find my blood-flecked arms are full
of hacked-up bits of bear and bull,
meat bundled up in bloody rags,
of boldly flown, but now abandoned flags,
and I have to add my bitter mother's cry
to this abattoir's black lullaby,
along with Klara and with Rosa,
each a *mater dolorosa*,
cradling Adolf's or Benito's tons
of other mothers' meat that once was sons,
and with Yekaterina, whose cradled darling
sucked milk, and then sucked blood as Joseph Stalin.[31]

The performance of *The Labourers of Herakles* took place less
than three months later, on 23 August. The story (or myth)
behind the play's genesis is that a lavish Festival was planned
for Delphi in 1995, and Harrison was 'promised' the resources
to bring over a whole company to perform his long-cherished
project of a version of Euripides' *Alcestis*. When all this fell
through, and the budget would scarcely stretch to ten people in
all, he determined to translate instead the *Alcestis* of
Phrynichus. Only one fragment of the play survives, the five
words which are the first heard in *Labourers*,[32] probably telling
how Herakles wrestled with Thanatos (Death) to save
Alcestis.[33] Eventually, *Labourers* included, for good measure,
nearly all of the fragments of Phrynichus, as gathered in volume 1
of *Tragicorum Graecorum Fragmenta*.[34]

This play is centrally concerned with the female chorus of
Greek tragedy. It starts from the 'fact' reported in the *Suda*
(quoted above) that Phrynichus invented the female role (or
'mask') in tragedy. A fine example of creative scratching
around in footnotes! The other basic 'fact' behind *Labourers* is
more firmly attested by Herodotus.[35] Soon after the Persians
had sacked Miletus in Asia Minor, a city with close ties to
Athens, in 494 BCE, Phrynichus dramatized this event in a play
(of which we have no fragments), probably called *Halōsis
Milētou* (*The Sack of Miletus*). Herodotus tells how the
Athenians fined Phrynichus a large sum and banned his play

from re-performance, because it distressingly showed 'their own, domestic troubles'.[36]

First, it is necessary once more to set the extraordinary scene.[37] The location was an excavation into some olive terraces in the grounds of the European Cultural Centre at Delphi, where it is hoped one day to build a new outdoor theatre. Round the rim stood nine cement-mixers that actually operated at various stages of the play. The cast consisted of five Labourers who are working on the site, using cement made by the Herakles Cement Company (a vast nationalized industry ubiquitous in Greece), whose huge silo, which turns out to be a kind of tube to the underworld, dominates the scene.

The stage directions refer to *'a "chorus" circle of nine cement-mixers'*; and later they say *'like a united chorus of mixers and men, the* Labourers *stand beside the turning mixers, beating a rhythm . . .'*[38] I think that 'anti-chorus' might have been a better term, since cement-mixers cannot feel and cannot articulate in words—they merely make a noise. Yet as Harrison himself has emphasized, the Greek chorus suffers and sings. In 'Facing up to the Muses'[39] he ties this especially to the *mask*: whatever terrible things happen, the mask stays upright with eyes and mouth open, it 'goes on speaking'. When in real life we would turn down or away and be reduced to silence or inarticulacy, the Greek chorus goes on witnessing and uttering, attempting to salvage some sense and to assert the will to survive despite all. So in so far as the circle of inarticulate machines seem to be like a chorus, this is, as it turns out, misleading.

The Labourers themselves are not very articulate; and they haven't got much time for theatre:

> No, there's nothing in the theatre for me.
> I'd sooner watch the fucking football on TV.[40]

When their feet get stuck in the concrete, this clearly signifies their mindless fixture in this attitude. It is the Spirit of Phrynichus (played by Harrison himself), raised by their recital of his meagre fragments, who gives them a lead towards liberation by pointing to the example of

> Phrynichos, who gave the theatre a start
> in redeeming destruction through the power of art,
> and, witnessing male warfare, gave the task
> of mourning and redemption to the female mask.[41]

This scene, near the end, interprets a puzzling sequence right back in the long 'dumb-show'—perhaps fifteen minutes' worth—which opens the play. During this the leading Labourer becomes possessed by the madness of Herakles and 'slaughters' a whole pile of cement sacks, finally coming on two further small sacks. As the stage directions put it: '*He impales their little bodies on the end of a pick. Red silk guts protrude from their gaping wounds.*' After his fit is over, the other four Labourers clear up the debris. Two of them

are like those who search the rubble of a gutted, devastated city looking for survivors or even something familiar, and eventually they are like mothers who search for their missing children [. . . .] Then with a terrible cry they recognise the tiny cement sacks that are the bodies of their children [. . . .] With a tragic shriek of recognition, Labourers 2 and 3 fall to their knees, and embrace and huddle to the cement sacks (their dead children) in their grief. They each pull from the gaping wounds of their babies a length of red silk, which becomes their robe and a classical female mask.[42]

They then deliver in ancient Greek the longest surviving fragment of Phrynichus, which is in fact four lines from his *Women of Pleuron* about an invading army that is setting fire to a whole coastal plain.

In the text it is explained that Labourers 3 and 4 '*become the two* **Women of Miletos**',[43] but in performance their metamorphosis into a pair of tragic women singing in ancient Greek is an enigma. It is only much later in the play that the Spirit of Phrynichus begins to make sense of the dumb-show. He tells the Labourers that enacting a play will teach them to face up to the horrors of the world:

> Cast aside mythology and turn your fearful gaze
> to blazing Miletos, yesterday's, today's.
> Once more the mourning women trudge the roads
> of murderous Europe. Look at them, and sing your odes![44]

Soon after, when Labourer 1/Herakles has put on his army-surplus camouflage shirt, and it becomes the agonizing 'shirt of Nessus', Labourers 2 and 3 again resume the voices of the female duet—'playing the other'—as they sing of the agonies of contemporary Europe.

> When all the men are massacred in Miletos, or elsewhere,
> who is left but women to keen in their despair?
> This was the truth that Phrynichos first knew
> when female masks first mourned *Halosis Miletou*.[45]

Before the beautiful closing song on this 'title with no play', a burning torch replaces the club of Herakles, who holds up that obsessive motif:

> The Greek shrines gutted by Persians, after Plataea,
> had their holy fires rekindled with the Delphic flame from here.
> The fire that burned Miletos and the flame
> that makes me writhe with anguish are the very same
> element that we hold up here tonight
> as a beacon for the future with its ambiguous light.
> This fire for the future that still comes flickering through
> drew its first flame from . . .
>
>   **All**
>   *Halosis Miletou*.[46]

The Labourers of Herakles is not likely to go down as Harrison's greatest theatre work. Both text and performance betray signs of being put together under pressure. At Delphi it met with a 'mixed' reception from its predominantly Greek audience. To some extent they may have been defeated by the characteristic verbal and dialectal virtuosity. But they may well have also found the didactic message of Phrynichus, played by the poet himself, too overt. And there was, arguably, an excess of esoteric allusions. Arguably, even, Harrison failed to fulfil his own admirable maxim: that the play should be self-sufficiently accessible, without requiring any homework or footnotes (no matter how many have gone into the *poiesis*.) This emerges most clearly in places, such as that discussed above, where the printed text with its stage directions is clearer than the performance. At the same time, *Labourers* is far from a hasty *jeu d'esprit*, and includes fine accretions to some of Harrison's most enduring themes, especially that of the chorus of grieving women, of Mams.

'The Chorus of Mams' brings me to the last, and first, example. *The Big H* is another work which has only been properly 'performed' once (so far as I know)—on BBC 2 on 26 December 1984. I foolishly missed it then, and have only seen a video once, in the lecture theatre at Delphi in 1985. A couple of hundred people were present, and, despite the unrelenting Leeds setting and dialect, many had tears openly streaming down their cheeks. I believe that this film deserves to be shown every Christmas as much as *The Snowman* (and far more than musicals of *A Christmas Carol*).

After the opening collage of Leeds coats of arms and of local place-names beginning with 'H', we hear a Primary School Teacher calling the register of boys. Each time a girl (the Chorus of Mams) sadly echoes the name: 'Our Roger!', 'Our Johnny!' At the end, Rachel, their leader, says:

> He were a lovely lad.
> And God alone knows why
> my baby had to die!

And Boy 12, who will turn out to be important, adds:

> We were bonny babies so say our mams
> but we all got murdered in our cots and prams![47]

I shall not attempt to give a résumé of this ever-shifting, mesmeric, moving and very funny work. Here already are the seed-pearls of some of the themes I have been threading together. For example, after both parts I and II, when the boys have turned into Herod's terror squad and massacred the innocents, attention turns to a 13th Mam—Herod's mother.

> Somebody put 'im to 'er breast
> and taught 'im ABC.
> In case you 'aven't already guessed
> that somebody were me.[48]

> A nice lad an' so sweet to me
> a dear when 'e were littler
> 'ow could I know e'd grow up to be
> an Adolf bloody 'itler!

> All swaddled in warm baby clothes
> 'is mother's little darling.
> Who'd know 'e'd grow mustachios
> and end up Joseph Stalin.[49]

Here, even down to the rhyme of 'darling' and 'Stalin', we have the infant forerunner of Faustina's great speech in *The Kaisers of Carnuntum*. In this earlier work, the 13th Mam insists that, none the less, every baby is special—'worth Gold, Frankincense and Myrrh'.[50]

Boy 12's refusal of the slaughter and 'orror, and his insistence that the owl on the Leeds coat of arms stands for wisdom, and not for 'owls of pain, leads to a redemptive ending in the Maternity Hospital (sign: 'H') at midnight on Christmas Eve. In many ways this is a far cry from the Trojan Women at the Greenham fence, the gobbets of meat in the Amphitheatre at Carnuntum, and the massacres of Miletos and of Bosnia evoked in *Labourers*. At the same time, the Chorus of Mams, who draw tears with their roll-call of massacred babes, have a future. 'Our Roger. Our Johnny. Our Frank. Our Malcolm. Our David. Our Jason. Our Ronnie. Our Michael. Our Peter. Our Tony. Our Mark. Our 'arry.'

I conclude with the wish that Our Tony's[51] future will bring him many more days and years of good health and good poetry. May he live out his own insight that, in the words of my favourite lines of all,

> it's the kumquat fruit expresses best
> how days have darkness round them like a rind,
> life has a skin of death that keeps its zest.[52]

And, when, one day in the distant future, greedy Thanatos comes to gulp down the oyster, I hope he chokes on all those immortal pearls.

12

Poetry or Bust: Tony Harrison and Salts Mill

Jonathan Silver

Salts Mill, built in 1853 by Titus Salt, is a grade-two listed complex of mill buildings near the River Aire at Saltaire, in West Yorkshire. I met Tony when the National Theatre performed *Trackers* here in 1990. We became friends, and I asked him if one day he might write a special piece for the mill. At the end of *Trackers*, on a crazy evening, he presented me with John Nicholson's *Collected Works*, in a Victorian edition, probably one of the only ones left, and I felt that somehow this would lead, as coincidences often do, to a dynamic conclusion. Don't ask me why, but sometimes the senses tell you something—or as Tony Harrison would say, the Muses were at work. There was plenty of coincidence here: John Nicholson was a poet, an ex-mill worker who scratched his verses in grease from the fleeces he was supposed to be sorting, and an Airedale man who drowned in the River Aire two minutes away from Salts Mill.

When *Poetry or Bust* happened in September 1993, it was a totally dynamic process, partly because Tony Harrison was hyper at the time, and I'm always hyper. We were in my studio one day when Tony noticed a Burmantofts plaque of Dante. Burmantofts is a local pottery in Leeds which I have collected for many years. Not much is known about this very unusual stylized faience pottery. It doesn't look English—more Isnik or Anglo-Persian—but it comes from an area of Leeds not far away from where Tony grew up. He collects images of Dante. His eyes lighted on it at the same time as mine (I had only bought it a couple of days before), and I said, 'If you write a piece for the mill, to be performed early in September [at the time I think it was July], then Dante can seal the deal!' Tony was immediately challenged, and perhaps enchanted with the idea. I lent him an old golfball typewriter and my home in Saltaire, thus effectively 'gating' him. He did not stop work until the last performance, and became more dynamic than ever, inevitably collapsing into delirium at the end. I think the pressure of the time-scale was a tonic for him.

Barrie Rutter, who had played Silenus in *Trackers*, was keen to do another play with Tony, and brought his Northern Broadsides company with him. Pace Micro Technology PLC, who occupy part of Salts Mill, agreed to be my co-sponsor for the production. Robert Fleming was having lunch in Salts Diner at the same time as Tony and me. I introduced Tony to him and within a few minutes he had agreed to co-sponsor the piece—another remarkable and delightful coincidence. They continued to come. In his quest for poetic immortality, John Nicholson had carved his name on rock near Eldwick, and always hoped that after his death there would be a bust to his memory. Moss had long since covered the carved name, and the bust erected in Bingley Park by his friends was almost immediately stolen. Tony Harrison located both the carved name and the vacant plinth on which the bust had stood, and incorporated them into the play. Soon after that, someone arrived with the plaster cast of Nicholson's features which he had commissioned on his abortive trip to London in 1827, and his portrait was retrieved from the obscurity of a vault.

The day before the first performance, David Hockney was in my Diner, and I asked him if he would illustrate the book. 'What book?' said Tony. Impulsively, I said, 'We'll print it through the night of 4 September.' Everyone laughed, but it happened—that's one of the reasons the book is completely uncorrected by Tony, and also explains the addendum. David Hockney simply drew the covers on Friday afternoon. I think they were proofed on Saturday, and printed through the night on 4 September. By this point, everything was moving so fast that I was quickly losing a sense of time. Tony himself painted the Aire, with its stepping stones, across the floor, and on Friday, when David Hockney first saw the set, he got out his brush and attacked the river, contributing some of his famous light reflecting on water effects. Rehearsals were still taking place a few hours before the play opened. As I said to Tony, 'Anything and everything is possible, as long as you want to do it!'

The flavour of the performance was caught by Michael Church's *Observer* review, which reported that we had 'galvanised' Bradford with a 'stirring tale' which 'bursts forth with appropriate wildness' and is played 'with authentic conviction'. As he said: 'Everything is revelled in—rhyme, Yorkshire speech rhythms, drumming feet, choral harmony. Poetry in its place.' And as he also said: 'There's nothing more powerful than a poem in its place'.[1] The *Guardian* described the play as 'ribaldly witty', and 'staged with heartfelt verve', adding that it wasn't 'just jolly knockabout—it has serious things to say about artistic integrity and human vanity'—among other things.[2]

Salts Mill had no licence to sell alcohol, but on 5 September, shortly after drowning in the Aire, John Nicholson (a.k.a. Barrie Rutter) revived, and in the spirit of Titus Salt, who despite his advocacy of Temperance, was patron to the alcoholic Nicholson, invited everyone to a free bar. The last-night party was total anarchy which swept from the painted river (now inhabited by a stuffed crocodile) to the gallery, and still lives in the minds of all who attended it. As the *Observer* review's headline put it: 'Immortality at last for Airedale's bust-a-gut poet'.

13

In the Canon's Mouth: Tony Harrison and Twentieth-Century Poetry

PETER FORBES

THERE has been surprisingly little discussion of Tony Harrison's poetics, as opposed to his subject-matter. The crossing of his classical education with his background has mesmerized many into thinking that's all there is to it. Douglas Dunn, a poet with whom Harrison has occasionally been linked to form a notional school (tagged 'Barbarians' after Dunn's book of the name, or 'Rhubarbarians', after Harrison's poem), has briefly considered Harrison's poetry on several occasions.

[H]is style is reminiscent of the sub-classical manner of Thomas Gray. Historically alert readers might also sense the pre-Augustan clarity of Dryden, or the varied urbanities of Virgil, Horace, Juvenal, Ovid and Martial.[1]

The pedal he presses consistently results in verse that could be called sub-classical, encrusted with Northern vernacular, sometimes demotic, but never populist [. . .][2]

It is significant, and I believe correct, that Dunn doesn't seek to place Harrison within a twentieth-century tradition. For Harrison is curiously at odds with his contemporaries. He rejects the burnished sonorities of Heaney, the eye-cramming images of Raine, the trickeries of Muldoon. For all their differences, most of his coevals partake of the contemporary *Zeitgeist*, enshrined in the Poetry Workshop nostrums: 'Show, don't tell'; 'Particular, not general'. These 'rules' derive from Pound's precepts and represent his lasting influence. Although Harrison wrote a poem ('Summoned by Bells')[3] to mark Pound's anniversary, and used Eliot's 'Journey of the Magi' to supply both epigraph and title for one of his Gulf War poems,[4] there's no evidence in his work for even the minimal Poundian influence that most contemporary poems display. ('Summoned by Bells' suggests that Pound 'helped to re-botch' the civilization he described in 'Hugh Selwyn Mauberley' as 'botched'.[5])

Not only is it difficult to place Harrison among his contemporaries, he doesn't often discuss them. He has expressed an impatience with what he sees as poetry's reduced horizons:

Poetry used to inhabit all the important arenas, the theatre, politics, that was where poetry operated. Then it retreated and shut itself away in the poetry magazines. What defeatism! What a pathetic decline![6]

That poetry *chose* its little-magazine parish rather than the wider arena is questionable, but the inverse correlation between public verse/clarity and coterie poetry/difficulty is well established. Because small groups can communicate successfully in codes that would be meaningless to a wider audience, increasingly esoteric poetry actually becomes favourably selected in such groups, thus diminishing the audience even further.

But when Harrison began writing he did not seem such a singular figure. At the end of the sixties a new generation of formal poets emerged—Douglas Dunn, Derek Mahon, John Fuller, Fleur Adcock, Kit Wright. These poets were more adventurous than the Movement generation, and Harrison seemed to belong among them. They shared a new *brio*, frankness in sex, regionalism—for all their different personalities, here might have been a new movement with Harrison one of its prime exponents. But the others sit quite happily in the twentieth-century canon—Auden is the figure behind them, in varying degrees certainly, but if any of them wrote a sonnet, it would be in awareness of 'Who's Who' ('A shilling life will give you all the facts'.)[7] A Harrison sonnet will be Miltonic, Wordsworthian, or Meredithian.

Tony Harrison has always had friends and supporters among the poets: whilst a student at Leeds he met Geoffrey Hill, Wole Soyinka, James Simmons, and Jon Silkin, who published his early work in *Stand*. Alan Ross published his first book-length collection *Loiners* at London Magazine Editions.

His fellow Yorkshireman Blake Morrison has been a staunch supporter. But the terms on which Harrison works—everything bar a few brief introductory essays in verse, no reviewing[8]—and his negative feelings about the poetry scene have inevitably led to a distancing.

The exception in terms of twentieth-century influence was the American poet Robert Lowell. The pungency of Lowell's early work provided an encouragement to Harrison. 'The Nuptial Torches' is the best example: a literary poem, unrelated to Harrison's experience, which imaginatively animates its epigraph: ' "These human victims, chained and burning at the stake, were the blazing torches which lighted the monarch to his nuptial couch." (J. L. Motley, *The Rise of the Dutch Republic*)'.[9] One could compare this with Lowell's 'A Quaker Graveyard off Nantucket', which doesn't have an epigraph but recreates the death of the sailors (in a sense the gravestone is the epigraph). Compare these lines from Lowell and Harrison:

> Light
> Flashed from his matted head and marbled feet.
> He grappled at the net
> With the coiled, hurdling muscles of his thighs;[10]

> Young Carlos de Sessa stripped was good
> For a girl to look at and he spat like wood
> Green from the orchard for the cooking pots.
> Flames ravelled up his flesh into dry knots[11]

Lowell's Grand Guignol rhetoric is observable throughout *Loiners*, but it is absent from Harrison's mature style, the dynamics of which I shall develop later.

In his early years the poet Harrison was most often linked with was Douglas Dunn. Critics and readers seem to like pairing poets off: Heaney and Hughes, Sexton and Plath, Auden and MacNeice, Armitage and Maxwell. Resemblances in these cases are more likely to be superficial than profound. Tony Harrison and Douglas Dunn share working-class backgrounds and an insistence on formal metrics, but I believe they are very different. Dunn is a social and civic poet who has adapted the inheritance of Auden and Larkin to his own ends. His *Barbarians* (1979) may well owe something to Harrison, but a poem like 'The Student' shows their essential difference.

Dunn's subject is an 'unknown student' figure from Renfrewshire in 1820:

> For our mechanics' Literary Club
> I study Tacitus. It takes all night
> At this rough country table which I scrub
> Before I sit at it[12]

Harrison's student is himself, sitting at a foldaway card table: *'Ah bloody can't ah've gorra Latin prose'*.[13]

I should like to enquire more deeply into the 'sub-classical manner of Thomas Gray' identified by Dunn.[14] I believe that Harrison's circumstances and aims made twentieth-century Modernism and its followers an unsuitable academy from which to learn, whereas a long-ignored eighteenth-century aesthetic suited him very well.

In 1985 Nicholas Bagnall wrote an innocuous sounding and little-noticed book under the misleading title *A Defence of Clichés*.[15] Bagnall's purpose was to question the overriding twentieth-century aesthetic imperative: Pound's 'Make it new'. Against this, Bagnall opposed the eighteenth-century notion that writing should be 'what oft was thought, but ne'er so well expressed',[16] that writers should use phrases that the reader has met before, rather than slow them down by making them try to unpick wholly novel phrases and allusions. He emphasizes the universal pleasure people take in shared catch-phrases and of course links the eighteenth-century practices to the enormous credibility the classics then had. To quote from the classics was a virtue in itself, so much so that the eighteenth-century goal could be said to be the exact opposite of the Poundian novelty principle: a well-used phrase was hallowed by such usage, not diminished by it.

The connection between all this and Tony Harrison is his classical education. I believe that Harrison has carried the traits of a classical education into his verse practice far more rigorously than other classically trained poets, Louis MacNeice, for example. MacNeice remained a practitioner of the classics, but, despite a few versions of Horace, his poetry is of the twentieth century, influenced by Auden, Eliot, and further back by Hopkins. Harrison's attitude to his masters is classical—he keeps them constantly in view. Milton and Wordsworth are classical touchstones for Harrison in a manner foreign to MacNeice. The names 'Milton' and 'Wordsworth' occur several times in Harrison's poetry, along with many others more incidental. You won't find the names of poets very often in MacNeice's poetry—Hopkins, a key influence, never appears at all.

If the names Milton and Wordsworth have an iconic force in Harrison's poetry unusual in the twentieth century so also do the words poetry and poet. Harrison reifies the concept of the poet to an unusual degree. For him it is the equivalent of the more solid and earthy trades he grew up among in Leeds. He is unlikely to share Miroslav Holub's view of the tenuous status of the poet (Yes, you wrote a poem once, but how do you know you'll ever write one again?). He has said: 'I wanted to make poetry a real job, and that's a question of hazarding the whole of your life on what you do'.[17]

A classical training of course is also a training in eighteenth-century thought processes. The classics have not changed and the Englishing of them reflects the period when they really mattered to us. What Harrison uniquely did was to graft on to classical notions of verse discipline his own vision of poetry as the equal of an industrial trade. Poetry to Harrison had to be at least as well made, not as prose, but as a leak-free plumber's joint. The man who parsed the Latin hexameters mutated into 'the man who came to read the metre'. Harrison has also sought to justify formal verse by pointing out that iambic pentameters occur regularly in ordinary speech—especially the speech of his parents: '*If you weren't wi' me now ah'd nivver dare*'.[18]

> But your father was a simple working man,
> they'll say, and didn't speak in those full rhymes.
> His words when they came would scarcely scan.
> Mi dad's did scan, like yours do, many times![19]

Some find the combination of a fierce working-class sensibility and classical learning in Harrison paradoxical, but in fact they reinforce each other perfectly. It is the upper middle classes who lost their faith in Latin tags and went whoring after novelty. Homeric epithet finds a ready echo in working-class life: Lofty-browed Homer becomes Dead-eye Dick.

The great Yorkshire fast bowler Freddie Trueman was once quoted by a journalist on the origins of his nickname. Trueman said that they called him 'Fiery' because 'it rhymes with Fred'. He was demonstrating his naive enthusiasm for poetry, alliter-ation being an inherently demotic art even if the word itself is unknown to the less well-educated. Sportsmen and women are always 'Gorgeous Gussie', 'Fiery Fred', or 'Typhoon Tyson' because finding likenesses in which the sound matches the sense is as instinctive a human activity as breathing.

What's more, the kind of everyday glum, undeceived, put-you-in-your-place rhetoric of working-class life isn't a million miles from Gray's Augustan language (making the appropri-ate transpositions, e.g. 'fly-blown dump' for 'ivy-mantled tow'r'[20]). A working-class neo-Augustanism seemed ready-made for Harrison, reinforced by both his background and his classical training. And in this language, the two poles which are consciously set apart in his poetry find a reconciliation. His insistence on his background and his classics dictated his verse style, and made him a neo-Augustan, perhaps without know-ing it.

The theorist of the Augustan age was Edmund Burke in his *A Philosophical Enquiry into the Origin of Our Ideas of the Sublime and Beautiful* (1756). The essence of Burke's ideas was that we all see and feel the same things, so that what the reader experi-ences in reading poetry is *recognition*: of the states and moods described, which are universal, and the language in which they are described, which is conventional but is learnt by every edu-cated person. Romanticism destroyed this notion; it sought unprecedented states, absolute individuality. Nothing that has happened since compares with the force of this change, not even Modernism, which can be seen as an extension of Romanticism in its insistence on the unprecedented, the extreme, even if it contradicts its metaphysics.

On one level, the difference between eighteenth-century and Modernist poetry can be summed up as: eighteenth-century poetry intends to communicate by using the common stock of ideas and phrases and moulding them into something harmo-nious—new but not startlingly novel; Modernism began in a revolt against bourgeois common values and deliberately eschewed the common stock of received ideas and phrases. We have become so used to Modernism (at least in its diluted form as practised by most contemporary poets) and its influence that of all the centuries the eighteenth now seems the most remote. Poets from Chaucer to Donne, and from Wordsworth onwards, are still alive for us, are chosen for *Poetry Please*, and still influence to some extent poetry today. But the practice of a poet like Pope seems to differ in a fundamental way from much of what preceded and followed it.

But if the eighteenth century is so unpopular today, how is it that Tony Harrison has come to write some of the most widely read contemporary poetry using its techniques? This paradox is explained by Harrison's subject-matter and diction. The formal principles of eighteenth-century verse are aimed at relatively easy understanding and a wide readership. The problem is that the subject-matter and sentiments expressed today seem impossibly pallid and low-key. But Harrison's poetry is blazingly passionate and aggressively up to date in its diction.

The eighteenth-century aesthetic has been important to Tony Harrison because of his passionately expressed desire to communicate to the widest possible audience. The Modernist's badge of pride in his alienation from the common herd is not for him: too aware of the alienation caused by his education, he wants to bridge gaps not widen them. Harrison's belief that poetry should appear in newspapers, on stage, and wherever the culture is vibrant has inevitable stylistic consequences. Despite seventy-five years in which acclimatization could have taken place, the wider public, even, say, the serious novel-reading or theatre-going public, have never really accepted *difficulty* in poetry. To be difficult has been to guarantee a small audience. Tony Harrison's early poetry, although not Modernist in technique, was knotty with allusion, and the syntax was often contorted. There has been a progressive ironing out, and his recent work has been much plainer than the earlier. It is no accident that when *v.* was subjected to attack by philistines, moral guardians, and the tabloid press, figures from the general arts culture such as Bernard Levin and Joan Bakewell rushed to its defence. These were people who had not often spoken up for contemporary poetry before. What made the difference was that here was a *cause célèbre*—and it was a poem you could understand! Not since Betjeman had there been a poet who so clearly wrote to be read widely, and to be read aloud. Closer in spirit to Harrison of course (if opposed in politics) is Kipling, a public poet, a political poet, and one who wrote in strong, archaic rhythms. Above all, Kipling is the poet recently voted the most popular amongst a wide audience (BBC1 viewers). In many ways Tony Harrison is the Kipling *de nos jours*.[21]

Several strands can thus be identified in the forging of Harrison's style: his classical training, which fosters respect for quotation and pre-digested phrase or modulation therefrom; the need to find a voice acceptable to a wider public; the conception of verse writing as a trade like any other, with its hallowed rituals and stereotyped procedures; his work in the theatre, with its requirement for clarity and strong rhythms; his unwillingness to accept the compromises made by his poetic contemporaries—writing reviews, judging competitions, running workshops, which has cut him off from the contemporary poetic *Zeitgeist*. All of these factors work in the same direction. They reinforce the tendency towards a taut, rhythmic style in which the diction doesn't depart too far from common usage, and isn't afraid to use conventional emotional expressions which receive an echo, if not in every bosom, in readers of the *Guardian* at least.

I am aware that Tony Harrison might not recognize himself in this picture. He acknowledges a debt to the seventeenth century rather than the eighteenth—particularly Donne, Marvell, and Milton. But Harrison's sensibility is not really metaphysical. Even when he writes in Marvellian mode in *Kumquat*, he doesn't attempt a 'green thought in a green shade':[22] his verse is closer to the flatter diction of Pope and Gray. It might not be too fanciful to trace a movement from seventeenth to eighteenth century in his verse, from the pungent and elliptical early poems—'The White Queen', *Newcastle*—to the more meditative and smoothly paced 'Following Pine', 'Cypress & Cedar', and, of course, *v.*

v. obviously suggests Gray's *Elegy* as a starting-point, and the parallels have been extensively discussed by Sandie Byrne.[23] But there are very obvious stylistic disparities between the poems. Gray's *Elegy* is a compendium of received wisdom expressed in received phrases: 'ivy-mantled tow'r', 'rugged elms', 'lowly bed', 'blazing hearth', 'yew-tree's shade', 'cool sequestered vale', 'purest ray serene'.[24] The leisurely pace of the poem and its strict metrics no doubt encouraged these sonorous phrases. No wonder Dr Johnson found that it 'abounds with images which find a mirror in every mind, and with sentiments to which every bosom returns an echo'.[25] To some extent the echo was built in. To be fair to the poem, some of it is far more original than this. Its quotable quotes: 'Far from the madding crowd's ignoble strife', 'Some mute inglorious Milton',[26] deserve their status. But in *v.*, as in all of Harrison's poetry, there are hardly any epithets at all, let alone cosy ones. His poetry is relentlessly substantive. He famously said that what was between him and his father were 'books, books, books',[27] and what his poetry is made of is 'nouns, nouns, nouns'. The vice of weak poets, to be always searching for flowery adjectives in an attempt to make a description more precise, never occurs to him.

When Harrison does use compound epithets, they are, like Gray's, from the common stock—'hard-earned treasures',[28] 'tart lemon's tang', 'dew-cooled surfaces',[29] or simply physically descriptive—'buried ashes', 'shored slack, crushed shale, smashed prop', 'unclaimed stone', 'blunt four-letter curses'.[30] Unlike Gray's, though, these epithets have no designs of 'poetry' on us; they are deflationary rather than uplifting. 'Gilded prayer'[31] is the only one remotely akin to Gray. They are the dystopian inverse of Gray's mildly rubefacient phrases.

Harrison's attitude to the canon of English poetry is enshrined in his verse. 'So right, yer buggers, then! We'll occupy | your lousy leasehold Poetry'.[32] Appropriation rather than homage: he takes just what he needs and no more. Metaphysical poetry provides him with 'Newcastle is Peru'; Louis MacNeice's 'The North begins inside' furnishes a handy epigraph.[33] Harrison needs the tradition because no poet can work without one, but he resents it because it is a canon written and selected largely by the southern upper middle class. The extent to which Harrison's poetics are indebted to eighteenth-century formal principles has been obscured by the ambivalence towards the traditional canon expressed in his work and by his aggressively contemporary diction. His classical interests are balanced by a knowledge of twentieth-century science and technology, particularly the technology of war. In his 'American' poems he comes over as a man at home in the modern world of materials. His knowledge of street idiom is also formidable. But the formal poetic use to which these materials are put would not have seemed eccentric to Gray (whereas some of the materials themselves certainly would).

If Harrison's work owes so little, not only to his contemporaries, but to twentieth-century poetry generally, could his work represent a paradigm shift, like Wordsworth and Coleridge's *Lyrical Ballads*, or Eliot's first poems? His poetic strategy is different enough and coherent enough to be so considered, but he has few obvious followers. Like William Blake, he may well be a complete one-off. It might be argued that Simon Armitage's poetry would not have been possible without Harrison's example, but it is highly debatable, given Armitage's avowed influences—Auden, Hughes, Frank O'Hara, Weldon Kees, Robert Lowell, and Huddersfield argot. Would northern poetry have remained of only regional significance without Harrison's example? It cannot be proven, but I imagine that the Huddersfield phenomenon would have emerged just the same without him. The set of factors that made Harrison the kind of poet he is were singular and are unlikely to be repeated:

> *How you became a poet's a mystery!*
> *Wherever did you get your talent from?*
> I say: *I had two uncles, Joe and Harry—*
> *one was a stammerer, the other dumb.*[33]

But it is now possible to discern a number of poets working in what might be called the New Plain Style—Harrison, Douglas Dunn, James Fenton, Carol Ann Duffy, Wendy Cope, Simon Armitage—as opposed to the postmodernist obliquities of Paul Muldoon, W. N. Herbert, Peter Didsbury, Selima Hill, Medbh McGuckian, Ian Duhig, Maggie Hannan. Sometimes Plain Style and postmodernist modes coexist within the same person. There are many ways of being plain, and the poets are unlike each other in most respects, but Harrison was the first post-war poet to write such emphatically Plain Style verse, and in that he has clearly been influential.

In the end, Harrison's achievement has been to bring a new directness into poetry. Neither the obliquities of Modernism nor the pre-digested formulations of Augustanism suit his purpose entirely, although he is much closer to the latter than the former. If poetry in the twentieth century has been largely metaphoric—seeing something always as, or at least like, something else—Tony Harrison has chosen such dramatically vivid material—the pathos of his estrangement from his parents' world, the skinhead's incoherent challenge to humanist pieties, the potential nuclear holocaust, the Gulf War and Bosnia—that the head-on approach has worked, while so many other poets were merely beating around the bush—the bush, of course, that they took so often for a bear.

14

Command of English

Bernard O'Donoghue

IN HOMAGE TO TONY HARRISON

'the thin, smoky beauty of vain eloquence'

Denis was always an hour late, or more.
He stammered so badly that the teacher
Gave up on him, and he didn't need
To learn anything. Johnny O'Connor
Was Down's Syndrome and cried when, every year,
He was kept back. He left junior school
At nineteen, still in high infants. When he
Pretended to recite, you couldn't tell
Whether or not what he was burbling was
'If all those endearing young charms.'

For all I know, I haven't seen him since.
He never took off his homemade cloth satchel
Or his coat, but he hypnotized us with
The pencil twiddled between his fingers:
So fast after fourteen years' practice
It was no more than an indistinct blur.
But Johnny had no luck to speak of.

T. W. in reverse, I would say 'luck'
For what the rest of them pronounced like 'look'.
And once at the bottom of an essay on
'What I would like to be when I grow up',
Was written 'Good command of English',
Which I didn't understand. Johnny sat late
Some nights, his ear six inches from
The HMV speaker, cronawning along

With Count John's rendition of 'Believe me',
His head on one side, balancing the dog's.

These days I'm better at interpreting,
Or so I fancy. In Johnny's remembered
Indecisive voice, I know every word
He meant: that *the heart that once truly loves*
Never forgets but as truly loves on
To the close, and further sentiments about
Gods and sunflowers and the setting sun.

15

Pericles in Tynemouth

DESMOND GRAHAM

I wrote 'Pericles in Tynemouth' among a sequence of poems bringing Shakespearean figures to the North-east. I thought I was putting his seafaring Pericles into landlocked retirement alongside people I had met here. The statue of Collingwood overlooking the harbour in the sixth line of my poem should have told me otherwise. Shortly after leaving Tynemouth station you come across a statue of Queen Victoria, Tony Harrison's 'Tynemouth Queen' in 'Ghosts'. One thing leads to another. I had been reading *Loiners* some weeks before writing the poem, preparing to write my prose piece for this book. So 'Pericles in Tynemouth', which is not about Tony himself, is full of the kind of intertextualities which I believe are a true homage: to Shakespeare, of course, and to Tony.

Pericles in Tynemouth
(After Shakespeare)

He could not stand the land.
There were incidents he talked of,
best forgotten, after the seventh pint
hit him, but most, something in the chip
of light beyond the north pier looking down
beside the Coastguards, from where Vice Admiral
Lord Collingwood surveyed the North Sea
and at his back the Tyne—that stripe
of light through darkness brought back what:
a rioting of islands, a visit to a king,
his daughter lost to London, found,
and lost again, or someone he tipped over—

it was rough enough for silence in the human world,
no human voice could break that roaring,
and the one he held and let slip gently
or maybe gave a push to—he will tell it over . . .
the pavement turns its sickly patterns,
semis passing him in darkness, starboard/
port, starboard/port, starboard/port—
the woman with his fortune in the backroom
off Front St., spelling the cards; the man
who offered him, unbuttoning her cardigan,
across the vinyl, his own wife; and the lunchtimes
drinking where the bars filled up like cabins
and the rats got out long before they sank in silence
through to dreary evenings. He wanders on
with seaman's tales of cargoes, landings,
wives in every port and all that stuff,
then the judder in his talk as if a wave
as high as Collingwood had hit him,
and he drifts home staring at the dome of Spanish City,
slipping between the ice cream stalls to the long tide
still trailing in and waits till its black
has landed—he who sized up Neptune
from the near side, landlocked, longing
for rough weather when you could not think.

Notes

INTRODUCTION

1. *SP*, back cover.
2. *TW*, back cover.
3. Quoted on *TW*, back cover.
4. Quoted on *SP*, back cover.
5. Quoted on *Bloodaxe 1*, back cover.
6. *Gorgon*, back-cover copy.
7. 'The Act', *Gorgon*, 20.
8. *Labourers of Herakles*, *P3*, 145.
9. *v.*, *SP*, 242.
10. Foreword (untitled), *Bloodaxe 1*, 9, repr. from a *Contemporary Writers* booklet published by the Book Trust in association with the British Council in 1987.
11. 'Agrippa', *Bloodaxe 1*, 33.
12. Foreword, *Bloodaxe 1*, 9.
13. 'When Shall I Tune My "Doric Reed"?', *Poetry and Audience*, 4/11 (25 Jan. 1957).
14. A. R. Mortimer and James Simmons (eds.), *Out on the Edge* (Leeds, 1958).
15. Anthony Cronin, Jon Silkin, and Terence Tiller (eds.), *New Poems 1960* (London, 1960).
16. A. R. Mortimer *et al.* (eds.), *Poetry and Audience 1953–60: An Anthology* (Leeds, 1961).
17. See especially the speeches of Silenus and the satyrs in *Trackers*.
18. Philip Larkin (ed.), *The Oxford Book of Twentieth-Century English Verse* (Oxford, 1973).
19. D. J. Enright (ed.), *The Oxford Book of Contemporary Verse 1945–80* (Oxford, 1980).
20. Seamus Heaney and Ted Hughes (eds.), *The Rattle Bag* (London, 1982).
21. John Heath-Stubbs and Davis Wright (eds.), *The Faber Book of Twentieth-Century Verse* (London, 1975).
22. Edward Lucie-Smith (ed.), *British Poetry Since 1945* (London, 1970).
23. For example, Kevin Crossley-Holland (ed.), *The Oxford Book of Travel Verse* (Oxford, 1986), which includes 'Prague Spring' and 'Brazil' from 'Sentences', and Tom Paulin (ed.), *The Faber Book of Political Verse* (London, 1986), which includes 'On Not Being Milton'. There are exceptions, such as Michael Schmidt (ed.), *Some Contemporary Poets of Great Britain and Ireland: An Anthology* (Manchester, 1983), which includes 'Thomas Campey and the Copernican System', 'The

Nuptial Torches', 'On Not Being Milton', 'Classics Society', 'National Trust', 'Book Ends', 'Continuous', 'Timer', 'Art and Extinction', and *Kumquat*.

24. Francis Palgrave, *The Golden Treasury*, 6th edn. updated by John Press (Oxford, 1994).
25. Margie Ferguson, Mary-Jo Salter, and Jon Stallworthy (eds.), *The Norton Anthology of Poetry*, 4th edn. (New York, 1996).
26. Price asked by The Poetry Bookshop, Hay-on-Wye, Jan. 1993.
27. See *Newcastle*, 16.
28. By now, as 'Them & [uz]' records, his own name, Tony (rather than T. W.) Harrison.
29. Beginning with 'The Curtain Catullus', *London Magazine*, NS 7/4 July 1967), 63–4.
30. 'Ghosts: Some Words Before Breakfast', *Poetry and Audience*, 7/22 (20 May 1960).
31. *Poetry or Bust*, *P3*, 51.
32. An image reinforced by the photograph (by Michael Childers) on the back cover of *Phaedra Britannica*, 3rd edn. (London, 1976), in which Harrison has long hair, wears a denim jacket, and is posed in front of a black-painted brick wall. (The text of *Phaedra* is also in *TW*.)
33. Acknowledgements, *Bloodaxe 1*, 6.
34. *Poetry or Bust*, *P3*, 55–7.
35. Walter Benjamin, 'Edward Fuchs, Collector and Historian', in *One-Way Street and Other Writings* (London, 1979), 359.
36. 'Working', *SP*, 124.
37. Ibid.
38. Diana Rigg and Alec McGowen.
39. *The Misanthrope*, 2nd edn. (London, 1975). (Also in *TW*.)
40. Tony Harrison and James Simmons, *Aikin Mata* (Ibadan, 1966).
41. The poets further collaborated in performance as the two halves of a donkey.
42. Rosemary Burton, 'Tony Harrison: An Introduction', *Bloodaxe 1*, 15.
43. Ibid. 21.
44. Oswyn Murray, 'Tony Harrison: Poetry and the Theatre', in *Bloodaxe 1*, 266.
45. See 'Facing up to the Muses', his address (as President) to the Classical Association, repr. in *Bloodaxe 1*, 429–54.
46. See, for example, *South Bank Poetry and Music* (London, 1971), which included 'On Not Being Milton'; *Planet*, 24/5 (Aug. 1974), which included three sonnets under the heading 'From "The School of Eloquence" ', and Allen De Laoch (ed.), *A Decade and Then Some* (London, 1976), which included 'The School of Eloquence', later retitled 'The Rhubarbarians'.
47. 'Heredity', *School*, 7.
48. *School*, 4 (acknowledgements page).
49. Harrison held the Northern Arts Literary Fellowship twice, in 1967 and 1976, and was Gregynog Arts Fellow at the University of Wales from 1973–4.

50. *A Kumquat for John Keats* (Newcastle-upon-Tyne, 1981); *U.S. Martial* (Newcastle-upon-Tyne, 1981).
51. Neil Astley, letter to S. Byrne (9 Feb. 1993).
52. His 'turn' in his father's flat cap could be read as both the literal swirl about before a mirror and a performance, implying that Harrison acts as a working-class male impersonator.
53. 'Turns', *SP*, 149.
54. See 'Social Mobility', *SP*, 107.
55. 'Interview', 233.
56. 'The Earthen Lot', *SP*, 179.
57. 'Poetry or Bust', *P* 3, 48–52.
58. 'Them & [uz] II', *SP*, 123.
59. His version of Karel Sabina's libretto for Smetana's *The Bartered Bride* was performed at the New York Metropolitan Opera in Nov. 1978, his film-poem *Arctic Paradise* was broadcast in Oct. 1981, and his music drama *The Big H* was broadcast on Boxing Day 1984.
60. Nicolas Tredell, 'Prizing Poetry', unpub. talk given at 'The Poetry Industry' conference, Oxford University, Feb. 1994.
61. Foreword, *Bloodaxe 1*, 9.
62. Astley, letter to Byrne.
63. Neil Astley (ed.), *Poetry with an Edge* (Newcastle-upon-Tyne, 1988), 19.
64. In publicity material and in *Bloodaxe 1*, 505.
65. Another of Harrison's poems, 'Voortrekker', had already been produced as a poster in 1972 (MidNAG Poster no. 17).
66. See *Palladas: Poems*, *SP*, 77–94, and Harrison's contribution to the translations in Peter Jay (ed.), *The Greek Anthology* (Oxford, 1973).
67. *The Oresteia* (London, 1981). (Also in *TW*.)
68. Bloodaxe is considering the possibility of marketing video recordings of Harrison's works, and in 1997 Faber and Penguin are to release a 3-hour audio cassette of the poet reading an extensive selection of his poetry.
69. Astley, letter to Byrne.
70. Described on the front cover as 'New edition with press articles' and on the copyright page as 'second edition'.
71. *v.*, *The London Review of Books*, 7/1 (12 Jan. 1985), 12–13. The poem was reprinted in the *Independent* (24 Oct. 1987) with an introduction by Blake Morrison.
72. See the press articles, letters, and House of Commons Early Day Motion repr. in *v.*, 39–79.
73. 'This second edition of his *Selected Poems* contains fifteen additional poems [. . .] and his remarkable long poem "v.".'
74. By Martin Booth, pub. in *Tribune*.
75. Sales figures kindly supplied by Neil Astley.
76. Richard Eyre, 'Such Men are Dangerous', *v.*, 38.
77. *The Northern Echo* (15 Jan. 1988), reproduced in *v.*, 79.
78. *The Big H*, *TW*, 335.
79. *Blasphemers' Banquet*, *Shadow*, 53.

80. James Meikle, Education Reporter, the *Daily Mail* (14 Jan. 1988), repr. in *v.*, 78.
81. *Coming*, back-cover copy.
82. 'Interview', 232.
83. Foreword, *Bloodaxe 1*, 9.
84. Photograph by Moira Conway.
85. Martin Seymour-Smith, *Robert Graves* (London, 1982).
86. *Loiners*, 7, repr. in *Bloodaxe 1*, 5.
87. The two poems were first published in the *Guardian* on 5 and 18 Mar. 1991.
88. 'Deathwatch Danceathon', the *Guardian* (12 Oct. 1994).
89. 'The Bright Lights of Sarajevo' and 'The Cycles of Donji Vakuf', the *Guardian* (15 Sept. 1995).
90. 'The Bright Lights of Sarajevo', the *Guardian* (15 Sept. 1995).
91. *Poetry and Audience* and *Stand*.
92. In 1987–8.
93. He reads and speaks, among other languages and dialects, French, German, Latin, Greek, Czech, Afro-Caribbean, Swahili, Yoruba, and Hausa.
94. See Judith Haber, *Pastoral and the Poetics of Self-Contradiction: Theocritus to Marvell* (Cambridge, 1994), 113.
95. 'The White Queen: I, Satyrae II', *Loiners*, 20.
96. 'White Queen: I, Satyrae II', *Loiners*, 22–3.
97. Ibid. 21.
98. Ibid. 22.
99. Thomas Wyatt, ['They fle from me that sometyme did me seke'], *Collected Poems*, ed. Kenneth Muir (London, 1949), 28.
100. Except that his possession of a name and history gives him an individual identity which the others lack.
101. *Trackers*, Delphi text, 69.
102. 'Turns', *SP*, 39.
103. *Trackers*, 132.
104. William Empson, *Some Versions of Pastoral* (London, 1995), 20–1.
105. Bruce Woodcock, 'Classical Vandalism: Tony Harrison's Invective', *Critical Quarterly*, 32/2, 50.
106. 'The Heartless Art', *SP*, 207.
107. Ibid. 208.
108. Ibid. 207.
109. Ken Worpole, 'Scholarship Boy', *Bloodaxe 1*, 61–74.
110. See Richard Hoggart, *The Uses of Literacy* (London, 1971), 273–90.
111. See the speech given to Silenus in the National Theatre text of *Trackers*, 124–5.
112. 'A Good Read', *SP*, 141.
113. 'Breaking the Chain', *SP*, 153, and 'Illuminations II', *SP*, 147.
114. *Chorus*, introd. v.
115. Ibid. After the showing of a forthcoming film based on the Prometheus myth at Delphi late in 1997, the screen is to be set on fire.

116. Carol Rutter (ed.), *Permanently Bard* (Newcastle-upon-Tyne, 1995).

1. THE BEST POET OF 1961

1. 'The Flat Dweller's Revolt', 1st pub. *Poetry and Audience*, 8/19 (10 Mar. 1961); *Ew*, 5–6.
2. 'Book Ends I', *SP*, 126.
3. I must acknowledge Neil Hairsine's help with 'last' here, and the extensive understanding of Harrison's work which he has shared with me while working on his doctoral thesis on *Loiners*, *Continuous*, and *v*.

2. TONY HARRISON THE PLAYWRIGHT

1. T. S. Eliot, 'Poetry and Drama', in *Selected Prose of T.S. Eliot*, ed. Frank Kermode (London, 1975), 145–6.
2. The film was broadcast on Channel 4 in Nov. 1987.
3. A project which has since come to fruition and will be shown as a Channel 4 film in the autumn of 1997.
4. Staged at the National Theatre in May 1996.

3. *V.* BY TONY HARRISON, *OR* PRODUCTION NO. 73095, LWT ARTS

1. 'A Good Read', *SP*, 141.
2. See 'The Queen's English', *SP*, 136.
3. See 'Me Tarzan', *SP*, 116.
4. *v.*, *SP*, 236.
5. Ibid.
6. Ibid.
7. Ibid. 237.
8. Ibid. 238.
9. Ibid.
10. Ibid. 240–1.
11. Ibid. 244.
12. Ibid. 246.
13. Ibid. 249.

4. ON NOT BEING MILTON, MARVELL, OR GRAY

1. 'THL', 56–7.
2. Ibid. 57–8.
3. See the Introduction above, and, for example, 'When the Bough

Breaks', *Poetry and Audience*, 4/15 (22 Feb. 1957) and 'What Plato Might Have Said', ibid.

4. *Poetry and Audience*, 7/1, 1–2. No date appears on the cover, but as the magazine was at the time produced weekly during term, and vol. 7, no. 2 is dated 23 Oct. 1959, the likely publication date of this issue was 17 Oct. 1959.

5. 'Agrippa', *Bloodaxe 1*, 33.

6. Wyatt, ['They fle from me that sometyme did me seke'], *Collected Poems*, 28. Wyatt's poem is, of course, three stanzas of rhyme royal, while this section of *The White Queen* (quoted in full in the Introduction) is composed of seven couplets.

7. We could, in turn, read this as mirroring the turn-and-turn-about relationships of power and ownership between 'original' and quoted texts.

8. *Newcastle is Peru*, 2nd edn. (Newcastle-upon-Tyne, 1974), introduction, 6. The poem from which the epigraph is taken, 'News from Newcastle', was at the time of *Newcastle is Peru*'s composition attributed to John Cleveland (e.g. in George Saintbury's *Minor Caroline Poets*, vol. 3) (Oxford, 1921)), but was later reattributed to Thomas Winnard (see *Poems of John Cleveland*, ed. Brian Morris and Eleanor Withrington (Oxford, 1967), p. xxxi).

9. See *Newcastle*, 2nd edn., introd., pp. 6–7.

10. Winnard, 'News from Newcastle', Saintsbury, *Caroline Poets*, iii. 88.

11. 'Thomas Campey and the Copernican System', *SP*, 13–14. (First pub. in *London Magazine*, NS 7/4 (July 1967).)

12. 'The White Queen 3: Travesties' has an epigraph: 'Distant Ophir (after Hieronymi Fracastorii, *Syphilis, sive Morbus Gallicus*, Veronae, MDXXX)' (*SP*, 29).

13. *Palladas: Poems* I, *SP*, 77.

14. 'Cypress and Cedar ', *SP*, 230.

15. *A Kumquat for John Keats*, *SP*, 192–5.

16. See John Donne, 'The Sunne Rising', *Poetical Works of John Donne*, ed. Herbert J. C. Grierson (Oxford, 1971), 10–11.

17'. 'The Heartless Art', *SP*, 206.

18. 'Facing North', *SP*, 179.

19. 'The Red Lights of Plenty', *SP*, 203.

20. Ibid.

21. Ibid. 192–3.

22. Ibid. 193.

23. *Newcastle*, *SP*, 66–7.

24. John Donne, Elegie XIX: ['Going to Bed'], *Poetical Works*, 106–8.

25. For example, 'Doodlebugs', *SP*, 20.

26. John Carey, *John Donne: Life, Mind, and Art* (London, 1981), 18.

27. See ibid. 37–41.

28. Personified by Mrs Florrie Harrison, knitting, in 'Jumper', *SP*, 165.

29. *Gorgon*, 19–21.

30. 'Durham', *SP*, 70. For an interesting definition of metaphysical poetry based on 'the problem of the One and the Many', which could also be

applied to this and other of Harrison's poems, see James Smith, 'On Metaphysical Poetry', *Scrutiny*, 2/13 (Dec. 1933), 227–8.

31. See William Empson, *Essays on Renaissance Literature*, vol. 1, ed. John Haffenden (Cambridge, 1993) intro., pp. 6–14.
32. See, for example, 'The Chopin Express', *Loiners*, 69–70, as well as 'Durham'.
33. See Frank Kermode, 'The Argument of Marvell's *Garden*', *Essays in Criticism*, 2 (1952), repr. in John Carey (ed.), *Andrew Marvell: A Critical Anthology* (London, 1969) 250–65.
34. *Kumquat*, *SP*, 192.
35. Andrew Marvell, 'Bermudas', *The Poems and Letters of Andrew Marvell*, vol. 1, ed. H. M. Margoliouth, 3rd edn., rev. Pierre Legouis and E. E. Duncan-Jones (Oxford, 1971), 17–18.
36. Andrew Marvell, 'To His Coy Mistress', *Poems and Letters*, i. 27–8.
37. 'Seize the day' and 'time devours'.
38. Kermode, 'Marvell's *Garden*', Carey, *Andrew Marvell*, 256.
39. Andrew Marvell, 'The Garden', *Poems and Letters*, i. 53.
40. *Kumquat*, *SP*, 194.
41. 'Following Pine', *SP*, 228.
42. See 'Me Tarzan', *SP*, 116.
43. See 'Ghosts: Some Words Before Breakfast', *SP*, 72–6.
44. See, for example, 'Giving Thanks', *SP*, 200.
45. See Henry King, 'The Exequy', David Norbrook and H. R. Woudhuysen (eds.), *The Penguin Book of Renaissance Verse* (London, 1992), 644–8.
46. 'Cypress and Cedar', *SP*, 233.
47. Marvell, 'To His Coy Mistress', *Poems and Letters*, i. 28.
48. *Newcastle*, *SP*, 65.
49. J. V. Cunningham, 'Tradition and Poetic Structure', *Modern Philology*, 51 (1953), repr. in Carey, *Andrew Marvell*, 218.
50. *Newcastle*, *SP*, 64.
51. Cunningham, 'Tradition and Poetic Structure', Carey, *Andrew Marvell*, 221.
52. 'Deathwatch Danceathon', the *Guardian* (12 Oct. 1994), 13.
53. See, for example, William Wordsworth, ['She dwelt among the untrodden ways'], *Poetical Works*, ed. Thomas Hutchinson and Ernest de Selincourt (Oxford, 1969), 86. For a discussion of the poem's 'a-logical structure', see Cleanth Brooks, *Modern Poetry and the Tradition* (New York, 1965), pp. xiv–xvi.
54. John Guillory, *Cultural Capital: The Problem of Literary Canon Formation* (Chicago, 1993), 88.
55. See *v.*, *SP*, 236.
56. See Woodcock, 'Classical Vandalism', *CQ* 32/2 (1990), 58 for an excellent comparison of Gray's and Harrison's use of iambics.
57. *v.*, *SP*, 236.
58. Geoffrey Harvey, *The Romantic Tradition in Modern English Poetry* (London, 1986), 14.
59. Ibid.

60. Guillory, *Cultural Capital*, 89.
61. Tony Harrison, 'All Out', review of Alan Bold (ed.), *The Penguin Book of Socialist Verse*, *London Magazine*, NS 10/12 (Mar. 1971), 87.
62. See Thomas Gray, *Elegy Written in a Country Churchyard*, in Roger Lonsdale (ed.), *New Oxford Book of Eighteenth-Century Verse* (Oxford, 1984), 354.
63. Guillory, *Cultural Capital*, 99.
64. 'I wanted to make poetry a real job [. . .] for more than fifteen years I've done nothing but write verse for a living. I wanted my job to be the whole enterprise, the whole risk' ('Interview', *Bloodaxe 1*, 246).
65. See 'Self Justification', *SP*, 172.
66. 'Poetry is all I write, whether for books, or readings, or for the National Theatre [. . . .]' (Foreword, *Bloodaxe 1*, 9).
67. Neil Astley, 'The Wizard of [Uz]', *Bloodaxe 1*, 10.
68. Ibid.
69. *v.*, *SP*, 241.
70. Ibid. 242.
71. See *The Big H*, *TW*, 321–61.
72. *v.*, *SP*, 241.
73. Gray, *Elegy*, 357.
74. *v.*, *SP*, 241.
75. Ibid. 242.
76. Ibid. 244.
77. Ibid. 242.
78. Ibid. 244.
79. John Storey, *An Introductory Guide to Cultural Theory and Popular Culture* (Hemel Hempstead, 1993), 121.
80. *v.*, *SP*, 243.
81. *v.*, back-cover copy.
82. Guillory, *Cultural Capital*, 91.
83. See *v.*, *SP*, 239.
84. Ibid. 246.
85. Ibid. 240.
86. Ibid. 239 ff.
87. Ibid. 248.
88. Ibid. 239, 244, and 245.
89. Ibid. 245.
90. Ibid. 247.
91. Ibid. 245.
92. Ibid. 246–7.
93. Empson, *Versions of Pastoral*, 11–12.
94. Percy Bysshe Shelley, *Queen Mab*, v. 137–42.
95. Empson, *Versions of Pastoral*, 12.
96. Harrison, 'All Out', 88.
97. Empson, *Versions of Pastoral*, 12.
98. *v.*, *SP*, 241.
99. Ibid. 242.
100. Ibid. 244.

101. Ibid. 245.
102. Charles Dickens, *A Christmas Carol* (London, 1843).
103. Gray, *Elegy*, 357.
104. 'Blocks', *SP*, 164.
105. 'Book Ends II', *SP*, 127.
106. Harrison, 'All Out', 88.
107. *v.*, *SP*, 247.
108. Ibid. 246. My italics.
109. John Lucas, 'Speaking for England?', in *Bloodaxe 1*, 354.
110. Gray, *Elegy*, 358.
111. *v.*, *SP*, 249.
112. Ibid. 248.
113. *The Prose Works of William Wordsworth*, ed. W. J. B. Owen and Jane W. Smyser (Oxford, 1974), 133.
114. *v.*, *SP*, 249.

5. OPEN TO EXPERIENCE

1. 'Interview', *Bloodaxe 1*, 227.
2. Ibid. 229.
3. 'The Pocket Wars of Peanuts Joe', *SP*, 16.
4. 'Pain-Killers II', *SP*, 170.
5. Gerard Manley Hopkins, 'Hurrahing in Harvest', *The Poetical Works of Gerard Manley Hopkins*, ed. Norman H. MacKenzie (Oxford, 1990), 149.
6. 'Study', *SP*, 115.
7. 'Conversation', *Bloodaxe 1*, 39.
8. 'Jumper', *SP*, 165.
9. 'Conversation', *Bloodaxe 1*, 43.
10. 'Jumper', *SP*, 165.
11. 'Conversation', *Bloodaxe 1*, 43.
12. 'A Good Read', *SP*, 141.
13. 'Interview', *Bloodaxe 1*, 237.
14. 'A Good Read', *SP*, 141.
15. 'Illuminations I', *SP*, 146.
16. 'Bye-Byes', *SP*, 163.
17. 'The White Queen 2: The Railroad Heroides', *SP*, 28.
18. 'The White Queen 5: *from* the Zeg-Zeg Postcards', *SP*, 35.
19. See *Newcastle*, *SP*, 63–8.
20. *Fire-Gap*, *SP*, 214.
21. Ibid. 218.
22. Ibid. 219.
23. 'Long Distance II', *SP*, 134.
24. 'The Gaze of the Gorgon', *Gorgon*, 62.

6. CULTURE AND DEBATE

1. 'Agrippa', *Bloodaxe 1*, 33–4.
2. *SP* 'Book Ends', 126–7; 'Long Distance', *SP*, 133–4; and 'Flood', *SP*, 135.
3. 'The Queen's English', *SP*, 136.
4. *v.*, *SP*, 248.
5. Richard Eyre, 'Such Men are Dangerous', *Bloodaxe 1*, 362.
6. Terry Eagleton, 'Antagonisms: Tony Harrison's *v.*', *Bloodaxe 1*, 350.
7. *v.*, *SP*, 238.
8. 'Them & [uz]', *SP*, 122–3.
9. *v.*, *SP*, 241.
10. Ibid. 241.
11. Romana Huk points out that Harrison's lyrics have an inner divisiveness, 'so strong that unified utterance becomes *dialogic*, dramatic, even 'polycentric' when the poet mediating between voices steps back to implicate his/her own role in their construction' ('Tony Harrison, the *Loiners* and the "Leeds Renaissance" ', *Bloodaxe 1*, 79). Huk cites Merle Brown, *Double Lyric: Divisiveness and Communal Creativity in Recent British Poetry* (London, 1980), 30.
12. *v.*, *SP*, 242.
13. Ibid. 244.
14. Ibid. 241.
15. Ibid. 244.
16. Ibid. 246.
17. Ibid. 248.
18. George Steiner, *Antigones* (Oxford, 1984).
19. 'Them & [uz] I', *SP*, p. 122.
20. 'Turns', *SP*, 149.
21. Huk, 'Leeds Renaissance', *Bloodaxe 1*, 82.
22. In his preface to *Aikin Mata* (Ibadan, 1966).
23. See 'The Songs of the PWD Man I, II', and 'The Death of the PWD Man', *SP*, 41–9.
24. *v.*, *SP*, 237.
25. Ibid. 240.
26. 'Bringing Up', *SP*, 166.
27. Bennett M. Berger, *An Essay on Culture* (Berkeley, 1995), 35.
28. *Trackers*, introd., p. xiv.
29. Ibid. introd., p. xii.
30. Ibid. introd., p. xxi.
31. Ibid. 84.
32. Ibid. 92.
33. Ibid. 96–7.
34. Ibid. 100.
35. Ibid. 105.
36. Ibid. 107 ff.
37. Ibid. 114.

38. Ibid. 117.
39. Ibid. 119.
40. Cf. Allan Bloom, *The Closing of the American Mind* (New York, 1987) 73 f.
41. *Trackers*, 120.
42. Ibid. 121–2.
43. Ibid. 124 ff.
44. Ibid. 127.
45. *Poetry TH*, 59.
46. *Trackers*, 129.
47. *Shadow*, 53.
48. Harrison is a poet-classicist indeed, and is exceptionally aware of the continuing value of a traditional canon. This is not just an academic matter—the framework of belief about the arts of any 'cultured person' will have its canonic component (however idiosyncratic), in the sense that there is a series of works of arts which count for him or her, to which he or she makes reference, and which provide some kind of standard. Palladas, for one, who shows the ironic satiric posture of much of Harrison's work exceptionally well.
49. Seamus Heaney, *The Redress of Poetry* (London, 1995).
50. Ibid. p. xiii.
51. Ibid. 4.
52. Ibid. 7 f.
53. *v., SP*, 248.
54. Humour is defined by Kundera as 'the divine flash that reveals the world in its moral ambiguity and man in his profound incompetence to judge others; humour: the intoxicating relativity of human things; the strange pleasure that comes of the certainty that there is no certainty' in his *Testaments Betrayed* (London, 1995), 32 f. He also has some wonderful things to say about the value of irony. See 201–3.
55. He goes on to point out that the 'School of Eloquence' (a name for the London Corresponding Society, an eventually banned radical organization of the 1790s) contains 'a thesis about political and linguistic oppression' (Blake Morrison, 'The Filial Art', *Bloodaxe 1*, 54–6).
56. Heaney, *The Redress of Poetry*, 7.
57. *Blasphemers' Banquet, Shadow*, 56.
58. *Blasphemers' Banquet* was itself censored in its film version. 'Under legal pressure the BBC removed [. . .] two quatrains from the film ' (*Shadow*, 64 n.). The two censored quatrains are restored in *Shadow*.
59. Ibid. 63.
60. Ibid. 60.
61. Ibid. 59.
62. Foreword, *Bloodaxe 1*, 9.
63. Neil Astley, 'The Riff-Raff Takes Over', *v.*, 2nd edn., 35.
64. John Deans and Garry Jenkins, 'Four-Letter TV Poem Fury' (*Daily Mail*, 12 Oct. 1987), *v.*, 2nd edn., 40–1.
65. The MP Gerald Howarth was also reported as describing Harrison as

'another probable Bolshie poet trying to impose his frustrations on the rest of us' (*v.*, 2nd edn., 41).

66. The IBA even considered 'bleeping out' the naughty words in the film of the poem. See 'Clear Road for Rude Ode', the *Observer* (11 Oct. 1987), *v.*, 2nd edn., 39.
67. Mary Whitehouse, letter to *The Times* (26 Oct. 1987), *v.*, 2nd edn., 59.
68. *v.*, 2nd edn., 60.
69. Hugh Hebert, 'Vindications of Mortality', the *Guardian* (17 Oct. 1987), *v.*, 2nd edn., 49.
70. Bernard Levin, 'An Adult's Garden of Verse', *v.*, 2nd edn., 52. Cf.: 'the poem is a scream of outrage against the degradation of thought, emotion, imagination and language' (David Isaacs, 'Ignorant Assault', *v.*, 2nd edn., 47), which may do justice to a theme, but is still in the expressionist spewing rather than the rational debate metaphorical area, given the 'scream'.
71. *v.*, 2nd edn., 52.
72. Ronald Butt, 'Disdain Verses Manners', *v.*, 2nd edn., 54–5.
73. Reported in the *Daily Telegraph* (13 Oct. 1987); *v.*, 2nd edn., 43.
74. Martyn Green, 'To Show V or not to Show V', *v.*, 2nd edn., 48.
75. Geoff Dyer, 'V Signs', the *New Statesman*, 30 Oct. 1987, *v.*, 2nd edn., 63.
76. Tom Phillips, letter to the *Independent*, 3 Nov. 1987, *v.*, 2nd edn., 69.

7. BOOK ENDS

1. 'Interview', *Bloodaxe 1*, 227.
2. 'Durham', *SP*, 70.
3. 'Bringing Up', *SP*, 166.
4. A *Kumquat for John Keats*, *SP*, 193.
5. See the introduction to the 2nd edn. of *Newcastle*. Harrison gives the source of the poem's title and epigraph ('Correct your maps: Newcastle is Peru!') as John Cleveland. In his statement of 1971, 'The Inkwell of Dr Agrippa', in *Bloodaxe 1*, he says that he read the lines in a poem he 'atttributed' to Cleveland. The source is the second line of 'News from Newcastle: Upon the Coal-pits about Newcastle-upon-Tyne', which Harrison most probably read in George Saintsbury (ed.), *Minor Poets of the Caroline Period*, Vol. 3 (Oxford 1921), 88:

> England's a perfect world, has Andes too;
> Correct your maps, Newcastle is Peru!

Saintsbury put this poem among 'Poems certainly or almost certainly Cleveland's but not included in 1653 or 1677 [editions]'. In *The Poems of John Cleveland*, eds. Brian Morris and Eleanor Withington (Oxford, 1967), the editors say that the poem is by Thomas Winnard (p. xxxi) and was first attributed to Cleveland in the edition *J. Cleaveland Revived: Poems, Orations, Epistles etc* (London, 1659), but give no further information about the attribution. The *English Poetry Full-Text Data Base* does not have 'News from Newcastle', but gives an interesting remote echo in John Davies's 'The Bien Venu': 'Great Britain's metamorphos'd to Peru' (l. 152).

6. Thomas Fuller, *The History of the Worthies of England* (1662), 135, quoted in *The Poems of John Cleveland*, ed. Brian Morris and Eleanor Withington (Oxford, 1967), p. xix.

7. 'I had a very loving upbringing; without question, a very loving, rooted upbringing' ('Interview', *Bloodaxe 1*, 246). It is interesting that Harrison goes on to say: 'Education and poetry came in to disrupt that loving group, and I've been trying to create new wholes out of that disruption ever since.'

8. 'The Rhubarbarians I', *SP*, 113; 'National Trust', *SP*, 121; 'Working', *SP*, 124.

9. A problem Harrison is well aware of and discusses eloquently in his interview with John Haffenden. 'Traditionally when you climb a ladder you are expected to kick the rungs away' ('Interview', *Bloodaxe 1*, 232).

10. The term was first employed by T. S. Eliot in his essay 'The Metaphysical Poets', *Selected Essays*, 3rd edn. (London, 1951), 288.

11. In his later essay 'Milton II', Eliot says 'that to lay the burden on the shoulders of Milton and Dryden was a mistake [. . .] the causes are too complex and too profound to justify our accounting for the change in terms of literary criticism' (*On Poetry and Poets* (London, 1957), 153). The scientific revolution and the Civil War were only two of these causes. Eliot's comments further justify use of the term away from its historical basis and into a more precise literary matrix.

12. Eliot, 'The Metaphysical Poets', 287–8.

13. Ibid. 288.

14. Ibid. 289.

15. 'Them & [uz] II', *SP*, 123.

16. Cf. 'But Wit, abstracted from its effects on the hearer, may be more rigorously and philosophically considered as a kind of *discordia concors*; a combination of dissimilar images, or discovery of occult resemblances in things apparently unlike' (Samuel Johnson, *Samuel Johnson: Rasselas, Poems, and Selected Prose*, ed. B. H. Bronson, 3rd edn. (New York, 1971), 358).

17. Conversely, recognizing the need for a humanist perspective, Harrison has tried to see his work under the title of Tragedy in order to give it a high life-affirming force: 'in an age when the spirit of affirmation has almost been burned out of us, more than ever we need what Nietzsche also called tragedy in *Ecce Homo*, 'the highest art to say yes to life' ('Facing up to the Muses' (Harrison's Presidential Address to the Classical Association, 1988), repr. in *Bloodaxe 1*, 440).

18. 'Me Tarzan', *SP*, 116.

19. Johnson, *Rasselas, Poems, and Selected Prose*, 358.

20. 'Curtain Sonnets 1', *SP*, 55.

21. In *SP* this follows a quote from E. P. Thomson's *The Making of the English Working Class*, and Milton's '*Ad Patrem*', on p. 111. Cf. 'Self-Justification', *SP*, 172.

22. 'Curtain Sonnets 2', *SP*, 56.
23. 'Curtain Sonnets 3', *SP*, 57.
24. *SP*, 52–3 and 54.
25. 'Curtain Sonnets 4', 'The People's Palace', *SP*, 58.
26. 'Curtain Sonnets 5', 'Prague Spring', *SP*, 59.
27. *Newcastle*, *SP*, 63.
28. Ibid. 64.
29. Ibid. 63.
30. Ibid. 64.
31. A transcript is given as introduction to the 2nd edn. of *Newcastle*.
32. Juan de Mena, *Laberinto de Fortuna*, ed. Louise Vasvari Fainberg (Madrid, 1976). Harrison is taking a liberty with the poem's organization: the protagonist is taken on an allegorical journey by Providence through seven concentric circles (based on the planets as in Dante's *Paradiso*), at the centre of which labyrinthine shape lie three vast wheels, two stationary which represent past and future, and the third of which represents the present in perpetual motion.
33. *Newcastle*, *SP*, 65.
34. John Donne, Elegy XVIII, 'Love's Progress', *Poetical Works of John Donne*, ed. Herbert J. C. Grierson (Oxford, 1971), 105.
35. John Donne, 'The Sunne Rising', *Poetical Works*, 11.
36. John Donne, Elegy XIX, ['Going to Bed'], *Poetical Works*, 107.
37. Donne, 'Love's Progress', *Poetical Works*, 105.
38. *Newcastle*, *SP*, 67.
39. Ibid.
40. Donne, 'The Sunne Rising', *Poetical Works*, 11.
41. *Newcastle*, *SP*, 64.
42. Ibid.
43. Ibid. 63.
44. Ibid. 65.
45. Ibid. 66.
46. Ibid.
47. Ibid. 67.
48. Ibid. 67–8.
49. The suggestion of Aeneas is Harrison's own, from his introduction to the 2nd edn. of *Newcastle*.
50. 'Durham', *SP*, 70.
51. 'Art & Extinction', *SP*, 182–9.
52. See 'The Rhubarbarians II', *SP*, 114.
53. See *Kumquat*, *SP*, 193–4.
54. Ibid. 194.
55. Ibid. 195.
56. See Rosalie L. Colie, *Shakespeare's Living Art* (Princeton, 1974), ch. 2, 'Mel and Sal: Some Problems in Sonnet-Theory', pp. 68–134. The fascination with these terms stems from their opposition in Petrarchan oxymora: *mel* (lit. honey) is love's sweetness, *sal* (lit. salt) is love's bitterness.

57. John Keats, 'Ode on Melancholy', *Poetical Works*, ed. H. W. Garrod (Oxford, 1970), 220.
58. *Kumquat, SP*, 193.
59. John Keats, Letter to George and Tom Keats, 21, 27[?] December 1817, in H. E. Rollins (ed.), *The Letters of John Keats, 1814–1821*, vol. 1 (Cambridge, 1958), 193.
60. *Kumquat, SP*, 193–4.
61. Nessus (*Inferno* xii); Athanas and Myrrha (*Inferno* xxx); Philomela (*Purgatorio* ix); Procne (*Purgatorio* xvii). Dante actually refers to Ovid's transformations in *Inferno* xxv.
62. *Kumquat, SP*, 194.
63. 'Wordlists II', *SP*, 118.
64. [Natural] place of [sensual] delight.
65. *Kumquat, SP*, 193.
66. As Harrison has said: 'My brain can tell me life isn't worth living, I would like to die; but my heart beats on. For me, it's the struggle and tension between what the head is saying and what the heart is feeling which is how I make my poetry' ('Conversation', *Bloodaxe 1*, 43).
67. Geoffrey Chaucer, *The Parliament of Fowls*, *The Riverside Chaucer*, ed. L. D. Benson, 3rd edn. (Oxford, 1987) 394.

8. TONY HARRISON AND THE *GUARDIAN*

1. Thomas Hardy, 'Channel Firing', *The Complete Poems of Thomas Hardy*, ed. James Gibson (London, 1976), 305.
2. Paul Fussell, *Killing in Verse and Prose* (London, 1988), 132.

9. DOOMSONGS

1. 'Agrippa', *Bloodaxe 1*, 32.
2. Ibid.
3. *Shadow*, 10.
4. *Coming*, 9.
5. 'Interview', *Bloodaxe 1*, 246.
6. See 'Rhubarbarians II', *SP*, 114.
7. 'A Close One', *SP*, 160.
8. Ibid.
9. Ibid.
10. 'Jumper', *SP*, 165.
11. 'The Morning After', *SP*, 157.
12. 'The Morning After II', *SP*, 158.
13. *A Kumquat for John Keats*, *SP*, 193–4.
14. For instance by Robert Crawford. See *Devolving English Literature* (Oxford, 1992), ch. 6.
15. Tom Leonard, 'On Reclaiming the Local', in *Reports from the Present: Selected Work 1982–94* (London, 1995), 38.

16. *Kaisers of Carnuntum*, P3, 77.
17. *Gorgon*, 62.
18. Ibid. 64.
19. Ibid.
20. *Labourers of Herakles*, P3, 143.
21. *Gorgon*, 60.
22. *Labourers of Herakles*, P3, 145.
23. Wilfrid Owen, *The Poems of Wilfred Owen*, ed. Jon Stallworthy (London, 1985), 135.
24. 'Conversation', *Bloodaxe 1*, 43. Harrison repeats this idea elsewhere. He comments in his interview with John Haffenden, for example, that he is drawn to verse because 'it's associated with the heartbeat, with the sexual instinct, with all those physical rhythms which go on despite the moments when you feel suicidal' ('Interview', *Bloodaxe 1*, 236).
25. An eloquent, representative proclamation is A. Alvarez's 'Beyond the Gentility Principle', his influential introduction to the Penguin *New Poetry* anthology of 1962. Alvarez's title makes clear the relationship of these ideas to a heavily revised and secularized Freudianism, a tradition to which Harrison's Thanatos-Gorgon might be related.
26. 'Interview', *Bloodaxe 1*, 235.
27. *Chorus*, 49–50.
28. 'Facing up to the Muses', *Bloodaxe 1*, 435.
29. *Bloodaxe 1*, 436.
30. Ibid.
31. Ibid. 445.
32. Ibid. 441.
33. Ibid. 448–9.
34. *The Oresteia*, TW, 242.
35. See Oliver Taplin, footnote to Harrison, 'The Oresteia in the Making: Letters to Peter Hall', *Bloodaxe 1*, 275.
36. See Martin Walker, *The Cold War and the Making of the Modern World* (London, 1993), 228–9.
37. E. P. Thompson, 'Notes on Exterminism, the Last Phase of Civilisation', in *Zero Option* (London, 1982), 71. The essay was first published in the May–June 1980 number of *New Left Review* and was hotly debated over the next two to three years. See E. P. Thompson, 'Exterminism Reviewed' (1982), in *The Heavy Dancers* (London, 1985), 135–52. For commentary on Thompson's overall contribution, see Fred Inglis, *The Cruel Peace: Living Through the Cold War* (London, 1992) and Meredith Veldman, *Fantasy, The Bomb, and the Greening of Britain: Romantic Protest, 1945–1980* (Cambridge, 1994).
38. *Aeschylus: Plays*, tr. G. M. Cookson (London, 1906) and *The Oresteian Trilogy*, tr. Philip Vellacott (Harmondsworth, 1956). For 'War Plan Trojan', see *Chorus*, 10.
39. *The Oresteia*, TW, 209–10.
40. Ibid. 238.
41. E. P. Thompson, 'Deterrence and Addiction' (1981), in *Zero Option*, 15–16.

42. See Thompson, 'Notes on Exterminism', *Zero Option*, 68.
43. Ibid. 69.
44. Raymond Williams, *Towards 2000* (London, 1983), 221.
45. In post-Cold War pieces like *A Maybe Day in Kazakhstan* (1994) and *Kaisers of Carnuntum*, Harrison produces images of 'new world order' states which represent little significant break from old dispositions. In his interview with John Haffenden, Harrison also stresses the gender politics of the ending and the way it marks a power shift towards a masculine 'new order': 'the crushing of the female principle is one of the great shortcomings of society in England and beyond' ('Interview', *Bloodaxe 1*, 241).
46. *Chorus*, p. ix.
47. 'The Ballad of the Geldshark', *SP*, 104.
48. *Palladas: Poems* (London, 1975), 8. The poems are also in *SP*. For 'The Murderer & Sarapis', *see SP*, 93–4.
49. Poem 11, *SP*, 79.
50. Poem 3, *SP*, 77.
51. Martin Amis, *London Fields* (London, 1989).
52. 'Interview', *Bloodaxe 1*, 235.
53. *v.*, *SP*, 238.
54. *The Memory of Troy*, BBC Radio 4 (28 Aug. 1988).
55. 'The Bedbug', *SP*, 54.
56. 'The Curtain Catullus', *SP*, 52.
57. *Loiners*, 69.
58. 'The Pocket Wars of Peanuts Joe', *SP*, 16–17.
59. Doris Lessing, *The Golden Notebook* (London, 1962).
60. Relevant poems are Ted Hughes, 'A Woman Unconscious', *Lupercal* (London, 1960), and 'Out', *Wodwo* (London, 1967); Thom Gunn, 'Adolescence' and 'Innocence', *My Sad Captains* (London, 1961); Philip Larkin, 'MCMXIV', *The Whitsun Weddings* (London, 1964); Geoffrey Hill, *King Log* (London, 1968).
61. *Gorgon*, 13, 14. One aspect of Harrison's account of war not covered in this essay is his attention to the First World War, especially in *Square Rounds* and *Chorus*. One reason why writers regularly turn to World War I rather than World War II to organize moral responses to warfare is that the first war inaugurates industrial killing as a modern technique, and is unclouded by the complicating moral and political perspectives of the 'just' war against fascism. Harrison (and Hill too) are unusual in sustaining their case in relation to the second war.

10. THE DRUNKEN PORTER DOES POETRY

1. *Loiners*, 7.
2. In a note to 'The White Queen', Harrison records that 'Hieronymus Fracastorius (1483–1553), the author of *Syphilis*, was born, as perhaps befits a true poet, without a mouth' (*SP*, 30).
3. 'Agrippa', *Bloodaxe 1*, 34.

4. See 'Conversation', *Bloodaxe 1*, 40.
5. 'Interview', *Bloodaxe 1*, 236.
6. 'Conversation', *Bloodaxe 1*, 43.
7. *Coming*, 10.
8. Ibid. 9.
9. Ibid. 11.
10. Ibid. 11–12. My italics.
11. Ibid. 14.
12. Ibid. 13.
13. Ibid. 14.
14. Ibid. 16.
15. See 'Them & [uz] I and II', *SP*, 122–3.
16. John Lucas, 'Speaking for England?', *Bloodaxe 1*, 359–60.
17. See 'Heredity', *SP*, 111.
18. 'Them & [uz] I', *SP*, 122.
19. 'Marked with D', *SP*, 155.
20. 'Them & [uz] II', *SP*, 123.
21. 'Interview', *Bloodaxe 1*, 233.

11. THE CHORUS OF MAMS

1. *Trackers*, 68.
2. Though written in 1985–6, his version of *Lysistrata* was not published in book form with this title until 1992. The version of Euripides' *Trojan Women*, its companion piece, exists only in a half-finished manuscript. The third play of the projected trilogy eventually emerged independently as *Square Rounds*.
3. I prefer this nice wordplay, used by Penguin, to *Dramatic Verse* (Bloodaxe) or the anodyne *Plays*, now adopted by Faber. Among the many ramifications of this subject which I shall not have space to explore, the translation of the *Oresteia* is only the most blatant.
4. Aristotle, *Poetics*, 1456a25–6.
5. This subject will be fully documented in a book by Peter Wilson to be published by Cambridge University Press; he has contributed a 'trail' to C. B. R. Pelling (ed.), *Greek Tragedy and the Ancient Historian* (Oxford, 1997).
6. I have in mind particularly John Gould, 'Tragedy and Collective Experience', in M. S. Silk (ed.), *Tragedy and the Tragic: Greek Theatre and Beyond* (Oxford, 1996), 217–24, and three essays in *Arion*, 3rd ser. 3/1 (1994/5): H. H. Bacon, 'The Chorus in Greek Life and Drama' (pp. 6–24); A. Henrichs, '"Why Should I Dance?": Choral Self-Referentiality in Greek Tragedy' (56–111); and C. Calame, 'From Choral Poetry to Tragic Stasimon: The Enactment of Women's Song' (136–54). Two formative influences behind this revaluation of the chorus were Claude Calame's two-volume *Les Chœurs de jeunes filles en Grèce archaïque* (Rome, 1977) and Jack Winkler's 'The Ephebes' Song: *Tragōdia* and *Polis*', in *Representations*, 11 (1985), rev. in J. J.

Winkler and F. Zeitlin (eds.), *Nothing to Do with Dionysos?* (Princeton, 1990), 20–62.

7. Gould, 'Tragedy and Collective Experience', 233.

8. Among others who have emphasized this recently, I would single out the extremely interesting, if ultimately unconvincing, article by Mark Griffiths, 'Brilliant Dynasts: Power and Politics in the *Oresteia*', in *Classical Antiquity*, 14 (1995), 62–129, esp. 119–20.

9. It is explicitly connected with Greek tragedy in his Classical Association lecture 'Facing up to the Muses', *Bloodaxe 1*, 429–54. For the link between audience and chorus, compare *The Labourers of Herakles, P3,* 133:

> No audience in Delphi, Athens, Epidaurus
> has ever been more useful than the helpless chorus.

10. There is a brief account of this with reference to the *Oresteia* in S. Goldhill, *Reading Greek Tragedy* (Cambridge, 1986), 51–5.

11. This is well treated by R. Just, *Women in Athenian Law and Life* (London, 1989).

12. For a straightforward account of this approach to the definition of the citizen by opposition to 'the other' see Cartledge, *The Greeks* (Oxford, 1993).

13. In fact the three best contributions, in my opinion, are not so recent any longer: John Gould, 'Law, Custom and Myth: Aspects of the Social Position of Women in Classical Athens', *Journal of Hellenistic Studies*, 100 (1980), 38–59; Helene Foley, 'The Conception of Women in Athenian Drama', in Helene Foley (ed.), *Reflections of Women in Antiquity* (London, 1981), 126–67; Froma Zeitlin, 'Playing the Other: Theatricality and the Feminine', in *Representations*, 11 (1985), 63–94, repr. in Winkler and Zeitlin, *Nothing to Do with Dionysos?*, 63–96, and repr. with revisions and additions in Froma Zeitlin, *Playing the Other: Gender and Society in Classical Greek Literature* (Chicago, 1996), 341–74.

14. Cf. Gould, 'Tragedy and Collective Experience', 237, n. 20.

15. *Tragicorum Graecorum Fragmenta*, ed. Bruno Snell (Göttingen, 1971), vol. I 3T1, 69: πρῶτος . . . γυναικεῖον πρόσωπον εἰσηγαγεν ἐν τῆι σκηνῆι—for Phrynichus see further below. The *Suda*, ed. A. Adler (Leipzig, 1928–38), is a tenth-century literary encyclopaedia which draws on earlier sources; its information can be unreliable, however.

16. This was *The Dramatic Festivals of Athens* by A. Pickard-Cambridge, 2nd edn., rev. J. Gould and D. M. Lewis (Oxford, 1968), 263–5. My pusillanimity was even recorded in an interview: see *Bloodaxe 1*, 243. I had, however, made up my mind before the appearance of the two significant—and contradictory—contributions by J. Henderson, 'Women and the Athenian Dramatic Festivals', *Transactions of the American Philological Association*, 121 (1991), 133–4, and S. Goldhill, 'Representing Democracy: Women at the Great Dionysia', in R. Osborne and S. Hornblower (eds.), *Ritual, Finance, Politics [. . .] for D. M. Lewis* (Oxford, 1994), 247–69 (I generally agree with the latter).

17. The contrast between this and the real carnage of the Roman

amphitheatre is a preoccupation of *Kaisers of Carnuntum*—see, for example, *P3*, 76:

> Where Greek tragic choruses bewailed their woes
> became for Rome a place where real blood flows.

18. See n. 13.
19. *Medea, TW*, 366–71.
20. Ibid. 431.
21. Ibid. 446.
22. Ibid. 447.
23. See *Chorus*, 40–1.
24. I think, for example, of the sonnets 'The Morning After' I and II, and of *The Mother of the Muses*. I am grateful to Tony Harrison for permission to quote from the *Trojan Women* draft.
25. Gould, 'Tragedy and Collective Experience', 217.
26. Visible in the photos in *P3*, 91, 105.
27. See *Square Rounds, P3*, pp. 82–4 and photos, 85.
28. The passage is Marcus Aurelius' advice on what to say to someone who is setting out to damage you: 'No, my child; we came into the world for other ends. It is not that I am harmed, but you are harmed, my child', in the translation by A. S. L. Farquarson, reissued in the World's Classics series (Oxford, 1990) 107. (The Greek text above corrects that in *P3*.)
29. *Kaisers, P3*, 84.
30. There is a scrap of Richard Blackford's score in *P3*, 112.
31. *Kaisers, P3*, 99–100. The combination of sucking milk and sucking blood, and the thought that murderers once were babies at the breast, surely have their intertextual root in the Clytemnestra of Aeschylus' *Choephori*.
32. *Labourers, P3*, 120.
33. σῶμα δ' ἀθαμβὲς γυιοδόνητον τείρει, which seems to mean something like: 'He [Thanatos?] wears out his [Herakles'?] fearless, limb-shaking body.' For discussion see A. M. Dale, *Euripides' Alcestis* (Oxford, 1954), pp. xiii–xiv. (In *Labourers*, Harrison tended, by the way, to use the Greek forms of proper names, such as Phrynichos, Herakles.)
34. *Tragicorum Graecorum Fragmenta*, i. 69–79. Most of the testimonia and fragments are reprinted with German translation and notes in R. Kannicht *et al.* (eds.), *Musa Tragica* (Göttingen, 1991), 40–9. I am gravely offended that the inclusion of ἐξώστρα (after no. 21 on 141) rejects my suggestion (*The Stagecraft of Aeschylus* (Oxford, 1977), 442 n. 1) that this word occurred in some other Phrynichus (contrast no. 15 on 140, which is—rightly—attributed to the later comic playwright of the same name)!
35. Herodotus, 6. 21. 2.
36. This is discussed (with full footnotes) by David Rosenbloom, 'Shouting "Fire" in a Crowded Theatre: Phrynichos's *Capture of Miletos* and the Politics of Fear in Early Attic Tragedy', *Philologos*, 137 (1993), 159–96.

37. This is greatly aided by the photos in *P3*, which can be supplemented by the designer's sketch and three other photos in *Arion*, 4/1 (Spring 1996), 143–6, especially the one on 144.
38. *Labourers, P3*, 113. The blurb on the back of *P3* also talks of 'a chorus of nine cement mixers', without any inverted commas.
39. *Bloodaxe 1*, 444–8.
40. *Labourers, P3*, 131.
41. Ibid. 143
42. Ibid. 122–3. The photo on p. 124 shows the scene (but without the red robes). The masks are strongly reminiscent of those worn by the chorus of slave women in the great 1981–2 production of *Choephori*. They were (of course) the work of the same supreme designer, Jocelyn Herbert.
43. Ibid. 123.
44. Ibid. 145.
45. Ibid. 147.
46. Ibid. 149.
47. *Big H, TW*, 325–6.
48. Ibid. 340.
49. Ibid. 348.
50. Ibid. 349.
51. Or, in keeping with the proper academic convention, Our 'arrison.
52. *A Kumquat for John Keats, SP*, 193.

12. POETRY OR BUST

1. Michael Church, the *Observer* (12 Sept. 1993).
2. Robin Thornber, 'Integrity or Bust', the *Guardian* (10 Sept. 1993).

13. IN THE CANON'S MOUTH

1. Douglas Dunn, 'Importantly Live: Tony Harrison's Lyricism', *Bloodaxe 1*, 255.
2. Douglas Dunn, 'Formal Strategies in Tony Harrison's Poetry', *Bloodaxe 1*, 130.
3. *Gorgon*, 24–5. The poem has an epigraph from Pound: 'The art of letters will come to an end before AD 2000 . . . I shall survive as a curiosity.'
4. *Coming*, 8: 'A cold coming we had of it.' The poem is also in *Gorgon*.
5. See Ezra Pound, 'Hugh Selwyn Mauberley, Life and Contacts', *Collected Shorter Poems of Ezra Pound* (London, 1952), 208.
6. Tony Harrison, quoted by Rosemary Burton, unpub. article.
7. See W. H. Auden, *The English Auden* (London, 1977), 150.
8. The three pieces that Harrison contributed to *London Magazine* in 1970–1 suggest that his decision to abandon this kind of work was a loss both to criticism and to himself: 'I am surprised that [George

MacBeth] has never translated this kindred spirit [Comte Robert de
Montesquiou Fezensac], of whose poetry it was said: "The possibilities of verse for this expression of fluent, contorted, and interminable
nonsense have never been more cogently demonstrated" ' (*London
Magazine*, 10/8 (Nov. 1970), 94).

9. 'The Nuptial Torches', *SP*, 60–2.
10. Robert Lowell, 'A Quaker Graveyard off Nantucket', *Poems 1939–49*
    (London, 1950), 18–19.
11. 'Nuptial Torches', *SP*, 60.
12. Douglas Dunn, 'The Student', *Barbarians* (London, 1979).
13. 'Me Tarzan', *SP*, 116.
14. Dunn, 'Harrison's Lyricism', *Bloodaxe 1*, 255.
15. Nicholas Bagnall, *A Defence of Clichés* (London, 1985).
16. Alexander Pope, *An Essay on Criticism*, ll. 297–8, *Poetical Works*, ed.
    Herbert Davis (London, 1966), 72.
17. John Haffenden, 'Interview with Tony Harrison', *Poetry Review*, 73/4
    (Jan. 1984), 30.
18. 'The Queen's English', *SP*, 136.
19. 'Confessional Poetry', *SP*, 128.
20. Thomas Gray, *Elegy Written in a Country Churchyard*, in Roger
    Lonsdale (ed.), *New Oxford Book of Eighteenth-Century Verse* (Oxford,
    1984), 355–6.
21. *The Kipling Treasury* gave Harrison's library its 'auspicious start'
    ('Next Door', *SP*, 129).
22. Andrew Marvell, 'The Garden', *The Poems and Letters of Andrew
    Marvell*, vol. 1, ed. H. M. Margoliouth, 3rd edn., rev. Pierre Legouis
    and E. E. Duncan-Jones (Oxford, 1971), 53.
23. See Ch. 4 above.
24. Gray, *Elegy*, 355–6.
25. Samuel Johnson, *Lives of the English Poets*, ed. G. B. Hill, 3 vols.
    (London, 1905) i, §51, 441.
26. Gray, *Elegy*, 355–6.
27. 'Book Ends I', *SP*, 126.
28. 'Clearing I', *SP*, 144.
29. *A Kumquat for John Keats*, *SP*, 192, 195.
30. *v.*, *SP*, 236, 237.
31. *v.*, *SP*, 237.
32. 'Them & [uz] II', *SP*, 123.
33. For 'Facing North', *SP*, 190. See Louis MacNeice, 'Epilogue for W.H.
    Auden', *Letters from Iceland* (London, 1937), 259.
34. 'Heredity', *SP*, 111.

The Contributors

MELVYN BRAGG is Controller of London Weekend Television, a novelist, radio and television presenter, director, and critic.

CHRISTOPHER BUTLER is an Official Student and Tutor in English of Christ Church, Oxford, and is the author of *After the Wake: An Essay on the Contemporary Avant-garde, Interpretation, Deconstruction and Ideology*, and *Early Modernism: Literature, Music, and Painting in Europe 1900–1916*.

SANDIE BYRNE is a Lecturer in English at Balliol College, Oxford, and is the author of *H, v., and O: Tony Harrison's Poetry*.

MARTYN CRUCEFIX is a reviewer and poet. He has published three collections of poetry, the most recent of which is *Madder Ghost*.

RICHARD EYRE was for several years the Director of the National Theatre and has directed a number of Tony Harrison's dramatic works, including *v*.

PETER FORBES is Editor of *Poetry Review*. He has contributed articles and reviews to many magazines and newspapers including the *Guardian*, the *Independent*, the *Financial Times*, and *Modern Painters*.

LORD GOWRIE is Chairman of the Arts Council of Great Britain.

DESMOND GRAHAM is Reader in English at the University of Newcastle, where he teaches the work of Tony Harrison to graduates and undergraduates. Two of his recent collections of poetry have been published by Seren, and he is the author of a study of the war poet Keith Douglas.

BERNARD O'DONOGHUE is a poet whose published collections include *Poaching Rights*, *The Weakness*, and *Gunpowder*, which won the 1995 Whitbread Poetry Prize. He has also written studies of medieval secular lyrics and the poetry of Seamus Heaney, edited the *Selected Poetry of Hoccleve*, and compiled a collection of essays on the courtly love tradition. He teaches Medieval English in Wadham College, Oxford.

JEM POSTER is Lecturer in Literature with the Department of Continuing Education, Oxford, and a Fellow of Kellogg College. He has edited a selection of George Crabbe's poems and is the author of *The Thirties Poets* and a collection of poetry, *By Some Other Route*.

ALAN RUSBRIDGER is Editor of the *Guardian* and has edited the collections *New World Order* and *Altered State*, and *Guardian Year 1994*.

RICK RYLANCE is Professor of Modern English Literature at Anglia Polytechnic University, Cambridge. He is the author of, 'Tony Harrison's Languages', published in Antony Easthope and John Thomson (eds.), *Modern Poetry Meets Contemporary Theory*, and of other articles and books including *Roland Barthes* and *Victorian Psychology and British Culture 1850–1880*. He is presently writing volume 11 of the *Oxford English Literary History*, covering the years 1930–70.

JONATHAN SILVER runs Salts Mill, Saltaire, Bradford, where several of Tony Harrison's plays have been staged, including *The Trackers of Oxyrhynchus* and *Poetry or Bust*.

OLIVER TAPLIN teaches Greek Literature at Oxford, where he is a Fellow of Magdalen College. His books include *The Stagecraft of Aeschylus*, through which he first crossed paths with Tony Harrison, *Homeric Soundings*, and *Comic Angels*.

N. S. THOMPSON is the author of *Chaucer and Boccaccio*, has translated several Italian novels, has published poetry in *New Writings 5* and elsewhere, and is the poetry editor of *New Poetry Quarterly*.

Select Bibliography

WORKS BY TONY HARRISON

Books

Earthworks (Leeds: Northern House, 1964).
Newcastle is Peru (Newcastle-upon-Tyne: Eagle Press, 1969).
The Loiners (London: London Magazine Editions, 1970).
The Misanthrope (London: Rex Collings, 1973).
Newcastle is Peru, 2nd edn., with an introd. by Tony Harrison (Newcastle-upon-Tyne: Northern House, 1974).
Palladas: Poems (London: Anvil Press, in assoc. with Rex Collings, 1975).
Phaedra Britannica (London: Rex Collings, 1975).
Phaedra Britannica, 3rd edn., with an introductory essay by Tony Harrison (London: Rex Collings, 1976).
Bow Down (London: Rex Collings, 1977).
From *'The School of Eloquence' and other Poems* (London: Rex Collings, 1978).
Continuous: Fifty Sonnets from 'The School of Eloquence' (London: Rex Collings, 1981).
A Kumquat for John Keats (Newcastle-upon-Tyne: Bloodaxe Books, 1981).
The Oresteia (London: Rex Collings, 1981).
U.S. Martial (Newcastle-upon-Tyne: Bloodaxe Books, 1981).
Selected Poems (London: Viking/Penguin Books, 1984).
The Fire-Gap (Newcastle-upon-Tyne: Bloodaxe Books, 1985).
The Mysteries (London: Faber and Faber, 1985).
Dramatic Verse 1973–1985 (Newcastle-upon-Tyne: Bloodaxe Books, 1985).
v. (Newcastle-upon-Tyne: Bloodaxe Books, 1985).
Theatre Works 1973–1985 (London: Penguin Books, 1986). Paperback version of *Dramatic Verse 1973–1985*.
Selected Poems, 2nd edn. (London: Penguin Books, 1987). Contains additional poems including *v.*
Ten Poems from 'The School of Eloquence' (London: Anvil Press, 1987).
Anno 42 (Scargil Press [private press], 1987).

v., 2nd edn. with press articles (Newcastle-upon-Tyne: Bloodaxe
   Books, 1989).
The Trackers of Oxyrhynchus (London: Faber and Faber, 1990).
   Contains both Delphi and National Theatre versions of the play.
A Cold Coming (Newcastle-upon-Tyne: Bloodaxe Books, 1991).
The Common Chorus, a Version of Aristophanes' Lysistrata (London:
   Faber and Faber, 1992).
The Gaze of the Gorgon (Newcastle-upon-Tyne: Bloodaxe Books, 1992).
Square Rounds (London: Faber and Faber, 1992).
Black Daisies for the Bride (London: Faber and Faber, 1993).
Poetry or Bust (Saltaire, Bradford: Salts Mill, 1993).
The Shadow of Hiroshima and Other Film/Poems (London: Faber and
   Faber, 1995).
Plays 3 (London: Faber and Faber, 1996).
The Prince's Play (London: Faber and Faber, 1996).
With James Simmons, *Aikin Mata* (Ibadan: Oxford University Press,
   1966).
With Philip Sharpe, *Looking Up* (Malvern: Migrant Press, 1979).
Translations in Peter Jay (ed.), *The Greek Anthology* (London: Allen
   Lane, 1973).
Permanently Bard, ed. Carol Rutter (Newcastle-upon-Tyne: Bloodaxe
   Books, 1995). An annotated schools' selection of Harrison's
   poetry.

Film and television works (does not include televised theatre productions)

The Blue Bird (1975). Song lyrics for George Cukor's version of the
   play by Maeterlinck.
Arctic Paradise, BBC 2 'World About Us Series' (Oct. 1981).
The Big H, BBC 2 (Dec. 1984).
Loving Memory, four-film series BBC2 (July–Aug. 1987).
   Letters in the Rock (July 1987).
   Mimmo Perrella Non è Piu (July 1987).
   The Muffled Bells (July 1987).
   Cheating the Void (Aug. 1987).
v., Channel 4 (Nov. 1987).
The Blasphemers' Banquet, BBC1 'Byline Series' (July 1989).
The Gaze of the Gorgon, BBC2 (Oct. 1992).
Black Daisies for the Bride, BBC2 (June 1993).
Maybe a Day in Kazakhstan, Channel 4 (May 1994).
The Shadow of Hiroshima, Channel 4, 'Witness' (Aug. 1995).

Poems cited in Tony Harrison: Loiner *which have not been collected*

'When Shall I Tune My "Doric Reed"?', *Poetry and Audience* 4/11 (25 Jan. 1957).
'What Plato Might Have Said', *Poetry and Audience* 4/15 (22 Feb. 1957).
'When the Bough Breaks', *Poetry and Audience* 4/22 (24 Apr. 1957).
'Two into One': 'The Beast with Two Backs' and 'Grog', 'Guardian New Poetry', the *Guardian* (12 Jan. 1994).
'Deathwatch Danceathon', the *Guardian* (12 Oct. 1994).
'A Celebratory Ode on the Abdication of Charles III', the *Guardian* (11 Jan. 1995).
'The Cycles of Donji Vakuf', the *Guardian* (15 Sept. 1995).
'The Bright Lights of Sarajevo', the *Guardian* (25 Sept. 1995).

WORKS CONTAINING MATERIAL ON TONY HARRISON

Bibliography

KAISER, JOHN R. (ed.), *Tony Harrison: A Bibliography 1957–1987* (London: Mansell Publishing, 1987).

Criticism

ACHESON, JAMES (ed.), *British and Irish Drama Since 1960* (London: Macmillan, 1993).
ASTLEY, NEIL (ed.), *Bloodaxe Critical Anthologies 1: Tony Harrison* (Newcastle-upon-Tyne: Bloodaxe Books, 1991).
BEER, GILLIAN, *Open Fields* (Oxford: Clarendon Press, 1996).
CORCORAN, NEIL, *English Poetry Since 1940* (London: Longman, 1993).
CRAWFORD, ROBERT, *Devolving English Literature* (Oxford: Clarendon Press, 1992).
EASTHOPE, ANTONY, and THOMPSON, JOHN O. (eds.), *Contemporary Poetry Meets Modern Theory* (London: Harvester Wheatsheaf, 1991).
O'BRIEN, SEAN, *The Deregulated Muse* (Newcastle-upon-Tyne: Bloodaxe Books, 1997).
PEACH, LINDEN, *Ancestral Lines: Cultural Identity in the Work of Six Contemporary Poets* (Bridgport: Seren, 1995).
PEER, WILLIE VAN (ed.), *The Taming of the Text: Explorations in Language, Literature and Culture* (London: Routledge, 1988).
SCHMIDT, MICHAEL, *Reading Modern Poetry* (London: Routledge, 1989).
SPENCER, LUKE, *The Poetry of Tony Harrison* (London: Harvester Wheatsheaf, 1994).

THWAITE, ANTHONY, *Poetry Today: A Critical Guide to British Poetry 1960–1984* (London: Longman, 1985).

WILMER, CLIVE (ed.), *Poets Talking: The 'Poet of the Month' Interviews from Radio 3* (Manchester: Carcanet, 1994).

Index